JUST AS WELL I'M LEAVING

Michael Booth is a journalist and travel writer.
He currently lives in Paris with his wife and
two children.

MICHAEL BOOTH

Just As Well
I'm Leaving

To the Orient with
Hans Christian Andersen

VINTAGE BOOKS
London

Published by Vintage 2006

2 4 6 8 10 9 7 5 3 1

Copyright © Michael Booth 2005

Michael Booth has asserted his right under the Copyright,
Designs and Patents Act 1988 to be identified as the author
of this work

First published in Great Britain in 2005 by Jonathan Cape

Vintage
Random House, 20 Vauxhall Bridge Road,
London SW1V 2SA

Random House Australia (Pty) Limited
20 Alfred Street, Milsons Point, Sydney,
New South Wales 2061, Australia

Random House New Zealand Limited
18 Poland Road, Glenfield,
Auckland 10, New Zealand

Random House (Pty) Limited
Isle of Houghton, Corner of Boundary Road & Carse O'Gowrie,
Houghton, 2198, South Africa

The Random House Group Limited Reg. No. 954009
www.randomhouse.co.uk/vintage

A CIP catalogue record for this book
is available from the British Library

ISBN 9780099477457 (from Jan 2007)
ISBN 0099477459

Papers used by Random House are natural,
recyclable products made from wood grown in
sustainable forests. The manufacturing processes
conform to the environmental regulations of the
country of origin

Printed and bound in Great Britain by
Bookmarque Ltd, Croydon, Surrey

To Lissen

'No son, no brother, can suffer more than I do – but it is just as well I am leaving: my soul is unwell.'

Letter from Hans Christian Andersen to his benefactor Jonas Collin on the second day of his journey to the Orient, 1 November 1840

Chapter One

COPENHAGEN

Somewhere in the wings of Odense Koncerthus, a technician reached behind Roger Moore's back, checked his batteries and flicked a switch. Moore's eyes fluttered into life, his spine stiffened and his right eyebrow spasmed into a quizzical arc. The operator pointed him towards the spotlights, waggled a toggle on the control panel, and out he strode onto the largest stage in Scandinavia.

At least, I can only assume this is what happened, out of sight, in the murk of the theatre's wings. For me and the rest of the two-thousand-strong audience, among them various members of the Danish royal family, local dignitaries, ordinary Danes, Hans Christian Andersen aficionados and maybe, who knows, even the odd Roger Moore fan, his serene detachment to the irrelevance of his speech could only have been explained by the fact that this was a marionette Moore, dispatched from the superstar's Swiss eyrie to help him bear the burden of his tireless work as an UNICEF ambassador. It was a speech that Roger Moores were giving from Bratislava to Burundi, quite possibly at that very minute.

Either that or Rog had become carried away with the slap and the sherry in his dressing room.

Anyway, while Moore slurred onward about the victims of famine, my mind had drifted. I was not the only one. I looked at my Danish in-laws, sitting on either side of me. I could see from their faces, fixed in polite perplexity, that Moore's monologue, which had long ago deviated from the work of UNICEF and was now focusing primarily on his career, was cause for some confusion. This bafflement was reflected in the other Danish faces around me. These sturdy, sensible people hadn't travelled from their sturdy sensible homes on the many islands, fjords and peninsulas of their sturdy, sensible country to listen to a luvvie's rambling reminiscences. They had come to pay homage to their most beloved writer on what was, in fact, a rather auspicious occasion.

This was Odense's annual Hans Christian Andersen Festival, which, when Roger finally ceded the stage, would comprise songs, readings, speeches and dramatisations of his work (Andersen's that is, not Roger's). Despite the fact that the world's best loved fairy tale teller fled this rural backwater on the island of Fyn for Copenhagen as soon as physically possible, his birth-place continues to burnish his memory with a fanatical zeal. Think Memphis and Elvis, or Liverpool and the Beatles, and you will have some idea of how important Andersen is to the people of Odense. He is their greatest international export, by an infinite margin.

Ordinarily, bearing in mind what he had put me through, I would probably rather have celebrated Roger Moore's life than Hans Christian Andersen's, but this year was different. Different, not just because this also happened to be the sixtieth birthday of the Danes' universally respected and adored Dronning Margrethe (Queen Margaret) – or 'Daisy' as the Danes call her when they know there are no informers around – and Daisy herself was sitting in the front row alongside her jovial French husband, Henrik, but also because the next act on stage was a woman dressed like a transvestite chicken – a Copenhagen costume designer's night-marish interpretation of how the clockwork bird from Andersen's fable 'The Nightingale' might look.

And that woman was my wife.

Lissen and I had met at a house-warming party in London just before Christmas two years earlier. By the time I arrived at the

Islington flat, home to a theatre critic friend, I had moved way beyond being louche and was now, as Lissen would recall, about as drunk as one can be while remaining conscious. It can't have been a pretty sight, as the drool stains on my lapels the next day testified. In my defence, I had spent the afternoon at the *Time Out* Christmas lunch, before meandering on to a Channel 4 party in Soho. (Is that a defence?)

I was introduced to Lissen by Suzy, a mutual friend (also a journalist; later to be my best 'man'), and, confronted with this innocent-faced, curvaceous Scandinavian beauty, with her lustrous light brown hair, bewitching blue-green eyes, and foxy purple leather trousers, I did my best to turn on the charm.

Later, Lissen told me that, such was my overpowering magnetism, I had still been on her mind as she left the party some hours later. 'Who was that creepy guy with his jumper on inside out?' she had asked her friend as they walked to the station. Crucially though, in a city where men threw themselves at her like lemmings in Velcro jump suits, the fact that I had appeared aloof – stand-offish even – yet simultaneously interested had worked a perverse kind of magic on Lissen. What I knew to be my increasingly desperate attempt to stop the room from spinning and creating a centrifuge in my stomach that would have resulted in the redecorating of my friend's new flat in a psychedelic scheme unlikely to have been to her liking, Lissen had taken to be enigmatic charm. In other words, while most men had collapsed in a dribbling heap at her feet, I remained upright and dribbling. I was, therefore, well on my way to being 'intriguingly different'.

From this, it was but a nod, a wink and a stumbling, apologetic phone call a few days later (along with some masterful and not entirely scrupulous matchmaking from my future best man), to our first date, ensuing courtship and wedding bells. Had I known it would all lead to relocation to a country with withering weather, coruscating taxes, bewildering social etiquette and entire meals of pork fat and pickled fish, I would . . . well, the painful truth is I would have done it all over again. Purple leather trousers do it for me every time.

Lissen's parents and I left Odense Koncerthus and walked to our car to wait for my chicken-diva wife to emerge in more sombre garb. My father-in-law, Peter, an inventor (and the creator of, among other things, those conical plastic collars that dogs are forced to wear when they are ill, which make them look like they've lost a fight with a satellite dish), attempted to extract meaning from, or at least some kind of justification for, the presence of Roger Moore at a joint celebration of their monarch and their greatest writer. I kept quiet, fearing that if I even tried to explain I would somehow be held responsible.

Instead, across the dark skies of my mind, my resentment flew with its now customary speed to the man responsible for my being dragged to this hostile and dispiriting country in the first place – dragged kicking and screaming (well, whining and whinging) away from my friends, my family and my career. The man we had been honouring that evening (and I'll give you a clue, it wasn't Roger Moore).

I held this man solely to blame for the fact that I couldn't see *Top of the Pops* on a Friday night, or listen to *Start the Week* in the bath. In Denmark there is no Radio 4, and baths are categorised as unconscionable environmental abuses comparable to dumping your fridge on a Galapagos island (in Denmark a bathroom is not a place of indulgence; it is a place of efficient – preferably in some way painful – cleansing). This was the man who stopped me from buying *Viz* in my local newsagent (there is no such thing as a newsagent in Denmark – I am not making this up), or diving into a silken pint of John Smith's in my local (welcome to the tyranny of the Carlsberg brewery). He was the reason I couldn't find double cream or proper orange juice in the pre-Glasnost-era, par-boiled rice and tinned vegetable warehouse that passed for my local supermarket. They didn't even have decent crisps, for the love of God!

There were many magnificent things about Denmark, of course, it is just that in my first year there they were all obscured by a fug of self-pity and social confusion. It didn't help that the Danes are a race of virtually unparalleled beauty, with (mostly) statuesque physiques and the highest educational standards in the world. Living among them was like living with an entire nation of head boys and girls.

They have their dark side, though. Due to this man's post-humous derailing of my life, I had learned through painful experience that the Danes have no word for 'please' and never, *ever* say sorry if they elbow you in the bus queue. Despite their oppressive obeisance to absurd rules of etiquette (serving smoked salmon on rye bread is akin to offering your guests baked beans from the tin, for instance; it must always be white bread), they were incapable of forming orderly queues. Hold a door open in a Danish department store, as I had done the previous day while out looking for an after-show gift for Lissen, and, at best, people will completely ignore you as, one after the other, they file past. At worst, the withering looks you will receive from hatchet-faced feminists oppressed by your chivalry will make you think twice about doing so again. They make the Hong Kong Chinese – up to that point by far the rudest people I had ever encountered – look like a bunch of librarians on an assertiveness training course. As an Englishman used to apologising when someone *else* treads on his foot, I took it all terribly personally and would often return home close to tears after a brief shopping excursion. (And though it is clearly wrong to generalise in this way about an entire race, the Danes are proud of being an unusually close-knit tribe, which is all the excuse I need.)

Thanks to this man, this antiquated children's writer with a face like a deep sea fish, I could muster no fellow feeling for my local football team (the Danes are generally far too mature to get excited about sports), nor for that matter could I find much cheer in the local music scene (when was the last time you *chose* to listen to Aqua CD?). Thanks to him and his damned bird, instead of the Ferraris and Bentleys in which I used to swan around London, courtesy of one of my freeloading, sorry, free-*lancing* jobs writing about cars for a national newspaper, I was now the proud owner of a puce-coloured Renault Kangoo – the car equivalent of an anorak from Millets. This because the Danish government, in its nannying wisdom, thinks that cars are bad things and impose import duties of 180 per cent, rendering them an absurd luxury that every Dane burdens themselves with debt for life to afford.

I had come to believe that Denmark exalted in its medioc-rity. You think I'm exaggerating? Well, let me tell you about *Jantelov* (Jante's Law), a unique Danish phenomenon. You'll be shocked, I promise.

Jantelov was the nickname given by the twentieth-century Danish satirist Axel Sandemose, in a novel he wrote in 1933, to the oppressive, small-minded spirit that he believed reigned across the land. It can be summarised by two of its commandments, as imagined by Sandemose: 'Don't believe you are anything special' and 'Don't believe you are better than us'. Similarly, another Danish saying – 'the further up a tree a monkey climbs, the more you see of its bottom' – also refers to their disapproval of conspic-uous achievement. (Think of it as a kind of tall poppy syndrome only with much lower corn, so that it takes only the slightest eccentricity or achievement to render oneself conspicuous.) Though it is fictional, there are actually some Danes who believe *Jantelov* to be a real doctrine, and many wholeheartedly endorse its insular, 'Who do you think you are to be eating smoked salmon, isn't fish paste good enough for you?' dogma. It remains one of the defining characteristics of even the most worldly, cosmopolitan Dane, and it was one of the most difficult things I had to come to terms with as a foreigner living there.

Some examples: if a man buys a new Mercedes, he will almost certainly have to endure jokes along the lines of: 'Did someone order a taxi?' from his friends and family every time he turns up at their house. If someone scores top marks in an exam, their tone will be almost apologetic when telling you. (The Danes consider it unseemly to brag about such things.) Flash clothing labels are a no-no, and few men wear suits and ties to work on a daily basis – even Danish politicians attend parliament in knackered old jumpers seemingly plucked from the dog basket. Posh restaurants are for very special occasions only, which explains why they have to charge such exorbitant prices: their 'regulars' only return for milestone wedding anniversaries every ten years or so. Buy yourself some nice new towels and the Danes will think you are Elton John.

I happen to have something of a Mercedes fetish, I dream of an Armani suit and love eating out. My fresh-towel addiction makes Elton look like St Simeon Stylites. It was clear from an early stage that I was going to have problems assimilating.

You can witness Jantelov at work on the streets of Copenhagen any day of the week: Danes will, to a man, wait at the crossing until the green man tells them to cross, even though they can see no cars for miles. I was once hissed at for crossing on a red and, in the end, concluded that, when it comes to dealing with traffic, the Danes simply cannot think for themselves. Listen carefully and you can hear them bleating as they cross.

Hans sodding Christian bloody Andersen – this delusional romantic masochist, my wife had explained some months earlier when she won the role in the musical, had fallen in love with the Swedish singer, Jenny 'the Swedish Nightingale' Lind, famed throughout Europe for her captivating vocal charms. Andersen, the bird-faced, big-nosed geek, failed to woo said songstress, vented his frustration with frequent masturbation sessions (methodically recorded with a '+' in his diary) and, in a last desperate attempt to catch her attention, wrote 'The Nightingale' about a pure, virginal bird displaced in the affections of a king by a vulgar mechanical replica. And thus Andersen, indirectly I grant you, had given my wife the excuse she needed to escape her South London misery.

Lissen hated living in London, I'm not really sure why; looking back, maybe I should have asked. I think it was something to do with the relentlessness of fitted carpets in English homes and the way your bogeys go black every time you open a window. That, and the daily risk of violent assault. But all the time that I was earning enough money to maintain our lavish consumer lifestyle (limitless supplies of Imperial Leather and After Eights eaten during daylight hours – that kind of thing), and she was only receiving unemployment benefit from Denmark, it was hard to justify a move. Admittedly, Danish unemployment benefit is a sizeable amount – comparable to an English primary school teacher's salary – but the likelihood of me finding work to support us in Denmark, at least work that didn't involve wearing a red uniform with stars to denote my skills with the deep fryer, was slim.

That had all changed when Lissen received the job offer of a lifetime from one of the most venerable stages in Denmark, the Folketeater (the People's Theatre). Now, she argued, we could move to Denmark, and she could support us. This would mean that I could finish that novel that I hadn't yet begun, but when questioned always claimed was my ultimate ambition in order to deflect further questioning regarding the vacuity of my normal work.

As well as the car-swanning-around-in, this other 'work' typically consisted of things like writing a history of the bikini for the *Radio Times*; television reviewing for *Time Out* (imagine being paid to watch TV all day!); a trip in search of the best beaches in the Philippines for one newspaper, and an important investigation into who was best, Leonardo da Vinci or Leonardo di Caprio, for *Tomorrow's World* magazine (now defunct, can't think why). Another typical assignment saw me fly all the way to Argentina to learn how to play polo, despite never having ridden a horse before (I do not recommend this); for another I went to Tokyo just to take a bath. And then there was the time I spent three days going slightly insane in the world's biggest shopping mall. Happy, pointless tasks undertaken in order to write happy, pointless and forgettable newspaper articles.

But now Lissen had called my egotistical bluff by offering me a chance to express my inner Updike. In response all I could do was to open and close my mouth like a beached guppy and then watch as my magnificent media career and PR-party-packed life in SW1 disappeared down the U-bend to be replaced by life in a dull, grey, little land with endless TV shows about cattle, an odd liquorice fixation, and, of course, the bleak mid-winter weather, which lasts around 300 days of the year.

Damn you, Andersen, I thought to myself, as I clambered, shivering, from the freezing fog of April in Odense into my Postman Pat van. Damn you and your puerile fables, damn your clumsy moralising and your ugly duckling (we get the self-reference). And most of all, damn your Little Mermaid, that pathetic love-sick fish whose statue I had recently seen for myself for the first time – having schlepped miles out of the city centre to find it – sitting slumped on some rocks across from the grimmest part of Copenhagen's run-down industrial harbour front mostly, it seemed, for the edification of Japanese cruise ship passengers and as an evening rallying point for local vandals.

Of course, looking back, I can see that the contempt in which I held the man I now realise to be unquestionably one of the greatest literary innovators of the nineteenth century was irrational, unfounded and verging on the pathological. Likewise, my rage at Denmark was distorted out of all proportion (although I still think the liquorice thing is weird). I would, in fact, come to love this man like a long-lost twin and yearn for Denmark as if it were a Bahamian paradise (well, almost). But at the time the bile was genuine, the targets, in my mind at least, wholly deserving.

Did I keep these gripes and moans to myself in our everyday life? Did I suffer stoically, putting on a brave face for the sake of marital harmony?

What do you reckon?

That night, back in Copenhagen, I continued to rant and rage like a toddler with a full nappy, as I did most nights, and most mornings come to that. I complained – again – about the way the Danes drive with a complete lack of courtesy (finding a space in the car park at Netto was like trying to find a safe bed as the Vikings rampaged through Lindisfarne); and wondered aloud for the umpteenth time why every bloody cake and confection had to have a wodge of marzipan hidden somewhere beneath an otherwise tempting exterior. And what was with the open sandwiches? Was there a bread shortage or something?

I was Eeyore that time everyone forgot his birthday and Albert Steptoe at his horse's funeral rolled into one, and my sulking was beginning to affect our marriage. Resentment was brewing on both sides of the bed. Lissen had taken to wearing ear plugs. What stopped her from calling the police and simply asking them to escort me to the airport, I will never know.

In order to show at least a token commitment to my adopted home I had recently begun learning Danish at an intensive language school in Nørrebro, an area just outside of the city centre popular with immigrants. The school was off the main high street, behind a Turkish grocer's and above an Indian restaurant, and went under the mysterious and cruelly misleading acronym KISS. To this day I have no idea what that stands for. I was far too busy coping with its boot-camp methods and the sadism of its teachers to ask.

Being treated like a retarded twelve-year-old had come as a violent shock to my twenty-nine-year-old system, as had the daily bicycle ride across the city, typically in weather conditions that would have had Amundsen shrugging defeat and asking someone to call him a cab.

The day after Lissen's royal command performance was a Monday. The rain acupunctured into my cheeks as I cycled up H.C. Andersen's Boulevard and past the giant statue of its eponymous author, looking like a daydreaming undertaker, in his stovepipe hat and long coat. As I crossed the vicious wind tunnel of the city lakes, the gusts billowed beneath my parka, making me look like an unhappy cross between Marilyn Monroe and the Michelin Man.

At school, I climbed the stairs to the second-floor classroom, experiencing my daily, spine-chilling schooldays déjà vu (how is it that all educational institutions, everywhere, smell exactly the same?), and took my seat around the long rectangular table between Ahmed, an Islamic fundamentalist Afghan refugee, and Ibrahim, a Pakistani accountant, also a refugee. Our merry band of students made up a virtual united nations of misfits in a country that would probably have preferred it if we had stayed at home: there was a Peruvian film student, two French women – one an air stewardess, the other a biochemist – an American lawyer, a Russian optician, an Iraqi doctor and a Serbian model, all here for one of two reasons: either they were refugees who had wanted to come to Britain but weren't allowed in or they had shacked up with a Dane. I think it is safe to say that none of us had woken one morning and said to ourselves: 'I don't like living here. Denmark seems so much more attractive!'

Break times became a forum for our shared exasperation with the Danes, whose supposed liberal attitude is one of the great myths of international political theory. As with their neighbours the Norwegians and the Swedes they are, in fact, raving nationalists; their compulsive flag waving makes Americans look like unassuming global peacekeepers. Ordinary Danes will haul up their flag – a white cross on a red background, which, if you ask them, they genuinely believe to be the most beautiful in the world – at the slightest excuse: to welcome friends back from holiday; to mark a child's birthday; even the buffet laid on to celebrate the cat's successful hernia operation will be decked out in paper flags and napkins with the *Dannebrog* on them. Every single home and business has a flagpole out front – even allotments have them. Danish friends tell me there is nothing sinister in this at all, it is merely a celebratory tradition, but I had even heard that, chillingly, it is *illegal* to fly a foreign flag on Danish soil.

As with many smaller European states, racism is on the rise here too. Sometimes it felt as if, given the choice and with no one looking, many Danes (I am thinking here of the ones who regularly vote for the 'send the Muslims home' party, which, terrifyingly, is the power broker in parliament) would prefer to remove the vertical part of the white cross on the Danish flag, and just turn it into the universally recognised No Entry sign.

The conversations with my classmates – many of them the target of racial discrimination, particularly when it came to trying to find work – were the only compensation for the myriad miseries of the Danish lessons. Their life stories were often remarkable and occasionally harrowing, although I had soon learned not to engage Ahmed in conversation for the simple reason that he might kill me.

The week before, when I had asked why he had left his homeland, he had claimed that his religious beliefs had been too extreme for the Taliban, who were in power when he had fled. Too extreme for the Taliban! I wanted to ask how this could be possible, but Ahmed had swiftly added: 'In my country if one man makes another angry, he kills him.'

'Oh, that's nice,' I said, trying to stop my bottom lip from quivering. 'Hmm, what *is* that over there on the other side of the room?'

And then there was the daily torture of The Sentences.

This was the essence of the KISS system: every day, at the end of each morning's lessons, we were given fifteen sentences in Danish, plus around two pages of vocabulary to learn. If we were unable to demonstrate that we were word perfect in The Sentences, both orally and in written form, the next day, the teacher would put a black mark against our name. Three black marks received over the course of each three-week module would mean that you had to repeat the entire module again. Gradgrind would have loved it.

This was humiliating and stressful enough, but the method

of daily testing, in which the teacher would randomly fire key words from each of the sentences to different students around the table like some Erasmusian sniper, and then expect them to fire back the entire sentence instantly, compounded the terror. The content of the sentences was the final drop of vinegar to sting the wound. Though many were of the innocuous 'Jan and Pernille take the train to Århus' kind, there were other, more sinister phrases clearly designed to brainwash the new arrivals. 'Danes don't drop litter' was one (as if this were a typifying characteristic of other nationalities); 'Danes never call in on someone without ringing ahead to let them know' was another helpful piece of social indoctrination. We were also asked to recite the questionable mantra: 'Danes welcome people of all races and colours'. But I drew the line, and took my black mark on the chin, when asked to chant out loud: 'I like rock music, especially Danish.'

I have to admit that, though their methods exhibited about as much humanity and compassion as a foie gras goose farmer, stuffing vocabulary and grammar down our gullets, the KISS system worked. However painful and humiliating their process, the KISS teachers managed to achieve something no one had ever been able to do before them: to get me to speak a foreign language. That it happened to be one of the least attractive languages on earth, every word stuffed with glottal stops like a Geordie tongue twister ready to trip the unwary into spittle-flecked, gob-flobbed linguistic knots, only heightened the sense of achievement.

When Danes speak it invariably sounds like they are telling you off. 'I love you' is '*Jeg elsker dig*', pronounced something like: '*Yiye ellskere die*'. When shouted it sounds like something a Viking might yell as he plunges his horned helmet into your guts for the umpteenth time. Danish is not the language of love; it's more the language of an angry farmer who has just caught you trespassing on his turnips. For an entire year I was simply unable to make out individual words. It just sounded like the prolonged throat clearance of a heavy smoker (which bearing in mind that many Danes – including their queen – smoke like laboratory beagles, might well explain it). At school we spent hours crossing out the letters and syllables lost to the ravenous glottal monster – usually losing half the word in the process: which helped actually. Slowly, I began to figure out the subject of conversations and, as my confidence built, I would occasionally jump, Eric Cantona-like, into a dinner-party mêlée, grasping completely the wrong end of the stick. 'Ah, yes, I once knew a girl with ginormous breasts too!' I would interject triumphantly to a group of people who turned out to be deep in discussion about Proust (which, trust me, sounds very similar to the Danish for 'breast'). And so my linguistic progress was very much of the 'two steps forward, one dinner-party invitation back' kind.

That Monday at KISS we were to be spared The Sentences. Instead, our teacher, Steen (think Torquemada in a chunky sweater), had prepared a spot of translation work. He had photocopied some stories for us, in Danish, which we were to read, translate into our own language and answer questions about in Danish at the end of the session.

I should of course have guessed that the stories would be by Andersen, and that I would be given '*Den Lille Havfrue*' ('The Little Mermaid'). I began reading with much accompanying eye rolling and tutting, like a stroppy thirteen-year-old (it's not easy reading and rolling your eyes at the same time, but I was pretty determined).

But then something quite unexpected happened.

To describe reading this story in Andersen's original Danish as a road-to-Damascus moment is perhaps overstating things (it was probably more like if St Paul had all his life refused to try Marmite, then someone had slipped some on a pitta and he had actually quite liked it), but it certainly made me reconsider my opinion of its author.

'The Little Mermaid' is a remarkable piece of work, about as far removed from the Disney film version as an Arctic nature documentary is from an episode of *Pingu*, and not at all how I remembered the works of Andersen I had read as a child. I didn't, for instance, recall the bit where, following some fairly poor negotiating on the mermaid's part, the witch cuts out her tongue in exchange for growing legs, and insists that she can never return to her family and must experience excruciating pain every time she takes a step. Or that the prince gives the fish the finger and falls for another woman (I guess her lack of tongue was always going to be a bit of a turn-off), leaving the mermaid high and dry. Or that the witch informs her that if she wants to return to the sea she must kill the prince and allow his blood to drop onto her feet to turn them back to a tail. And I am sure that in Uncle Walt's version she doesn't end up as a 'daughter of the air', doomed to float around ethereally for 300 years in order that one day she might obtain an immortal soul. In fact, it all seemed uncannily similar to a Lars von Trier script.

The mermaid's yearning is so raw and intense that it must surely have been taken directly from Andersen's life, yet at the same time he also describes the awakening of a teenage girl's sexuality with a vivid authenticity. The viewpoint is sympathetically feminine, yet at times strongly misogynistic, if not downright sadistic. And is it me, or could there be a hint of the homoerotic in the subtext of a forbidden, silent love? Certainly there is an erotic charge that, in the context of a supposed children's story, quite makes one blush – 'She remembered that his head had rested on her bosom, and how warmly she had kissed him,' Andersen writes, and let's not forget, the mermaid is naked most of the time.

Meanwhile, you could spend all day hypothesising about the symbolism of the story. When the mermaid's newly formed feet bleed with her every step, is this a loss of virginity or the onset of menstruation? And I shudder to think what Andersen was getting at when he described the sea witch as 'allowing a toad to eat from her mouth . . . and ugly water snakes to crawl all over her bosom.' Beatrix Potter it ain't.

My curiosity was well and truly aroused. What kind of man could have written something like this?

On the way home from school that afternoon I stopped at the bookstore on Rådhuspladsen (the town hall square) and picked up an anthology of Andersen's stories, plus his autobiography. I read through the afternoon and into the night, peeling away the layers of each story, marvelling at their humour, their wisdom and their striking modernity.

I read 'The Steadfast Tin Soldier', a poignant hymn to the disfigured and the different of society in which a one-legged tin soldier endures a traumatic journey to return to his true love, the figurine of a ballet dancer, only to be cruelly thrown into a fire by a little boy 'just as things were going nicely for them'. 'The tin soldier stood there dressed in flames. He felt a terrible heat, but whether it came from the flames or from his love he didn't know.' At that moment the dancer is also blown into the fire and they burn together. I don't know about you, but I am a sucker for this kind of thing (Charlotte's death scene in *Charlotte's Web* does it to me every time). Andersen gives great pathos; as I was to discover, it was one of the defining qualities of his life.

The conspiracy of ignorance in 'The Emperor's New Clothes' is still a universally recognised scenario today, invoked by critics of everything from Damien Hirst's pickled cattle to New Labour – 'I know I'm not stupid,' the Emperor's official thinks when he is unable to see what the swindlers are weaving, 'so it must be that I'm unworthy of my good office. I mustn't let anyone find out.' – but a world of satire and wit emerges if you return to the original text.

I was astounded to discover that 'The Princess on the Pea' – one of his most iconic stories (and, you might say, a precursor to F. Scott Fitzgerald's assertion that the rich 'are different from you and me') – is just one page long, seven paragraphs in all. It is virtually haiku; if brevity is the soul of wit, Hans Christian Andersen is the James Brown of story tellers.

Had it been written any time after 1965, you might assume 'The Marsh King's Daughter' was created under the influence of hallucinogens, what with its psychopathic frog-girl princess and talking storks, while 'Clumsy Hans', the story of a young man's successful attempt to woo a princess with a dead crow, some soil and an old shoe, is nothing short of Pythonesque (actually, there's lots of Python in Andersen, from the naked Finnish women in 'The Snow Queen' who write to each other on bits of dried cod, to the chamberlain in 'The Nightingale' 'who was so grand that if anyone of lower rank dared speak to him, he would only say: 'P!'').

There is a ghoulish anarchy to many of his stories – people are garrotted, have their brains scattered about and endure other wonderfully arbitrary and brutal deaths, sometimes to the extent that you can't help feeling a good many of these tales are wholly inappropriate for children. In 'The Stork', for instance, the eponymous birds plot a grisly revenge on a boy who has taunted them: 'In the pond there is a little dead baby, it has dreamed itself to death, we will take it to him, and then he will cry because we have brought him a little dead brother.' While the moment in 'Little Claus and Big Claus' where little Claus dresses up his dead grandmother verges on the Hitchcockian.

Yet amid all the horror and fantasy, the telling details make it all seem somehow strangely real – like the walls rubbed with witches' fat to make them shine in 'The Elf Hill'; or the way the moon sees a Hindu maiden, 'the blood coursing in her delicate fingers as she bent them round the flame to form a shelter for it' in 'What The Moon Saw'.

In stories like 'The Shadow' (about a man haunted by his own shadow) Andersen raises existential questions every bit as knotty as those posed by his contemporary Copenhagener, Søren Kierkegaard. I was taken aback to discover here a tone of black pessimism that thrusts, with rapier accuracy, to the heart of the human condition. Clearly this was a man wrestling with a deep spiritual uncertainty.

He also seems to have been a keen observer of the pretensions and absurdities of the class system. In 'The Flying Trunk' we meet a quill pen with delusions of grandeur: 'There was nothing exceptional about it except that it had been dipped too far down in the inkwell. But because of this it now put on airs.' While 'The Happy Family' features some snails who look down upon slugs because they have no houses.

Another aspect of the stories that must have been revolutionary at the time (and I must admit, I am writing with hindsight here; I know it *was* revolutionary) was their informal, conversational style. They often begin with a gag – 'In China, as you know, the emperor is a Chinaman' ('The Nightingale') – or the literary equivalent of a smack on the back of the head: 'Come, pay attention! We are going to begin. When we reach the end of our story we shall know more than we do now; for we shall learn that once upon a time there was a wicked gnome of the very worst kind, the devil himself' ('The Snow Queen'). They continue in a chatty, direct style, free of periphrase and waffle, full of onomatopoeic exclamations, and often ending with an unceremonious abruptness: 'Shall we read the story once again from the beginning? It will be no different' ('The Snail and the Rosebush'). And as with all the best children's writers and performers, Andersen never condescends to his younger audience.

He was a true modernist. At a time when most people's idea of children's entertainment was to give them a stick and point them towards the nearest mud, and most children's books were intended to pummel them with facts, literature that spoke directly to them, that had the power to grab them by the shoulders and make them laugh out loud like this, was a seismic shift.

And I defy anyone – even, say, Vladimir Putin – to read 'The Little Matchgirl' and not blub like a pansy.

There had been fairy-folk tales before, of course – 'Sleeping

Beauty', 'Aladdin', 'Jack and the Beanstalk' and hundreds like them had been handed down orally for generations. Germany's Brothers Grimm – Jacob and Wilhelm – had been collecting such stories for their anthologies since the turn of the nineteenth century. Charles Perrault had performed a similar curatorial function in France, where flowery, girly romantic fantasies like 'Beauty and the Beast' had long been popular. And a Dane, Just Matthias Thiele (later to become one of Andersen's benefactors), had done the same in his country.

But as I read on I learned that, not only did Andersen imbue the form with a fresh literary vision and a subtle wit, he did something none of those other collectors of tales had done: he dreamed up entirely new stories.

According to the Andersen scholar Elias Bredsdorff, 144 of the 156 stories Andersen wrote were 'entirely his own invention', yet in many instances they have supplanted the old fables in the minds of millions, and are showing all the signs of having a shelf life to match.

His very first 'from scratch' story was 'Little Ida's Flowers', which, together with 'The Princess on the Pea', 'Little Claus and Big Claus' and 'The Tinderbox' (these last three had their source – albeit heavily reworked – elsewhere) constituted his first collection of fairly stories, published in an unbound pamphlet in May 1835. 'Little Ida's Flowers' showcased several of Andersen's most abiding innovations: the personification of inanimate objects (in this case Ida's flowers and toys, which come alive and dance at a ball); the chatty, 'read aloud' style; the subtle humour and a hint of darkness (the story ends with the flowers' funeral).

In volume after volume of *Eventyr* (folk tales) all the way to his last, the creepy 'Auntie Toothache' of 1872, Andersen would develop and refine these revolutionary ideas and introduce yet more. In doing so he elevated a peasant pastime into a literary genre – a genre of which he remains the king to this day. In short, he did nothing less than give birth to children's literature itself.

Without him there could well have been no *Winnie the Pooh*, no *Wind in the Willows*, no *Alice in Wonderland*, and – unthinkably – no *Tales of Mrs Tiggywinkle*. There would be no *Shrek*, no *His Dark Materials* and, dare I say it, even *Harry Potter* wouldn't quite be the same. Several of the characters through the wardrobe in Narnia, Lemony Snicket's anarchic disregard for the conventions of happy endings, the fact that *The Gruffalo* is as entertaining for its adult readers as for young audiences – all of this we can trace back to Andersen. And while we are at it, we can safely say that there would probably also be no Disney (and therefore no Christina Aguilera, Britney Spears or Justin Timberlake – but just as we cannot directly blame Wagner for the rise of the Third Reich, neither can we blame Andersen for this).

The universality of his tales is exemplified by the fact that Marxists, feminists, Jungians and Freudians have all claimed him as their own. And many of the stories are now so deeply ingrained in the global consciousness that their titles alone – 'The Emperor's New Clothes', 'The Ugly Duckling', and 'The Princess on the Pea' – are used as a shorthand to this day by people from the Bronx to Beijing to describe social phenomena, human weakness or improbable circumstances.

Did you know his works have been translated into 145 languages, or that Chairman Mao was such a fan that he put Andersen's stories on the syllabus of every school in China? Did you know his fairy stories were a great influence on, among others, Oscar Wilde (who was inspired by Andersen to contribute to the genre himself with 'The Happy Prince' and other stories), and that Thackeray, Priestley, Auden, Strindberg, Thomas Mann and Dickens were also fans? Did you know that Unesco has named him the world's 'most read' author?

It was all news to me.

Later, I discovered the reason why the notion of Andersen as a revolutionary literary genius had completely passed me by. When Andersen's fairy stories were first published in Danish, a rabble of opportunistic translators, like Mary Howitt and Charles

Boner, scrambled to produce English editions, despite not being able to understand Danish properly. They meddled with, embellished, bowdlerised and disfigured Andersen's delicate, precise prose so that his stories ended up with all the elegant clarity of the English-language instructions for a Made-in-Korea video recorder (which is why you probably know 'The Princess on the Pea' erroneously as the 'Princess *and* the Pea').

But why should the Victorians have influenced my experience of Andersen? For the simple reason that, amazingly, *scandalously*, the nineteenth-century translations remain the main source for English-language readers of Andersen's work, and there have been precious few faithful translations since. Even in Politikken, the largest book store in Andersen's adopted home city, the only English anthology I could find was a translation dating from 1899. So, many, if not most English-language readers will have experienced only a bastardised, woefully outdated version of Andersen.

While I was still reeling from all this, I found a copy of the 1950 Danny Kaye biopic, *Hans Christian Andersen*, for sale on the Internet. I wasn't expecting a scrupulous biography – the fact that people burst into song every few minutes does tend to mitigate against realism – but even I could tell this was a risible fantasy. The plot is only tangentially concerned with the facts of Andersen's life (the fact that everybody calls him 'Hans' is a giveaway; he was only ever 'Hans Christian' or, to close friends, 'Christian', never Hans). About the only thing the film gets right, as I was to discover, was the casting of the closet homosexual Kaye in the lead role. Great songs, though.

(Later on, while looking through the archives at the Hans Christian Andersen Museum in Odense, I came across original documents and letters about the film. It seems the Danish government was so upset by its inaccuracy that they complained to the United Nations, and the producer Sam Goldwyn was forced to add a caveat at the start of the film: 'Since he always turned everything into a fairy tale, perhaps it is not unlikely that he would have cast a benevolent and amused glance in the direction of this last, this ultimate fairy tale that we are telling now.' There is also a very anxious, as I would later find out, a very *Andersen-esque* letter, from Kaye: 'I do hope no dire consequences result from the commotion which has been raised in the papers and that at some time or other I will be able to get into Denmark without having stones hurled at me.')

When I turned to more reliable sources of information on Andersen I discovered his true life story to be far more outlandish than Hollywood's saccharine, sanitised version, and just as compelling as his fiction. His unprecedented, against-all-odds rise from being the illiterate son of a poverty-stricken washerwoman and a cobbler father (who died when he was eleven), to a globally acclaimed writer, friend of royalty and 'The most famous man in Europe' – as the writer Edmund Gosse called him – is one of the most, if not *the* most extraordinary life stories of any literary figure.

So what do we know about this man's life? Well, a great deal, as it happens. He wrote four versions of his autobiography, which is in itself indicative of the pathological self-obsession that was one of his defining personality traits. The first was in 1832, aged a Kenneth Branagh-beating twenty-seven, but was only published fifty years after his death; the second was published in 1847; followed by an update in 1855; with a final whitewash in 1869, six years before his death. I say 'whitewash' as all of his autobiographies should generally be read with a pinch of salt. Tellingly, he changed the title from *The True Story of My Life* to *The Fairy Tale of My Life* along the way. Andersen was a compulsive self-mythologiser and he skirted many of the unpalatable truths of his childhood – his mother's illegitimate daughter, for example, and the fact that his parents married hastily two months before he was born – preferring to focus on a more romantic story of an innocent talent rising from hardship and obscurity.

Far more revealing are the lengthy, detailed letters he wrote

to friends virtually every day of his adult life (many of which
survive, along with their replies); and the diary he kept, on and
off, from the age of twenty to the day he died, aged seventy, in
1875 (although, even the diary seems to have been written with
the assumption that it would one day be published – as one
biographer put it, he was 'a curator of his own existence'). As
well as this, Andersen gathered ephemera, like the autographs
and dedications of the famous people he met on his travels, in
a massive scrapbook, and from 1838 to 1871 he even took the
trouble to note down for posterity – on which he clearly had
his beady eye from a young age – the bare bones of each day
in an almanac.

So, as well as the precise dates on which specific events
occurred in his life, we know whom he met and when, his
thoughts, his feelings, his ambitions and his disappointments. And
from the crosses he makes in his diary and almanac we even
know the ins and, mostly, the outs of his ejaculatory habits (he
often complained about a sore penis the next day, seemingly
oblivious to the cause).

Here are some of the salient facts: Hans Christian Andersen
was born at one o'clock in the morning of 2 April 1805, in the
city of Odense on the island of Fyn. He was the only child of
Anne Marie and Hans Andersen. Dad was a shoemaker, mum a
scrubber – in both senses of the word: she was a tad promis-
cuous – who, unusually for the times, was around ten years older
than her husband.

Anne Marie was from peasant stock; she was a practical, hard-
working and, towards the latter part of her life, hard-drinking
woman, utterly devoted to and protective of her son. Hans
Andersen was rather a different kettle of characteristics, in fact,
it is a wonder he and Anne Marie ever hooked up in the first
place. Hans was a frustrated student who yearned for an education and mocked his wife's folklore superstitions. 'One day he
closed the Bible with the words, "Christ was a man like us, but
an extraordinary man!" These words horrified my mother and

she burst into tears. In my distress I prayed to God that he would forgive this fearful blasphemy in my father,' Andersen recalled. Hans was an autodidact and introduced his son to the tales of the *Arabian Nights*. The two were extremely close: 'I possessed his whole heart,' wrote Andersen in his autobiography. 'He lived for me.'

Hans' great hero was the self-made emperor, Napoleon, and in 1813, with Denmark siding with France against England, he enlisted in the army as a musketeer, earning his family desperately needed money by taking the place of a wealthier conscript. As it turned out, Hans Andersen saw no action, but the time he spent as a soldier ruined his health and he died two years after he returned home, in April 1816, aged just thirty-three. 'That was the first day of real sorrow which I remember,' Andersen recalled.

Hans Christian withdrew into a world of dolls and puppets. An effeminate, freakishly tall boy, with heavily hooded eyes and a great beak of a nose, he was the butt of local humour, teased at school and, later, bullied in the factory where he was sent to work like all the other young boys. 'I very seldom played with other boys,' he once wrote. 'My greatest delight was in making clothes for my dolls . . . I was a singularly dreamy child.' It hardly helped that his paternal grandfather, Anders Andersen, was the village idiot (well, with a name like that it was virtually predestined).

He knew he was special from the start. In *The True Story of My Life*, he tells of the time his mother and he were chased from a field by a cantankerous bailiff wielding a whip. Andersen lost his wooden shoes, and the bailiff caught up with him: '[he] lifted his whip to strike me, when I looked him in the face, and involuntarily exclaimed: "How dare you strike me, when God can see it?"' The bailiff was instantly pacified, and when Andersen related what had happened to his mother she was astonished: 'He is a strange child, my Hans Christian; everybody is kind to him: this bad fellow has even given him money.'

'I will become famous,' he once told his mother. 'People have at first an immense deal of adversity to go through, and then they will be famous.' When told, as he often was, that he should find a trade like all the other boys of his class, he responded solemnly: 'That would actually be a great sin.' From this singular self-belief was born his extraordinary will to succeed, which first manifested itself when he would stand on some open ground near his home and sing at the top of his soprano voice for anyone who would listen – earning him the nickname the Fyn Nightingale.

Odense was the only town in Denmark outside of Copenhagen that had a theatre and his visits there made a great impression on him. If he could not afford a ticket, he would blag a play-bill and imagine an entire drama from the play's title and the list of characters (one of the first he saw was *The Little Lady of the Danube* by Kauer). 'The more persons died in a play, the more interesting I thought it,' he later wrote and, soon, he was inspired to produce his first ever piece of creative writing, a play based on a song about Pyramus and Thisbe, called *Abor and Elvira*. 'I desired now that everybody should hear my piece. It was a real felicity to me to read it aloud, and it never occurred to me that others should not have the same pleasure in listening to it.'

His various talents earned him invitations to the homes of influential local families – 'the peculiar characteristics of my mind excited their interest' – and so he became even further removed from the normalities of childhood.

There survives a wonderful first-hand report of Andersen during these times from a girl who witnessed a performance of the 'Master Comedy Player', as she calls him, at the bishop's house. 'For two whole hours the little gentleman played parts from various comedies and tragedies; as a rule he did well, but we were much amused whether he succeeded or not, the gay parts were the best, but it was most absurd to watch him doing the part of a sentimental lover, kneeling down or fainting, because just then his large feet did not look their very best; well, perhaps they can improve their style in Copenhagen, perhaps in time he will make his appearance as a great man on stage. In the evening we had sandwiches and red fruit jelly, our actor joined us, but in a hot haste so as not to lose any time parading his talent. At half-past ten the bishop's wife thanked him for coming, and he went home.'

I love that 'hot haste' description; she also describes him 'bustling out the door like some dandy' – clearly he was so wrapped up in his own talents that he had no idea how foolish he appeared to others.

Having rapidly outgrown Odense, at the age of fourteen he gathered up his possessions and the savings he had earned from singing for the toffs, and travelled alone to Copenhagen to, as the fairy tale cliché has it, seek his fortune.

We'll leave his life story there for now. I'll tell you this though (and I hope it doesn't spoil things too much), but it never really had a happy ending.

For starters he was, as I have said, no oil painting. He was unusually tall – six feet one, or 185 cm – at a time when the average was 166 cms. Massive clown's feet, equivalent to a size 14; a vast expanse of forehead; over-inflated lips, plus of course the biggest hooter since Cyrano completed what was a uniquely unprepossessing physical specimen.

One friend likened him to a giraffe; another, the Swedish writer Carl Dahlgren, wrote after his death: 'I always called him the Crane, for I have never seen any human being more akin in appearance to a crane than him. Imagine a tall person . . . with long, thin legs and a long, thin neck on top of which a head has been placed like a knob; imagine this figure with a stooping, protruding back and in his gait never walking but hopping along almost like a monkey, or like a tripping crane; and finally, imagine his long arms hanging down like a couple of straps along his sides, and an ugly face . . . big lips, light blue eyes, dark hair and long teeth, like tusks.'

He was also pathologically ambitious, which usually ends in tears. He craved fame and recognition with every fibre of his being. 'My soul yearns to be recognised like a thirsty man for water!' he once wrote in his youth. But if the reviews were negative, as they often were in Denmark, his spirits nosedived as if a kamikaze pilot had grabbed the controls.

On one famous occasion, while staying with Charles Dickens at his house in Kent, Andersen had received news of a bad review back home in Copenhagen. His response was to throw himself face down on the front lawn and blub hysterically. The reaction was out of all proportion to the criticism and showed little awareness of appropriate house guest behaviour. It was childish, hypersensitive, attention seeking, needy and theatrical. What kind of a grown man would behave in this way?

Well, it wasn't easy to admit this to myself at first, but I suppose that were my wife and family to read this, they would right now be exchanging knowing glances. It is true, I do tend to react to criticism fairly badly and though I have yet to hurl myself onto the lawn of a leading novelist and make like a garden sprinkler, I am afraid I do sometimes lack a sense of proportion about things, particularly where criticism is concerned. I also – and it is not without some embarrassment that I admit this – cut out and keep *every single article* that ever appears with my name on it, whether it is in a national newspaper, a parish newsletter, or, as once happened, *Vogue South Korea* (not easy to get hold of, that one). I still have my cycling proficiency certificate: it's framed.

I was beginning to sense that – revolutionary literary talent, and giraffe legs aside – I had more in common with the architect of my exile than I might initially care to admit. And though we do part company temporarily where Andersen's rumoured bisexuality is concerned (although, who knows, maybe I just haven't found the right man yet) the similarities kept on coming.

His neuroses were legion. He appears to have been the prototype drama queen. This was a man who slept with a note beside him that read 'I only appear to be dead' to prevent someone accidentally burying him, and travelled with a nine-metre length of rope in case he got trapped in a building on fire. 'Trifles, such as whether he had paid too much or too little for a tram ticket or for some stamps at a local post office, could worry him for days,' wrote Elias Bredsdorff. 'An evening at the theatre could be ruined at the thought that he might have forgotten to put out the light in his apartment or lock the front door.'

He was also a dedicated hypochondriac. On one occasion, for example, he became convinced he had swallowed a pin while at dinner, as his friend, William Bloch, recounted: 'That evening and the following day he was very worried about the conse-quences. His anxiety was so pronounced that it had completely removed his fear that a little spot above one of his eyebrows might grow into a large excrescence which would cover the eye, which in turn made him forget that he might possibly rupture himself because I had touched his stomach lightly with my walking stick, which again made him abandon the thought of having hyrdarthrosis of the knee, something he was concerned about when he arrived.'

But then again, who among us hasn't mistakenly troubled our doctor with an ailment – say, a suspected brain tumour – and then spent months pestering him with repeated, increasingly hysterical visits, before, eventually, persuading him to refer them to a specialist for a brain scan and when that showed nothing, taking blood tests and stool samples to send to a laboratory in Geneva, before someone finally pointed out to me, I mean *them*, that they were perhaps sitting a little too close to their computer screen and maybe should get my eyes looked at? I mean, *one's* eyes . . .

Less excusable was Andersen's incorrigible toadying. He had a remarkable gift, a genius even, for making friends in high places and grovelled before, and often befriended, an impres-sive tally of European monarchs, crown princes, dukes, counts and lords. The English novelist Mary Russell Mitford was not alone in being 'completely disgusted' by Andersen's social mountaineering. '[He] uses fame merely as a key to open drawing-room doors, a ladder to climb into high places,' she snorted.

In short, Hans Christian Andersen was the neurotic Princess, the vainglorious Dung Beetle (who, snubbed at the royal court, sets off in search of honour elsewhere), the lovelorn Little Mermaid and the Ugly Duckling rolled into one. As one critic put it, 'He made more self-portraits than Rembrandt.' But, of course, we should be eternally grateful that the man was such a monumental mess, as it is precisely these personal conflicts, his social and sexual alienation, his doubts, resentments and deep, deep unhappiness, that give his stories their distinctive, troubling, challenging edge.

If he hadn't spent his life in restless pursuit of glory, the Fir Tree would have been content to stay in the quiet forest instead of yearning for the bright lights of the city; if he hadn't been such a neurotic, the Princess would have slept soundly; if he had not been troubled by a deep seated nihilism 'The Shadow' would have been just another doppelganger farce; if he hadn't felt such an outsider, we would never have had 'The Ugly Duckling'; and if he hadn't himself wrestled with a sexual duality and known countless unrequited loves then he could never have written 'The Snowman'.

'The Little Mermaid' would have been an everyday tale of boy-meets-fish.

Andersen first arrived in Copenhagen on Monday, 5 September 1819, a day so auspicious for him that he celebrated it as a second birthday for the rest of his life. The city was in the midst of its last pogrom. In his naivety Andersen simply assumed the uproar was the norm.

He couldn't afford the ticket to the centre of Copenhagen, and so was dumped unceremoniously a few miles out of town, walking the rest of the way.

His first stop was the Kongelige Teater (the Royal Theatre)

on Kongens Nytorv, which would become the centre of his world, the scene of some of his greatest triumphs as well as his most humiliating professional disasters. While standing staring up at the walls, he was approached by a ticket tout and gladly accepted what he thought was a free ticket. 'Where would you like to sit?' asked the tout. 'Oh, anywhere!' replied the grateful boy, at which point the tout lost his temper and snatched the ticket back.

He immediately set to work knocking on the doors of the city's artistic elite and 'bustling' into their front rooms to launch into a song or a dance before they had a chance to turn him away. As improbable as this sounds now, initially he planned to become a dancer and in his autobiography he describes the first of these guerrilla auditions, for Madame Schall, the ballerina: 'I confessed to her my heartfelt inclination for the theatre; and upon her asking me what characters I thought I could represent, I replied Cinderella . . . In the meantime I asked her permission to take off my boots, otherwise I was not light enough for this character; and then taking up my broad hat for a tambourine, I began to dance and sing . . . My strange gestures and my great activity caused the lady to think me out of my mind, and she lost no time in getting rid of me.'

He tried the same thing at the home of Thiele – the collector of Danish folk tales. Thiele describes looking up from his work to see 'an upstart boy with quite peculiar looks standing by the door with a deeply theatrical bow towards the floor. His cap he had already thrown off by the door, and when that lanky figure in a worn-out grey coat whose sleeves did not reach his emaciated wrists rose, I saw a pair of small, Chinese eyes, that needed a chirurgical [surgical] operation, in order to get a clear view from behind a large, protruding nose . . . in short a surprising character, who became even more surprising when he, taking a few steps forwards and repeating his bow, began to speak in a pathetic way: "May I have the honour to express my feelings for the theatre in a poem I have written myself?" In my astonish-

ment I did not even start to move before he was in the middle
of the declamation.' (Around this time Andersen was nicknamed
the Little Declamator.)

Unable to interrupt him in full theatrical flow, Thiele was
forced to sit and listen until Andersen finally finished, gave several
theatrical bows, grabbed his cap and disappeared back down the
stairs.

He received a stinging rejection from the Royal Theatre: 'When
the supplicant presented himself before the board about nine
months ago with a wish to be employed in the Theatre, he was
found, after having been tested, to lack both the talent and the
appearance necessary for the stage . . .' Desperate for money –
by this time his trousers hung well short of the tops of his shoes
and he was skeletally thin – he was forced to find work as an
apprentice cabinet-maker, but his colleagues ribbed him mercilessly just as they had in his home town. In Odense, on one
occasion, his co-workers in a factory had pulled his trousers down
to make sure he wasn't a girl. He wasn't about to let the same
thing happen to him in Copenhagen: 'I took the resolute determination not to remain a single day longer in the workshop. I
went to the master therefore, and told him that I could not stand
it; he tried to console me, but in vain: I was too much affected,
and hastened away.'

But then, slowly, his luck began to change.

The next door he knocked on was that of the director of the
Academy of Music, an Italian called Siboni. By chance, his dinner
guests that evening included a renowned composer and a poet,
who were both so amused by Andersen's histrionics – he burst
into tears at the end of his recital – that they agreed to help
establish a small fund to assist in his education. Siboni pledged
singing lessons. All was going swimmingly until Andersen's voice
broke shortly after, and he was again thrown out into the world
with advice to learn a trade ringing in his ears.

Like the most hapless of *Pop Idol* contestants, Andersen was
rejected and mocked, humiliated and driven to the brink of

starvation by Copenhagen's artistic establishment over and over
again. He found numerous supporters, but invariably betrayed
their faith in him through his own flightiness. With one last,
desperate roll of the dice, he asked a new acquaintance, the physicist H.C. Ørsted – who discovered electromagnetism – for help.
Ørsted suggested Andersen apply to Jonas Collin (pronounced
Colleen), the administrator of a royal fund for artists and a socially
progressive philanthropist.

A meeting was arranged with the man who was to become,
in Andersen's words, 'a second father', though initial impressions
did little to encourage the young ingénue: 'His conversation was
grave and in few words. I went away without expecting any
sympathy from this man . . . I regarded him rather as an enemy
than a protector.'

But, like a gruff, grey fairy godmother – Henry Higgins to
Andersen's Eliza Doolittle – Collin arranged for an annual royal
stipend that would allow Andersen to attend a grammar school
in the town of Slagelse, fifty-seven miles west of Copenhagen.
Here he would benefit from the same education as the boys of
the Danish upper classes – being drilled in classical history, Latin
and maths as well, it was hoped, as being shaped into a useful
member of society.

Three years after arriving in Copenhagen – three years of
desperate self-promotion and bruising setbacks including the
rejection of several plays submitted to the Royal Theatre and, in
1822, a self-published work, *Youthful Attempts* (of which only 50
copies were sold) – he had secured his short-term future and
found a surrogate family into whose lives he would wangle and
weave his fate.

Things were hardly plain sailing thereafter though. His new
headmaster was the fat, failed poet Simon Meisling. This tyrant
despised Andersen's airy-fairy ways, was jealous of his talent and
did everything to make his school years a misery. He branded
the poetry Andersen had begun to write 'sentimental, idle trash'
and told him he was 'a stupid boy, who'll never be any good'.

Andersen later recalled this period of his life in *The True Story of My Life*, the emotions still raw: 'The rector, who took a peculiar delight in turning everything to ridicule, did not, of course, make an exception in my case . . . I was as if paralysed with anxiety when he entered the room . . . To me he stood there as a divinity. I believed unconditionally every word he spoke.' In return Meisling bullied, pilloried and ridiculed the royally sponsored boy, as did the other students.

Andersen, now seventeen, had found himself in a class with a group of privileged eleven- and twelve-year-olds. They immediately scented a vulnerable quarry ('". . . he's too big and queer!" said the duck who had bitten him. "So he has to be pushed around."' – 'The Ugly Duckling'). It was, he wrote, 'the darkest, the most unhappy time in my life'. He began writing a diary and, not for the last time in it, he implored God to take his life.

When Meisling moved jobs to a school in Helsingør he somehow persuaded the cash cow Andersen to follow with a few unexpected kindnesses. The town – Hamlet's Elsinore – is situated at the point closest to Sweden, at the mouth of the Oresund Strait, and at that time it was a busy port visited by ships from around the world. It gave Andersen his first real taste of the exotic: 'What traffic! What liveliness . . . here some fat Dutchmen speak their hollow language, there I hear mellifluous Italian, further down coal is being unloaded from an English brig so that I think I can almost smell London . . . and I felt inexpressibly happy.'

This happiness was short lived as Meisling returned to his old, bullying ways. Eventually Collin intervened and removed Andersen from the school. Meisling's last words to the young boy were to tell him that his verses 'would grow mouldy on the floor of the bookseller's shop and that I myself should end my days in a mad-house'.

(In *The True Story of My Life*, Andersen claims to have met Meisling – though he never actually names him in the book – years later, just after his first novel had been published: 'He offered me his hand in a conciliatory manner, and said that he had erred respecting me, and had treated me wrong.' But up until his death Andersen was still recording nightmares about Meisling in his journal.)

By 1827 he was back in Copenhagen and worming his way into the Collin family. He dined with Jonas, his wife and their five children – Ingeborg, Gottlieb, Edvard, Louise and Theodor – once a week and came to think of them as the closest thing he had to a family. Initially he and Ingeborg became friends – she teased him and he loved the attention – but it was Edvard, three years younger than he, to whom Andersen would attach himself most strongly, eventually falling in love.

He took private lessons with a teacher who lived on the outskirts of the city. It was a long walk each day from his lodgings to the island of Amager (a bleak, windswept island, today home to Copenhagen airport), but it bore fruit in the form of his first piece of comic fantasy writing: *A Journey on Foot from Holmens Canal to the Eastern Part of Amager in the years 1828–1829* – the joke being that Andersen's story was about a walk he took over the course of New Year's night 1828–1829.

Two things are worth noting of this first, dazzlingly inventive novel: one is its ambition, he didn't play safe with it and indeed, it features elements, such as talking inanimate objects – in this instance a tower that can recite passages from *Hamlet* – that would prove revolutionary in his fairy tales (the final chapter consists only of exclamation marks and dashes); the second is that this first significant piece of writing was also a kind of travel piece.

The story was rejected by Copenhagen's publishers, so Andersen published the pamphlet himself. To his great delight, the initial print run sold out. The publisher Reitzel took up the option on the second edition, which also sold out. 'Everybody read my book,' Andersen recalled. 'I heard nothing but praise; I was a student – I had attained the highest goal of my wishes. I was in a whirl of joy.' Andersen's first theatrical success, *Love at Nikolai Tower*, was another strikingly modern piece in which the

audience voted via whistles or hisses to decide the outcome. It
was staged to some acclaim at his hallowed Royal Theatre.

While other successful debutante playwrights might spend their
box office receipts on wine and women, the first thing Andersen
did with all his newly accumulated wealth was to travel. In May
1830 he took off to Jylland, using the grand country homes of
Denmark's wealthiest families as stepping stones throughout the
journey, something he would continue to do during a lifetime
of travelling. In one town he was delighted to have his arrival
reported by the local newspaper (clearly a quiet day for cats stuck
in trees). A poem he had published while at school – 'The Dying
Child' – and *A Journey on Foot* had made him famous.

Crucially, this first journey brought him the two things he
desired most in life: public recognition and love. Well, a brief
infatuation at least.

The object was the twenty-four-year-old Riborg Voigt, the
dark-haired sister of a school friend from Copenhagen. She lived
in the small town of Faaborg, thirty miles south of Odense.

Faaborg is Lissen's home town and I know it well. The Voigts'
house, with its orange stucco, half-timbered walls, still stands close
to the high street, and in the yard to the rear is a statue inspired
by one of Andersen's short stories – 'The Top and the Ball'.

'The Top and the Ball' – in which a high-class ball spurns the
advances of a low-born top, only for the ball to end up in the
gutter and the top a much-loved toy – was inspired by Voigt's
rejection of Andersen and the bitterness that lingered when he
met her years later as a middle-aged mother. 'When the sweet-
heart has been lying in the drainpipe oozing water for five years
you can never recognize her again!' the story concludes.

In April 1831, his ego severely bruised, Andersen decided to
go travelling again, this time to Northern Germany. It was the
first time that he used travel as an escape from his unhappiness,
but not the last. His world, he wrote, 'expanded so astonishingly'
during this visit. He had found a new love, one he could rely
on to remain constant: 'Oh, to travel, to travel . . . I feel as if the

world is my home, and I shall, I must, frolic in this home!' he wrote at the time.

And frolic he would.

His first travel memoir *Skyggebilleder* (*Shadow Pictures*) resulted from the German holiday. Blending reportage with biography and short stories, it sparkles with energy and freshness. It also contains his first, brief mention of a mermaid legend but, more importantly, it was the prototype for a far more ambitious travel book that he was to write a decade later.

And this is where things started to get particularly interesting for me. From this moment on Hans Christian Andersen essentially became a nomad – homeless, rootless, without a family – a social exile from his own class but never accepted into the higher echelons. With little to anchor him in Denmark, and much to spur him to leave, he turned to travel.

You could argue that his momentous journey from Odense to Copenhagen was the first sign of the wanderlust that came to characterise his adult life, but it was really after those first trips to Jutland, Germany and Italy that he became increasingly obsessed by the promise of travel, the release of escape. Between the ages of twenty-five and sixty-eight, he visited most of the countries of mainland Europe and Scandinavia – many of them several times – and got as far as setting foot on African and Asian soil. He travelled abroad twenty-nine times, spending a total of nine years outside Denmark; he was even planning a trip just two weeks before his death, despite being barely able to walk.

When he wasn't off on one of his regular foreign trips – with his portmanteau, trunk, hat box, carpet bag, walking stick, umbrella, scrapbook, shoe tree, plus of course the nine metres of emergency rope, his own pillowcase (actually, not a bad tip, that . . .), banknotes sewn into the lining of his clothes and, later in life, miniature replicas of all his orders and decorations – he was invariably planning the itinerary and budget for the next one right down to the amount he would be giving in tips. Even when he was at home in Denmark, he was more often than not to be found staying with his aristocratic friends in their country retreats rather than living in his rented rooms. He never owned his own house, and only bought his first piece of furniture – a bed – in 1866, when he was sixty-one (and only then after having been pressurised into it by a friend). 'It terrifies me,' he wrote at the time, 'I am being weighed down with furniture . . .'

Andersen assumed everyone felt this way: 'Oh travel, travel! that is the happiest fate! That is why we all travel . . . even the dead in their silent graves fly with the earth around the sun. Yes, to travel is an obsession of the whole universe . . .' Of course he indulged his urge rather more than most. Even dinner was a peripatetic affair, as he recorded in a letter to one of his best friends, Henriette Hanck, in 1838: 'My dinners are as follows: Mondays at Mrs Bügel's, where the dinner is always as if for a big party; Tuesdays at the Collins' where the eldest son and his wife also dine on that day, and therefore we get something special; Wednesdays at the Ørsteds', who always invite their guests on that day; Thursdays again at Mrs Bügel's; Fridays at the Wulffs', where Weyse always comes on the same day and plays his fantasies on the piano after dinner; Saturday is my day off, then I dine wherever I happen to be invited, or at Ferrini's [a restaurant]; Sundays at Mrs Læssø's, or in the students' union . . .'

'To travel is to live' is one of Andersen's most famous and enduring quotations, at least in Denmark where they know all about his travels, but I knew nothing of all this until I started reading about him and it both puzzled and intrigued me. Considering how debilitating his everyday neuroses were – even at home where the food was safe and he understood the language he was aquiver with anxiety most of the time – it was hard to imagine a *less* likely transcontinental nomad than Andersen. I kept asking myself how this towering neurotic, a man who was afraid of his own shadow, managed to muster the courage to cross the road, let alone a dangerous continent in the midst of turbulent, revolutionary times. And, more to the point, *why*?

Travelling in Europe in the mid-nineteenth century was a

perilous, arduous affair – involving bone-shaking, cramped, cold, horse-drawn diligences and unsurfaced roads, not to mention the constant threat of robbery and the very real risk of contracting a whole host of fatal diseases. In Italy and Germany in particular, such was the splintered nature of their myriad kingdoms and provinces that borders, tolls and passports made travel an infuriatingly complex affair – which must have been especially troubling for a man who would often lay awake the night before a foreign trip with what he called his 'passport angst'.

Andersen's knowledge of foreign languages was shaky at best; his German was okay, but his Italian was virtually non-existent, and both his English and French were largely unfathomable for natives (Dickens asked him to speak Danish, which he claimed to understand better than Andersen's mangled Danglish).

Though several Danish painters of the time knew Europe well, most of his fellow writers, like the playwright Johan Ludvig Heiberg, the poet B.S. Ingemann and the philosopher Søren Kierkegaard, were content to stay at home and wallow in their Danishness. As Andersen wrote in his notebook – yet another receptacle for his reflections, ideas, jokes and observations – the Danish were not the most outward looking of peoples: 'No nation has more prejudice, I think, than the Danes . . . We strike our bosoms and say, "I thank you God, that I am not like the others!" We consider ourselves so modest, so open-hearted! It has become a saying among us: We are the good people. But to deride and sneer, to watch for the weak points in our neighbours, that is our evil nature. And that I have it and say so, proves that I am Danish.'

At that point, nothing was guaranteed to endear Andersen to me more than learning that the Danes got up his nose too, but this unexpected hostility is also a significant clue to Andersen's lust for travel. Though he is, effectively, the Danish national poet – their most famous export, the writer of one of their most beloved national hymns, 'I Danmark er Jeg Født' ('I was born in Denmark'), and the man who, in a 2004 Danish newspaper poll that gave new meaning to the term 'foregone conclusion', was voted the all time 'Greatest Dane' – his feelings about his home country were decidedly mixed.

Of course, he had far greater reason to resent Denmark than me, with my whinnying about the weather and their excessive use of marzipan, but I was immediately taken by his solution. 'If you can't beat them, leave them' seems to have been Andersen's motto. To escape what he saw as the unjust persecution of the Danish critics, as well as innumerable disastrous love affairs, professional failures and the awful weather, he turned to travel.

In February 1840 Andersen's play *The Mulatto* – an inter-racial love story that would challenge a few taboos even today – debuted to almost universal acclaim. His joy at a rare critical success was only partly undermined when another critic realised that Andersen had pinched the story from a French drama; his was not the 'original romantic drama' he claimed it to be in the programme notes. It was just the stick the Copenhagen literati – headed by Ludvig Heiberg, a former champion of Andersen's writing – were looking for to beat him with. Andersen felt these criticisms keenly and they fuelled his already raging persecution complex. In part to answer the criticism of plagiarism he hurriedly dashed off a second, markedly inferior work – *The Moorish Girl* – that was entirely his own. He had written the play with one actress specifically in mind: Heiberg's wife, Johanne Luise, the most famous actress in Denmark at the time. But she rejected it and Andersen was forced to give the role to someone else, unwisely bad-mouthing the Heibergs to anyone who would listen.

'I was conscious of being overlooked and badly treated all the time,' Andersen later remembered. 'I felt hurt, a combination of unpleasant circumstances occurred: I felt ill at ease at home, was half sick – was unable to stand this any longer – and I left my play to its fate; in a suffering and melancholy mood I hastened to go away.'

What with his trouble at the theatre and his various romantic misadventures leading up to that point (one object of his desire, Jonas Collins' daughter Louise, was about to be married) life in Copenhagen had again become unbearable for this highly strung, thin-skinned thirty-four-year-old. So he did what he always did in such circumstances. Without waiting to see how *The Moorish Girl* fared and, so, not even sure if he would have enough money to complete his journey (this time he had the more ambitious goal of the Orient in his sights) he left, or, as he put it, 'quitted my country in distress'.

In October he embarked on what would turn out to be the longest, most challenging, and exciting journey of his life, travelling south through Germany on one of the first steam railways, then by carriage to Florence, Rome and Naples, from where he took a steam boat to Malta, Greece and Turkey before returning home up the Danube, via Hungary, Austria, Prague and Germany. It was a route fraught with danger which was to include some genuinely uncharted territories: a real test of his endurance. It was as if Enid Blyton had taken it upon herself to canoe up the Zambezi.

He wrote about this fantastical adventure through pre-revolutionary Europe in an epic travel memoir, *En Digters Bazar* (*A Poet's Bazaar*), partly inspired by the French writer Lamartine's *Souvenirs d'un voyage en Orient*, published six years earlier.

When I first heard of this book I knew I had to get hold of a copy, and, having drawn a blank in Copenhagen's book shops, found one on sale via the Internet at a bookshop in New Jersey. It was the 1871 New York edition published by Hurd and Houghton, translated – unfortunately – by Mary Howitt.

It arrived a few days later with a sweet note saying: 'Glad to be returning this to its rightful home, Denmark!' I opened the green, hardback cover to see a library form declaring it the property of Hornell Library ('for every day the book is retained beyond two weeks, the holder will be fined two cents' – the last date stamp was September 1975). Ignoring this (come get me, bounty hunters!) I opened it, took a deep breath of its evocative dry-damp old book smell, and began to read. I don't think I looked up until I had turned the final page.

Blending reportage, memoir, philosophy, the odd theatre review and pieces of fantastical fiction *A Poet's Bazaar* is nothing less than a lost classic of travel writing. It sparkles with vivid observations, genuinely funny anecdotes, stories and an exotic cast of real-life characters – including famous composers like Liszt and Mendelssohn; monarchs and ambassadors; as well as pashas, priests, prostitutes, Persians and princes (and even some people who don't begin with 'p', like whirling dervishes and lackadaisical leech salesmen).

Unlike his often quite sub-standard plays and rambling, melo-dramatic novels (I've read them so you don't have to), it was immediately clear to me that travel writing was a facet of Andersen's literary talent that had been woefully neglected by the non-Danish-speaking world. *A Poet's Bazaar* was every bit as original and entertaining as his fairy tales. What's more, it was all true. (Or mostly true, as I was to discover.)

Later that night in bed, I excitedly told Lissen what I had discovered. For her, 'Hans Christian Andersen Actually Quite Good: Shock' was hardly a front pager, of course, but she seemed pleased that I was showing an appreciation for Danish culture at last, instead of just doing bad impressions of their newsreaders. What I didn't mention was that an escape plan was already fermenting in my mind.

Literally hundreds of books have been written about Andersen. His life and work have been combed more finely than Donald Trump's hair but so many questions remain unanswered. It seemed to me that this insatiable urge to travel lay at the heart of the many paradoxes and conundrums of Andersen the man – his neuroses, his sexuality and his myriad other demons – yet, repeatedly in the books I read about him, I found that his travel writing was either given no more than a cursory glance or glossed over entirely. There had been a couple of academic essays on specific elements of his journeys, but little else.

As far as I could make out no one had ever retraced any of his journeys and having read *A Poet's Bazaar* I became gripped, *consumed*, by the notion that if I were to do so, it might just bring me a little bit closer to this perplexing, captivating man. If I could marshal the wealth of detail that exists from this brief but, I believe, pivotal eight months of his life – using his diaries, letters, almanac and autobiographies, much of which has only ever been published in Danish – perhaps I could throw new light on his life and work.

In short, by undertaking this journey – by seeing the things he saw, standing in the places he stood, meeting for myself the peoples he described – maybe I could engage with one of the greatest literary innovators and most extraordinary men of the Victorian era in a way no one had ever done before.

I decided there and then that I would mark the two hundredth anniversary of his birth in 2005 by travelling by land and sea from Copenhagen to Hamburg, Leipzig, Rome, Naples, Malta, Athens, Istanbul, Budapest, Vienna, Prague, Dresden and home. If all else failed, I might at least meet a few interesting people, see places I had never seen before and enjoy a better quality of pastry.

Lissen seemed surprisingly enthusiastic about me embarking on a journey far from home lasting an indeterminate period of time.

Chapter Two

GERMANY

And that was how I found myself, a few weeks later, perched self-consciously on the edge of my chair like a vicar at a swingers' party, in a small, low-ceilinged, candle-lit room on the first floor of a Hamburg brothel, chatting with a nice woman called Sandra.

Prostitutes are something of an unknown quantity for me but they figured with surprising frequency in Andersen's travels, a discovery that seemed both significant and not a little troubling (a bit like finding a gimp costume in the Archbishop of Canterbury's wardrobe). Hamburg was just one of many foreign cities in which he had encountered women of easy virtue and, as it was my first stop and boasts one of the most famous red-light districts in the world, I set about tracking down a 'research assistant'. I had a few questions I wanted to ask Sandra that I thought might help get the sticky topic of Andersen's murky and dissembled sexuality out of the way early on. Theories abound about him – that he was homosexual or quite possibly bisexual, while Andersen himself claimed that he remained a virgin till his death, and I was determined to find some answers. I had no idea what to expect of a professional sex worker, or how she might react to my line of enquiry but, surely, if Andersen could brave a brothel, as he actually did later in life, so could I.

That first early February day of my trans-European footstepping had begun in the rather more salubrious surroundings of Copenhagen central station. The immaculately clean concourse was already bustling at 6 a.m., as I sat on a bench, my stomach on spin cycle with my usual pre-travel butterflies.

Like Andersen – who was invariably ready and waiting, bags packed and rope coiled hours before departure time – I tend to assume that all manner of unlikely events will conspire to prevent me catching my train, boat or plane, and set out hours earlier than necessary, patting my pockets every few minutes to check that my passport and tickets haven't somehow leaped out and scampered down a gutter. This drives Lissen crazy. She loves the thrill of a last-minute dash without a single wasted moment, and will contrive to find a number of urgent tasks to do at precisely the point that I have decided we should leave in case we encounter some unexpected flash flooding. (I once found her re-arranging my sock drawer ten minutes before we were due at a party on the other side of town, for instance, and the time we arrived at Gatwick instead of Heathrow, where our flight was actually departing from, and had to race around the M25 with seconds to spare was, I swear, one of the high points of her life.)

So there I sat, fifty minutes early, watching Copenhagen's commuters going through their mechanical motions, as I checked my passport for the twentieth time.

This being a characteristically deep-frozen, Danish winter's morning, there was a high fur coat and ski boot count. Not for the first time I was struck by the extraordinary wealth-in-depth of this classless society. When Andersen was born, Odense was known as the 'beggar city', on account of its high proportion of inhabitants living below the poverty line, while the bourgeoisie were almost exclusively confined to Copenhagen. These days, Denmark officially has the least disparity between rich and poor in Europe, which has its good and bad sides. On the plus side, people swanking about in Rolls-Royces and top hats and getting up everyone's noses is rare; crime is low and everyone – whether they be lawyer or bin man or, as most Danes seem to be, teacher – rides a bike (though not the queen, this isn't *Holland*). If equality at any cost is what you are after, this is the country for you.

On the down side, everyone wears the same clothes, eats the

same food, drives the same type of car and lives in the same kind of house, which can make it a rather somnolent place if, say, you have moved from London. If variety is the spice of life, Denmark is an extra mild chicken korma.

The Danes passing my bench all seemed to be sleep-walking, avoiding bumping into each other presumably via bat-like sonar. As with commuters the world over they looked anxious and preoccupied and were text messaging as if their very lives depended on it. A wave of liberation swept over me as I thought about the journey ahead. If all went well, my 'necessaries were embarked' (as local boy Laertes once memorably declared) on what would be the longest overland journey of my life, through twelve countries, and more than twenty cities – many of which I had never set foot in before.

Andersen had left Copenhagen on 31 October 1840, aboard the steamship *Christian VIII*. At the quayside his beloved Edvard Collin, the long-term unrequited object of his desires, planted a kiss on his mouth: 'Oh, it was as if my heart would burst!' Andersen wrote in his diary. But as soon as he arrived in Kiel, having endured a stormy, twenty-four-hour journey by steamship, together with a troupe of homeward-bound Spanish dancers who had recently taken Copenhagen by storm, Andersen had written a plaintive letter to Edvard's father Jonas expressing his deep-seated discontent. 'It is just as well I'm leaving, my soul is unwell,' he wrote. 'Even to those dearest to one, one dare not express that which weighs heaviest in one's mind.' Was he writing about his love for Edvard, perhaps?

Unfortunately, as I was to learn the hard way later in my journey, virtually all of the sea routes that existed on Andersen's journey – routes that in those days were crucial for transporting goods and passengers with the railways still at the novelty-ride phase – no longer exist, having been rendered obsolete by the jet engine. For an obsessive footstepper this was deeply discouraging. The closest I could come to replicating this first leg of his journey was to take the train south from Copenhagen to the Danish island of

Lolland. There was, however, some consolation in the fact that at Lolland the train would, I was told (but still couldn't quite believe), actually drive *onto the ferry* to Puttgarden, in northern Germany.

When the ticket clerk had told me this the previous day I had emitted a squeak of delight and she had looked at me as if weighing up whether or not to summon help. The whole concept of a train driving onto a boat was very exciting indeed.

For an Englishman, Danish trains are inconceivably luxurious and efficient and I eagerly clambered up into the toasty warm compartment of the 06.15 train from Copenhagen to Hamburg. There were seats! They were free of mysterious brown stains, and they reclined! There was no tumbleweed rolling down the aisles! It was almost too much to take in. Having found my seat, facing forwards by the window – Andersen's preference – I commenced the first of many wrestling bouts with my large rucksack and coat, looking like a tortoise fighting a wasp while demonstrating the latest dance craze.

As we chugged through the city's dispiriting southern suburbs – where the Danes corral their African and Asian immigrants, spoon-feeding them colossal social welfare payments in the hope that they will just stay there and be quiet – I looked out of the window at the icy blue sky. On clear days such as this, the sky always seems to me somehow *higher* in Scandinavia. It was really rather breathtaking but I suspect I only appreciated it because I was leaving.

My first destination, like Andersen's, was Breitenburg Castle on Lünenburg Heath, Holstein. In 1840 this was still part of Denmark and the house was the hereditary home of Count Conrad von Rantzau-Breitenburg. The count, who was prime minister of Denmark at the time, took a keen interest in the arts, funding several Danish artists, composers and writers, and he was one of Andersen's earlier social-climbing conquests. Never one to pass up a chance to schmooze nobility, Andersen decided to pay the Count a courtesy call on his way south.

'He belonged to that class of men who immediately inspire you with confidence,' Andersen wrote of his first encounter with the Count. 'He besought me to visit him, and frankly asked me whether there were no means by which he could be of use to me. I hinted how oppressive it was to be forced to write in order to live . . . He pressed my hand in a friendly manner, and promised to be an efficient friend.'

The castle, which dates from the twelfth century, is still the Rantzau family home and is not open to the public, but I had phoned earlier in the week to see if it might be possible to take a look round the grounds. Okay, okay, I admit it, I wanted a bit of the toff action myself, but I had still been a little taken aback when a descendant of Count Conrad, Count, or *Braedo* zu Rantzau-Breitenburg, to give him his proper title, had answered the phone himself. We chatted about Andersen and my project and he invited me to come and have a look around the house. He wouldn't be there, he'd told me, because he was off doing something horsey but his housekeeper, a Mrs Schmidt, would show me around. I tried not to take offence.

Soulless suburbs gave way to fresh-tilled, perma-frosted fields that undulated gently, like endless scoops of chocolate-chip ice cream. Denmark is still mostly farmland, with a few population hotspots like Århus on the gnarled phallus known as the Jylland (Jutland) peninsula; Andersen's birthplace, Odense, on the island of Fyn; and Copenhagen, on the eastern island of Sjælland (Zealand). Denmark's fertility was a major reason why the Germans invaded in 1940 (it was nicknamed Germany's larder), and today farming is still a mainstay of the economy, with pigs, famously, a speciality (although, Andersen must have been about the only Dane not to eat pork – he was terrified of catching trichinae). Pigs are said to outnumber Danes, but, spookily, you never, *ever* see any. The only living thing I spotted from the train was a lone horse standing mournfully, gazing into the middle distance which, it seems to me, is how horses spend almost all of their time.

As the train *shwooshed* silkily onwards I could see wood smoke spiralling from the frosted white roofs of isolated farmhouses. Where low fields by the railway line had flooded, the water was now frozen. It was an 'Ice Maiden' landscape.

I thought of the patterns that Andersen recalled forming on the frozen window panes of his childhood home, patterns that had foretold the passing of his father when Hans Christian was just eleven years old. The winter before, his father had pointed out a shape on the window that looked like a woman with outstretched arms: '"She is coming to fetch me," he said in jest. And now, when he lay dead on the bed, my mother remembered this, and it occupied my thoughts also,' he wrote in his autobiography.

Occasionally, a church whizzed past, whitewashed, with a crenulated gable, a simple tower and built on a slight mound, as most are in Denmark. Elsewhere the monotony was enlivened by a few clusters of woodland and the odd row of gargantuan wind power generators, among the thousands erected all over these flat, windswept isles to generate clean electricity. (Once, while researching an article on the environment, I had asked the spokesman for the Danish Environment Ministry why that year's wind-sourced electricity production had been down on the previous year's: 'It was a bad year for wind,' he'd told me, which, to this day, makes me laugh, despite the fact that it obviously means we are all doomed when the oil runs out.)

Aside from these futuristic power generators the Danish countryside must look pretty much as it did in Andersen's day. Actually, the windmills help make it a dead ringer for the place where the *Tellytubbies* live, though I have yet to see any gambolling intergalactic hermaphrodites with TV aerials on their heads (not while sober, at least).

We arrived at the port of Rødby where the train really did drive onto the ferry. In my excitement I regressed to around six years of age, pressing my face against the window – I even took a photograph.

The ferry crossing went without a ripple, unlike Andersen's journey. 'One sea after the other washed over the deck,' he writes in *A Poet's Bazaar*, 'once or twice the steamer seemed to stand still, as if bethinking itself whether it were not best to turn back. The decanters and plates, although they were lashed fast, trembled as if with fear or by instinct.'

Now, I have lived close to the Danish sea all the time I have been in Denmark – I can even see some of it from my living-room window. I have crossed it using boats and bridges at various times of the year and even, following intense peer-group pressure, swum in it without my pants on. But not once have I ever seen it storm-tossed as he describes here. In fact, rarely is it anything other than mill-pond smooth. Not that I am suggesting for a minute that Andersen would ever have exaggerated the reality to add spice to his narrative. But still . . .

At the first German stop, my carriage was joined by a bunch of young sailors, a mass of fuzzy bum fluff, acne and huge green duffel bags. Some wore their naval uniforms, with gold buttons and white hats. One of their number, a freckly ginger-haired boy with round glasses, sat opposite me and stared glumly out of the window. After a while the others began taunting him in girls' voices. They left at the next stop in a cloud of belches and potent aftershave.

My instinct was to tut loudly and roll my eyes at them (taking care that they didn't actually see this of course) but I had made a promise to myself to give Germany a break on this visit; to try to see it through Andersen's eyes, rather than as someone who has sat through – oh what is it now? – *three* penalty shoot-out humiliations in his lifetime.

Germany was Andersen's cultural fountain, its literature was a major influence on his work and the country became a second home for him after he began to be published there in the late 1820s. He claimed to feel more at home in many German towns than in Odense, maintaining that the critics were kinder to him there than in Denmark.

He always felt unappreciated in his homeland, and with good reason. The Danish critics, many of whom knew him personally and had witnessed his less appealing characteristics at first hand, were often scathing towards Andersen. What's more, in Germany he was able to mingle more easily with the higher echelons of society without being judged by the social baggage of his childhood. (The same was true in England where, so beyond the realms of class categorisation was this weird man-child who barely spoke a word of their language, that the upper classes were completely unable to pigeonhole him.) Indeed, in its latter stages, his auto-biography becomes a litany of meetings and friendships with German Grand Dukes, Emperors, Princes, Chancellors and Counts (including, memorably, the Countess Hahn-Hahn, so good they named her twice). At one point, so divided would Andersen's loyalties become between his home and its neighbouring land that he would become the focus of a kind of royal tug of love between the German and Danish monarchs, each intent on currying his favour during a time of tension between the two nations. And, as we will discover, Germany also provided Andersen with one of his most mutually rewarding love affairs: with one of its leading noblemen.

Breitenburg is a friendly, welcoming white stucco manor surrounded by a moat, trees and rhododendron bushes, and built on a slightly raised piece of ground, close to the river Stor (one of the flattest parts of Germany).

'The dishes smoked on the table, and the champagne exploded. Yes, it was certainly enchantment! I thought of the stormy sea, of the solitary heath, and felt that a man may, nevertheless, be at ease in this world,' Andersen writes of his arrival at the castle in *A Poet's Bazaar*.

The pungent odour of horses filled the air as I approached the imposing wooden front door and rang the bell. Mrs Schmidt turned out to be a very jolly lady in her thirties, dressed in a leopard-print top and jeans. She led me around the house, telling me some of its history as we went. Her English was better than my German, so we spoke English (which, cunningly implies that I speak some German, when the truth is my language skills make

Andersen look like James Joyce; I know only one German phrase, of limited use: '*Schnell, schnell, ich habe geburstag!*' – 'Quick, quick, it's my birthday!'). Breitenburg is still very much a family home, with muddy wellies by the door, wood-chip wallpaper on many of the walls and a broken-down TV in the hall.

Andersen spent three nights at Breitenburg, being fed and watered and wandering around the gardens lamenting the end of autumn. 'I have a beautiful room and a pleasant bedroom,' he writes in his diary. 'His Excellency took me into the chapel and above in a kind of banqueting hall with portraits of all his forebears . . . To dinner came the post master Herr Krogh and his three beautiful daughters, I sat beside the second eldest, she was very interesting . . . I read my *Moorish Girl* [his latest play] and told some of my fairy tales.' Unfortunately, Andersen's peace was shattered that night by the noise of the count's mad brother banging constantly on his door. 'Even when he dies you will still believe you hear his banging,' he complains to his diary.

Sadly, Mrs Schmidt did not know where Andersen had slept, and nor was there any tangible remnant of his visit. I did get to see the portrait gallery, where she pointed out the painting of Josiah Rantzau, rumoured to be the father of the French King Louis XIV. Josiah would seem to have been one of life's less fortunate characters, either that or he was pioneering some kind of radical weight-loss programme. By the end of his life he had a wooden leg and was missing his left forearm, an eye and an ear.

Near by was a portrait of the Countesses Amorne, who introduced the Christmas tree to Schleswig-Holstein. It was one such Breitenburg Christmas tree that is said to have inspired Andersen to write 'The Little Matchgirl' (although others claim it was a painting by J.T. Lundbye). On arriving at the manor for Christmas on another visit Andersen saw the lavishly decorated tree through a window from the frozen courtyard outside and imagined himself as an impoverished pre-pubescent, female matchseller, hallucinating as she slowly froze to death one Christmas Eve. As you do.

The matchgirl peers into the window of a grand house, where
the festivities are under way, and is tormented by the food, which,
in her weakened state, she imagines dancing before her. Finally
the spirit of her dead grandmother carries her to heaven. For all
its manipulative sentimentality, it was still a fairly damning attack
on the complacency of the middle classes of the period.

The Victorians loved a good child death scene and, like
Dickens, Andersen was a master at them, employing pathos with
a shameless skill. Mothers and their dying children were certainly
a preoccupation. He had lifelong recurring dreams about dying
children, including one in which a child died in his arms leaving
only its skin behind, and it is a recurring motif throughout his
work ('The Child in the Grave' and 'The Story of a Mother'
are two further examples).

Perhaps this obsession stems from the fact that one of his first
great successes came with the poem 'The Dying Child', written
in 1826 (against the wishes of the tyrannical Meisling), when he
was twenty-one.

Even today, I guarantee it will open the floodgates:

Mother, I'm so tired, I want to sleep now;
let me fall asleep and feel you near.
Please don't cry – there now, you'll promise, won't you?
On my face I felt your burning tear.
Here it's so cold, and winds outside are frightening
But in dreams – ah, that's what I like best:
I can see the darling angel children,
When I shut my sleepy eyes and rest.

Mother, look, the angel is here beside me!
Listen, too, how sweet the music grows.
See, his wings are both so white and lovely:
Surely it was God who gave him those.
Green and red and yellow floating round me,
They are flowers the angel came and spread.

Shall I, too, have wings while I'm alive, or –
Mother, is it only when I'm dead?

Why do you take hold of me so tightly,
Put your cheek to mine the way you do?
And your cheek is wet, but yet it's burning –
Mother, I shall always be with you . . .
Yes, but then you mustn't go on sighing;
When you cry I cry as well, you see,
I'm so tired – my eyes they won't stay open –
Mother – look – the angel's kissing me!

Even copying it out here, my bottom lip began to wobble and
it had pretty much the same effect on the rest of Europe. The
poem first appeared in a Copenhagen newspaper and was translated into German and French, enjoying lasting success through
most of the rest of the century. No one had thought of recording
a death from the child's perspective and it gave the poem a rare
emotional potency. Indeed one recent biographer has gone as
far as to describe the poem as an 'epochal text' on account of
its radical use of the child's perspective.

Mrs Schmidt's tour ended at the library, a magnificent, high-
ceilinged room lined, as is the custom, with books – 20,000 in
all. In the centre of the room was a hammer clavier once owned
by Mozart. Conrad had bought it direct from Mozart's widow,
Constanza, which you would think was good enough prove-
nance, but two experts had recently cast doubt on whether
Mozart ever played it. It seems that Constanza, who married a
Dane after the death of her first husband and moved to
Copenhagen, was possibly in the habit of selling counterfeit 'as
played by my Wolfie' pianos.

From Breitenburg Andersen sailed south on the River Elbe
towards Hamburg. One of his fellow passengers was a young
woman ('of what we call the lower class', he writes – hark at
the washerwoman's son!), who was carrying a child. She seemed

impatient and restless during the journey, and we soon find out why: she is on her way to meet her husband, returning from America. He rows out from his ship and the couple embrace.

A morose, lovelorn Andersen, perhaps thinking of the recent marriage of Louise Collin (after a seven-year engagement), looks on enviously: 'That was a kiss! That was the bouquet of a long year's sweet longing . . . the boat swung up and down, as if with joy – but we sailed away, and I looked on the flat and naked shores.'

. . . And I looked out on a flat and naked stomach. Sandra's.

There was a serious investigative motive behind my next stop – Hamburg's infamous (yet entirely legal) hooker street, Herbert Strasse, just off the Reeperbahn. I wanted to lance the boil of Andersen's sexuality, so that I could continue my journey focusing on higher-minded pursuits, like the socio-political movements of eastern Europe in the mid-nineteenth century, the influence of Renaissance art on Andersen's writing, and who makes the best cakes – Italians or Austrians.

I had a hunch Sandra might be able to shed some light on this (the sex thing, that is, I didn't ask about the cakes), but Andersen's sexual urges would turn out be a whole new can of tumescent worms – as if the lancing-a-boil image wasn't disturbing enough.

One thing is certain, travel liberated his libido. Something strange seemed to come over Andersen as soon as he began to head south; it was as if, away from prying eyes back home, he could open the door to his caged sexuality and let his urges fly free. Reading his diaries of these trips I lost track of the times he notes his 'sensuous' feelings and his 'feverish' nights, or describes the various attractive people he encounters – from muscle-bound oarsmen in Constantinople to a twenty-year-old monk with bare feet in Italy, to the pretty girls he flirts with from behind his mask during the carnival in Rome; he even notes a foxy nun he spots in church (and speaking as someone who was traumatised by these fearful creatures at school, my mind especially boggles at this. How randy must he have been *that* day?).

Travel gave Andersen the horn. For him Viagra was a ticket on a steam ship and a hotel reservation, and I believe this is one of the major explanations for his insatiable hunger for foreign lands.

Not only that, but, as I mentioned, this erotic deliverance seemed to occur most often in connection with prostitutes. Andersen had his first encounter with street-walkers on his first trip to France and Italy in 1833, but he would meet them again on virtually every trip thereafter, including his 1840 *Poet's Bazaar* journey. His diaries, almanac and even his autobiography tell of meetings – both on the streets and in brothels – with professional ladies in Hamburg, Paris, Rome, Naples, Istanbul, Athens and Vienna. But here's the strange thing: Andersen went to his grave proclaiming his sexual innocence. His biographers all seem to agree that this passionate man who fell in love with the regularity of the seasons, this expert on the red-light districts of Europe, this diarist who detailed his carnal desires and his every masturbatory interlude with the diligence of an actuary, never *ever* achieved physical intimacy with another human being. This, despite the fact that those same biographers also agree that Andersen's entire life was focused on forging an immortal legacy based on both his life and his work, *and* that he wrote his diary knowing full well that it would be read after his death. All of which makes it especially odd to me that they have always been prepared to accept Andersen's word that he died a virgin.

You can understand why the fans and scholars are united in their desire to think of Andersen as chaste to the grave. We would all rather our favourite children's writers were asexual or, if they must insist, happily married but avowedly celibate. As we read aloud the story of little Fluffy Bear and her cuddly kitten friend, none of us wants to imagine the author in the throes of sexual ecstasy, their faces contorted by orgasmic spasms. Have you ever actually *seen* a picture of Beatrix Potter? Can you imagine her 'at it like a train'? Not an edifying thought, is it? What about

A.A. Milne? Try picturing him engaged in the beast with two backs, Eeyore staring stoically from the shelf or, worse, somehow *involved* – doesn't bear thinking about, does it? And you, at the back with the Harry Potter book, you can wipe that smirk off your face *right* now.

Of course the reality is that children's writers are just as mixed up as the rest of us, if not more so. *Alice in Wonderland*'s Lewis Carroll, whose relationship with the young Alice Liddell would have got the *News of the World* camping on his doorstep had it occurred a few decades later, being a notable case in point.

In his diaries, Andersen often tried to excuse the sexual surges that, at times, virtually incapacitated him by blaming them on the heat of places like Naples and Rome. Again, the biographers are happy to go along with this (the implication being that chilly northerners are above the mucky animal antics of those over-heated Latin types). But the truth was he got the hots in the shadow of a snow-capped Vesuvius, when he was frozen in his lodgings in Rome, and when he was trawling the brothels of a wintry Paris. It had *nothing to do with the weather*; virtually every time he crossed the Danish border he became as randy as a rabbit on day release from rabbit prison.

Andersen left the innocence of childhood behind him the moment he set foot in Copenhagen in 1819. Though both his mother and grandmother were, like many women of their class, not averse to using their sexuality to survive – to the extent that they were actually not far off being prostitutes themselves (Anne Marie had given birth to an illegitimate daughter, Karen Marie – the naughty girl in 'The Red Shoes' is named after her – six years before Hans Christian was born, while his beloved grand-mother had three illegitimate children with three different men) – he had enjoyed an unusually sheltered childhood in Odense, playing with his dolls and doing his turns in the houses of the bourgeoisie. But on his arrival in Copenhagen he moved into an attic room in the notorious brothel street, Ulkegade (today Bremerholm), behind the Royal Theatre, and found himself in the thick of the city's sex-for-money milieu. Not that he knew it at the time. 'I found myself in the midst of the mysteries of Copenhagen,' he wrote, 'but I did not understand how to interpret them. There was in this house a friendly young lady, who lived alone, and often wept; every evening her old father came and paid her a visit. I opened the door to him frequently . . . He always drank his tea with her, and nobody dared to be present, because he was not fond of company: she never seemed very glad at his coming.' Years later, as Andersen begins to socialise among the higher echelons of Copenhagen society he sees the man again, at a party – he is 'a polite old man covered with orders [medals]' and clearly no more the girl's father than I was Sandra's son.

As well as this, his mother's sister, Christiane, was a brothel keeper. Soon after Andersen arrived in Copenhagen he went to see her to ask for support. 'She received me tolerably well,' he recalled in an early autobiography (the story was airbrushed out of later editions), 'but she was very hard on my poor mother . . . She finished by saying: "And see, after having behaved so badly to me, she now saddles me with her child! And a boy as well – if only it had been a girl!"'

In Copenhagen, as in every other European city at that time, prostitution was just another retail trade. Visits to prostitutes by the middle-class men who were to become Andersen's peers were far more acceptable than today to the extent that, as we will discover, several of Andersen's most respectable friends and even two of his doctors, actively encouraged him to visit brothels. But, tellingly, it wasn't until his first visit to Paris, hundreds of miles from Copenhagen, that Andersen finally began to feel the tug of temptation.

'Paris is the most lascivious city under the sun,' he wrote in a letter home while on his second foreign journey in 1833–34. 'I don't believe there is an innocent person there, incredible things happen, in daytime in the most respectable streets I have been offered "a beautiful girl of sixteen"; a young lady with the most innocent face, the most acceptable behaviour stopped me yesterday and in the most lovely manner asked us to visit her, saying that she would subject herself to any kind of examination first, that there was nothing the matter with her, etc. Everywhere there are bawdy pictures, everywhere lecherousness is referred to as something demanded by nature, etc. so that one's modesty is almost beaten into submission. All the same I dare say frankly that I am still innocent, though hardly anyone who knows Paris will believe it.'

Actually, in this instance I do tend to believe him. This was only his second time abroad and though he was by then twenty-eight years old he was still very naive – 'the gawping northern puritan' as Wullschlager puts it – and far too timid to have dared taste such illicit fruit. Paris would later be the scene of his most adventurous sexual encounters and the setting for one of his sauciest stories, 'The Dryad', but on this occasion the very idea was anathema to an aspiring poet still consumed by the romantic ideals of pure, marital love.

A few months later, on the same journey, he arrived in Rome and fell in with a crowd of expat artists and writers, among them the painter Albert Küchler. Küchler obviously knew an interesting face when he saw one and asked if he could paint Andersen's portrait. During one visit to his studio, Andersen was accidentally exposed to a pair of pert breasts belonging to a young artist's model. His reaction was instant and involuntary: 'I was there when a young model of about sixteen came in with her mother. Küchler said he wanted to see what her breasts were like; the girl seemed to be a little bashful because I was there, but the mother said "Fiddle-faddle" and loosened her dress and pulled it and her shift all the way down to her waist. There she stood then half-naked, with somewhat dark skin, arms a bit too skinny, but beautiful round breasts. As the mother exposed her, I could feel my whole body tremble. Küchler saw that I went pale and asked if there was anything wrong with me.'

'Nothing a good seeing to wouldn't sort out' is the tempting reply, but even amid all this nudity, with his almost daily encounters with pimps and prostitutes during his walks in the red-light districts of Rome, and the roister-doistering of his compatriots, Andersen claims to have remained a virgin.

His friends – many of them shameless punters themselves – goaded him about this. The Norwegian landscape painter, Thomas Fearnley, and Andersen's great friend, Bertel Thorvaldsen (the famous Danish sculptor and a long-time Rome resident), discussed trying to abduct him and take him to a brothel. 'Fernley [sic] talked to Thorvaldsen about seducing me from my innocence' is all Andersen says of this incident in his diary, but it was obviously a traumatic event as he recalled it in 'The Psyche', in which an artist's friends try to distract him with loose women after he has fallen in love with the model for one of his statues.

Andersen's under-the-collar temperature was to rise several degrees more during this first Italian trip as he headed further south. Male tourists couldn't go anywhere in Naples without being accosted by hookers and their employers. 'In the dusk of the evening I was surrounded by a bunch of pimps, who wished to recommend me a *bella donna*,' he wrote in his diary. 'I've noticed that the climate is affecting my blood – I felt a raging passion but resisted. God only knows what Hertz [his travelling companion] was up to when I got home! The room was locked and when I knocked on the door he came out and, speaking to me outside the door, apologised for the fact that I couldn't come in ... I left and was pursued in the street where I live by somebody who asked if I wanted to have a *ragazza*, or a *ragazzo*.

'I had no peace from the pimps,' he continues. 'A boy ten or twelve years old pursued me down the length of the street, speaking of this *donna multa bella, excellenza*! I became quite aroused, but still resisted the temptation anyway. If I am still innocent when I get back home, I'll stay that way.'

Three days after that, he is ambushed again: 'The boy with the white hat, who keeps trying to seduce me, couldn't praise his *donna* enough: "O, multa bella!" he said. She was only thirteen years old and had just this week given herself over to carnal pleasure. Finally I got tired of him and turned into a side street; suddenly he darted ahead of me because it happened to be precisely the street where she lived. He showed me the house, begged me to just take a look at her and said I wouldn't be able to resist. "Exactly", I thought and said "No! No! No!" as I walked to the next street . . . Experienced people will laugh at my innocence, but it isn't really innocence, it is an abhorrence of this thing which I dislike so much.'

It is not, then, the sex act itself that seems to repulse him, but the morality of using prostitutes, particularly young girls. 'I don't regard this gratification as a sin, but I find it disgusting and dangerous to do it with such creatures, and an unforgivable sin, with an innocent,' he writes.

But still, Andersen always seemed to find himself drawn to the streets where these women walked, like a randy moth to a red light. Though he often protests at their attempts to seduce him, I can't help feeling that he does rather seem to go looking for trouble.

On his *Poet's Bazaar* journey, six years later, he 'chanced upon' prostitutes in Rome, Naples, Athens and Vienna, but still claims in his diary to have resisted. In fact, it is usually assumed that the first time Andersen plucked up the courage actually to enter a bordello came over twenty years later, at the grand old age of sixty-one, while visiting Paris on the way back from a trip to Portugal.

He had already been tempted on the way there, having watched the comings and goings of a nearby brothel from behind the net curtains of his Paris hotel room. ('A woman wanted me to come up and see a small girl for ten francs, I thanked her and did *not* go up there,' he wrote in his diary.) His strength of will was tested to the limit in Portugal too. He had stayed in Lisbon with an old friend, Georg 'Jorge' O'Neill, a respectable man – he was the Danish consul in Lisbon – who, again, used prostitutes routinely. Jorge invited Andersen along on his brothel visits on several occasions, but he declined every time and retired to his room with a glass of cold water, '[which had] a fairly good effect on my warm blood'.

But the seed had been planted. On his way home from Portugal, after having spent the day in Paris visiting Alexandre Dumas and his daughter, Andersen went back to his hotel room, knocked down a glass or two of wine, left his hotel and marched straight into a brothel.

He confessed all to his diary that evening: 'For the entire journey I have been considering visiting a prostitute. How tired I was of it, I decided to see something of this; went up in a house; a lady who sold human flesh came in, four prostitutes lined up before me, the youngest was, she said, eighteen years old. I asked her to stay, she was virtually wearing just her shift and I felt so sorry for her. I paid the Madam five francs . . . but didn't do anything, just looked at the poor child who completely stripped and was surprised that I only looked at her.'

Even Kenneth Starr would struggle to describe this as a sex act, but it was sufficient to play on his mind for many months afterwards, ultimately luring him back to Parisian brothels no less than *three times* in the next year and a half. On the first occasion he used the Great Exhibition of 1867 as his pretext to visit the city, and was accompanied by a louche young friend, the editor Robert Watt. Though he had clearly had them in mind before he set out, Andersen still describes these brothel visits in his diary as impulsive affairs (which, again, suggests that he wrote with posterity in mind).

On that occasion, whipped up into a frenzy by Watt's tales of debauchery, Andersen took off into the night intent on his second brothel visit: 'After dinner I paced up and down in a sensual fever and suddenly took myself off to a People Boutique [Andersen's euphemism for a brothel]; one of them [the prostitutes] was covered with powder; the second, ordinary; the third woman was alright, I talked to her, paid twelve francs and left, without having sinned in the flesh, though I dare say I did in my thoughts [echoes of Jimmy Carter, while we are on the subject of Presidential peccadilloes]. She asked me to come back, said that I was indeed very innocent for a man. I felt so light and happy when I left that house. Many will call me a fool – have I been one here?'

On his final recorded visit to a Parisian brothel, in May 1868, Andersen spent some time with a young prostitute called Fernanda, again claiming in his diaries that nothing passed between them but small talk: 'I was only talking to Fernanda, the little Turkish girl, while E. [Einar Drewsen, his travelling companion] amused himself. She was the loveliest of them, we spoke about Constantinople, her native city, about the illuminations there on Mohammed's birthday; she was very insistent *pour faire l'amour*, but I told her I had only come to talk, nothing more. "Come again soon," she said. "But not tomorrow, for that's my day off." Poor girl!'

So there you have it, the sum total of Hans Christian Andersen's sexual adventures: four chaste visits to brothels and a lifetime's loitering in Europe's red-light districts.

Except for one thing. When I began to dig deeper and read some of the many studies of Andersen's life, and to (slowly) work my way through his diaries (in Danish), I learned of several less well-known – one might almost say, 'hushed up' – cryptic almanac references to other, possibly more action-packed visits to prostitutes. Interestingly, with regard to the *Poet's Bazaar* journey, the first came just a month before he boarded the *Christian VIII*, in October 1840.

Here we learn that he visited a prostitute with the initials 'MD' together with his doctor, Theodor Collin, the youngest son of Jonas Collin.

These are the entries:

22.9 Wild sensual mood[+]
23.9 Sore penis. WH [Wilken Hornemann, an appropri-
        ately named doctor friend] strongly advises me to take
        a prostitute.
24.9 Walked around all evening with sensual thoughts.
25.9 Th [Theodor Collin] will arrange a prostitute for me
        tomorrow.

27.9 Th has tonight arranged MD for Tuesday.

28.9 Didn't sleep well.

29.9 Feverish all day . . . half sick in the theatre, went with
     Th to MD trial. Ate at Ferrinis.

30.9 Light headed. Nerves tense. Nearly not slept all night.
     WH visited this morning. Sleepy and affected.

1.10 6.30 first G. Visited by Th, felt extremely well! Rich
     in thoughts.

2.10 Disturbed sleep! Annoyed with Th's dejection. Afraid
     of getting sick. Wilken cheered me up.

Love for L.C. [Louise Collin] awoken strongly. Decide to
travel with Holst.

Again, here in this last entry comes the link between carnal lust,
unrequited love and, ultimately, travel as a means of escape. The
entries for the days after this are full of brief comments such as
'sensual mood' and 'passionate' and of course there are the crosses
that so often turn his journal into something resembling a military cemetery. Whatever MD did to him it certainly worked him
up into a lather as, on the fifteenth, he notes that he felt the
need for a return visit, but his courage failed him: 'went up to
MD's door but didn't go in'.

Finally, the day after that aborted visit to MD, he sets a time
frame on leaving Denmark, which has an immediate calming affect:
'Decided to travel at the end of the month. Relaxed and happy.'

As a footnote to all this, three years later, in December 1843,
there is another enigmatic almanac entry: 'Was at Theodor's, who
promised to get me an F. – Sensual.' The F stands for 'Fruentimmer'
the Danish colloquialism for a prostitute but, again, we have no
way of knowing precisely what they got up to.

What do you think? I was beginning to understand why
everyone preferred to think of Andersen as a virgin.

It could be, however, that Andersen never expected his almanac
to become public property in the way that he clearly hoped his
diary would, and so this is the more reliable source. Certainly in

his diaries he protested his innocence to his dying day. On one occasion he even directly refers to the Copenhagen visits: 'It turned out that Wilken's [Hornemann] advice was not followed either at home or away, I will die as I am, without having followed his or my own blood's voice, maybe that is best for me.'

All of this set me wondering. How common is it for men to visit prostitutes just to talk? Could a fully functioning, hetero-sexual male, as, on a good day, I like to consider myself, really resist a no-strings, on-a-plate bit of how's-your-father with a skilled professional? And was it true that they never kissed on the lips, as my friend Keith Woolly had once claimed when as thirteen-year-olds we had had a heated debate on the subject, resulting in him trying to kiss Jennifer Tart – a fifth-former judged by us to be the closest thing to a sex worker that we had to hand on account of her name – and having his ear smacked so hard he couldn't hear for the rest of the day?

If you've never been, and I'm sure you haven't, Herbert Strasse is a short, cobbled street that runs parallel to the famous Reeperbahn, where the Beatles churned out rough-and-ready rock'n' roll covers before Ringo joined and transformed them into the greatest band of all time with his visionary musical genius. They also shagged anything that moved by all accounts; they certainly picked the right place.

Only Herberts over eighteen are allowed to pass through the high, graffiti-covered metal barriers at each end of the street, but beyond them they will find themselves, as I was, confronted with a street lined on both sides by quite ordinary terraced houses: ordinary except for the fact that sitting behind a plate-glass window in each front parlour sits a skimpily dressed temptress beckoning them towards an hour or two of lusty pleasure.

Thankfully, on a cold, battleship-grey Friday afternoon in February, there was just one other customer, a young man, aged about twenty. We passed briefly at the barriers. His shoulders were hunched, his head disappearing into his parka, his eyes fixed determinedly on the ground. Unsure of punter etiquette, for a moment I considered a polite nod and a 'Fruitful visit?', but quickly decided against it.

Entering Herbert Strasse was like walking onto a deserted film set, with its pristine rows of houses and shiny cobbles. And then the Sirens commenced their calling.

I span around from a semi-hypnotised contemplation of the first thing that had caught my eye – one of the largest pairs of bosoms I had ever seen, adorning a leather-clad dominatrix on my left – as a blonde in a pink and white silk bikini called to me in English with a heavy German accent. 'You come hello? You speak English?' (How could she tell?) Bolting through her beaded curtain like a frightened ferret (this is not a euphemism), I then stood adjusting my eyes to the murk.

Lord knows why, but I had removed my wedding ring before I had entered Herbert Strasse, as if that would save anyone's feelings or lessen my shame. Even though I had intended the visit to be chaste from the outset, and it had Lissen's blessing, I had still wrestled with guilt and anxiety beforehand. Strangely, the fact that I was visiting with the intention of asking questions made me feel even more nervous. Unlike Andersen, I was new to this and was worried that my interviewee would have me forcibly ejected as a weirdo by the burly, tattooed pimps I assumed were watching through peepholes. I envisioned my flailing carcass, by that stage resembling a pin cushion but with dildos rather than pins projecting from every orifice, rebounding from one garbage can to another in a dark, urine-stained alley, as they had their sport with the pervy Englishman.

Somehow, if I had just been going for sex like everyone else, the whole thing would have been so much more acceptable for all involved.

Luckily, Sandra was a professional in every sense and was entirely unfazed by my opening gambit: 'Hello, I don't actually want to do anything, I'm writing a book about Hans Christian Andersen, you see.' And for fifty euros up front, she had all the answers.

Looking back, I realised that, of course, she was used to dealing with strange requests from furtive, out-of-breath men, and after I had handed the notes over she invited me to take a seat as she sprawled disconcertingly before me on the red satin bedspread.

I explained a little more, and asked if many of her clients came 'just to talk'. 'Not so often,' she said. 'Many of my guys come for just a short blow job. Many work around here and come after work or at lunch and don't have so much time. Some want to talk, they want to stay longer, drink something.' How long do they stay? 'Three or four hours, but in the last thirty minutes I usually say, "Don't you want to do something?" and we usually . . .' She tailed off, leaving the rest to my most torrid imaginings. 'Young men want to talk,' she continued, warming to her theme. 'They are a bit scared. Older men want more special things. It is a safe place to come, but there is still the excitement.' She did, however, remember one client who came up to five times a month just to sit and talk. Apparently he came while his wife was visiting a doctor near by.

My mind was still on the 'special things' as I looked around the room at the three-tiered shoe rack — full of knackered red, white and black stilettos mainly — at the end of the bed.

'They want to kiss my feet, they like stockings, many men like shoes,' she explained.

The blinds were drawn but I could still make out the rest of Sandra's equipment scattered about the room: dildos the size of bollards (I gulped), whips, handcuffs, a fake zebra-skin carpet, a low-level sink by the door, various creams, lotions and a roll of kitchen paper by the bed. It was a dispiriting place, about as sexy as a Chinese restaurant.

She showed me into an adjoining S&M room, dominated by a stirrup chair. Opposite was a mirror and on all four window-less walls hung fearsome black vinyl costumes, whips, chains, thigh-length boots and a gas mask. The floor was covered in smooth, wipe-clean, grey vinyl.

I asked Sandra for a final guess of how many men actually

leave without so much as a quick grope. 'Maybe one out of every ten that says they only want to talk when they come,' she told me, an infinitesimally small number of the total.

I had rather feared I might be tempted myself, and had brought along an unbent paper clip to stick in my palm in case of arousal – a trick I had heard Alistair Campbell used to stem his anger when he was being questioned by the Hutton Inquiry (though he may well use it to dampen his ardour too, who knows). If I am really honest, I can't say for sure that I would not have taken things further had Sandra been more my type, but as it turned out, far from being a question of whether I could keep the old feller tethered or not, there was barely a tickle from down under (and I will never, *ever* disclose what prompted that).

I ascribe my lack of arousal to several things: firstly, and I realise it is hardly gallant of me to say so, Sandra was not quite as beguiling close up as she had seemed after that first, panic-stricken glimpse from the street. She was no longer in the first flush of youth, in fact her youth had probably disappeared down the U-bend around about 1985. She was the picture in Goldie Hawn's attic, and no amount of heavily applied foundation and eye shadow, or even her admittedly well-toned body, was going to distract from that. Sandra was very nearly old enough to be my mother – and thus I could never afford the psychotherapist's bills that a bout of whatever she had in mind would entail. Secondly, I found the whole experience of visiting Herbert Strasse, from having to stand in public while being beckoned by its saleswomen, to taking the plunge through the beaded curtain, to the squalid, dark room (which I couldn't help imagining had just been vacated by a greasy Ernest Borgnine lookalike with herpes, who had masturbated furiously and left in a cloud of dandruff), a sure recipe for erectile dysfunction. Even in its prime my equipment is never likely to impress a woman of the world such as Sandra, but in the state Herbert Strasse had reduced it to she would have needed powerful bifocals and the persistence of a milkmaid.

I had felt guilty before visiting Herbert Strasse, and I felt guilty when I left. The only difference being that when I left I felt guilty towards Sandra, and this was not just some vestigial Catholic angst. I felt guilty that I had used her, not as a sex object, but as a research subject – which was almost as bad – and most bizarrely of all, guilty that I had not succumbed to her charms. She had seemed rather deflated when I had left, in contrast to the smiling, welcoming professional hostess who had so swiftly put me at ease as I stood in the entrance hall. I don't know if this sadness I sensed was the inevitable, hard-bitten melancholy of someone who has worked in a gruelling and degrading trade for many years (she had told me eight), or that, as preposterous as this might sound, bearing in mind she had just earned fifty euros for a half-hour chat instead of, well, whatever it is she usually gets up to, she might have felt just a little rejected. Whatever, I hoped Sandra would swiftly recover from being spurned by the sweaty Englishman.

I don't think I took breath between Herbert Strasse and the Reeperbahn, and once there I bolted for a bar to compose myself. The Reeperbahn is a fantastically ugly post-war thoroughfare, busy and wide as a motorway, and lined with kebab shops, theme bars and, for some reason, shops selling cheap shoes (although maybe they're not so incongruous after all, now I think of it). The air smells of fried chicken and old fat.

Apart from a salutory glimpse into the dark underbelly of the sex trade, what had I discovered about Andersen's sexuality from my visit? Well, if Sandra was to be believed, and she had no reason to lie, some men actually do visit prostitutes just to talk, but the numbers were small.

I could imagine Andersen, who was, despite his outward frailty and broad portfolio of neuroses, an intrepid and endlessly curious man, visiting a brothel once for 'research purposes'. But what drove him to return repeatedly during his life to red-light districts and brothels? It is hard to imagine it was the small talk – if he was looking for stimulating conversation, the bourgeois salons of Copenhagen, Paris or Rome, with which he was familiar, would seem to be more fertile hunting grounds. And I don't believe that it was the excitement of going somewhere forbidden and 'naughty'. As we know, some of his most respectable friends were actively encouraging him to go. The forbidden-fruit frisson would have been very faint indeed.

On the other hand, we know for sure that he had a healthy libido. His need to note down every masturbatory episode with a cross in his almanac is one of the more unsettling aspects of his self-obsession. Perhaps he was concerned there might be deleterious health consequences to such behaviour and he wished to keep an eye on it; maybe he saw it might kickstart the latent madness he feared he had inherited from his grandfather. Salvador Dali kept a similarly conscientious record of his masturbation, in his case indicative of a monstrous ego that felt his every ejaculation worthy of record – maybe Andersen's own pathological narcissism led him to do the same. Who knows?

And let's not forget, Andersen chose his prostitutes from a line-up, so one has to assume that, unlike Sandra and me, they *were* his type.

Many have claimed that Andersen's sheer terror of his own and others' sexuality outweighed his desires and curiosity, that in returning again and again to houses of ill-repute he was merely trying to pluck up courage. What really went on at the residences of 'MD' and 'F'? If nothing, how do you explain the fears he expressed soon after that he might have caught something? No one seems to be prepared to hazard a guess.

You know what I think? I find it very hard to believe that all 'MD' and 'F' administered was a light massage and some aromatherapy. Could it be that – without wishing to get too mechanical – Andersen favoured the Clintonian definition of sexual relations, as meaning only penetrative sex? If this is the case and if 'MD' and 'F' had merely given him a hand job, he would have felt able to write with a clear conscience that his virtue remained intact.

Alternatively, was the true purpose of these visits to try to *test* his own sexuality? If he feared he was homosexual, as many have suggested he was, were they part of his attempt to decode his own feelings?

Of course, unless a great, great, great, great grandchild comes forward with a positive blood test (and, oh boy, are they in for a windfall if they do), this will remain one of the many missing pieces of the Andersen sexual jigsaw. I decided, for the meantime at least, to dwell on the subject no longer, but I had a suspicion that it would return to haunt me more than once during the journey ahead.

After my actually very cordial half hour with Sandra I spent the rest of the evening walking around the city. I do hope the goodly Hamburgers don't take this the wrong way, but I thought their city was one of the most dispiriting, ugly and tasteless places I had ever visited – and that includes Jakarta, Ulan Bator and Sheffield.

Every other shop window boasted a bewildering range of terrifying sex toys and the kind of eye-watering porn that would make Heidi Fleiss blush. I don't consider myself a prude (although I understand if by now you have formed another impression), but after a while, being visually bludgeoned by twenty-inch dildos and dominatrix costumes at every turn becomes a little wearing. You can't pop out for a pint of milk in Hamburg without discovering at least one new way in which to be penetrated. Whether this indicates a healthy, open attitude towards sex on the part of the locals, or a diseased society on the brink of apocalypse I wouldn't like to guess, but I had had my fill and after a bite to eat at McDonald's (I swear it was the first and last visit to the golden arches on my trip, and at least it was, technically, locally themed food), I hastened to my guest house above a grubby nightclub near to the central station, and then to bed.'+' (I'm *joking*.)

★   ★   ★

Old pop groups never die, they work out their purgatory touring Germany. I was reminded of this the next morning, as I waited for the train to Leipzig, reading a station billboard that threatened the imminent arrival in Hamburg of Leo Sayer, Showaddywaddy and Boney M. Andersen had fared rather better in his choice of musical entertainment while in the city, attending a concert by Franz Liszt at the Hotel Stadt London.

In *A Poet's Bazaar*, so overcome does Andersen profess himself to be by the electrifying talents of the charismatic Hungarian pianist – 'one of the kings in the realm of tone . . . the modern Orpheus . . . who with magic fingers defines the boundaries of his art in our age!' – that he dedicates the Hamburg chapter to him. He reports on the hypnotic effect the 'demonic' pianist has on the audience, particularly the ladies, and claims, slightly implausibly, to have met politicians who believe Liszt capable of inciting revolution through his playing.

Liszt's next gig is in London, and Andersen regrets that the two are heading off in opposite directions: 'Shall I again meet him? was my last thought; and chance would have it that we should meet on our travels – meet at a place where my reader and I least could imagine; meet, become friends, and again separate.' Just in case the reader can't bear the suspense, he adds, 'but it belongs to the last chapter of this flight.' (In fact, his real impressions of Liszt are revealed in a letter to a friend a few weeks later. His envy of a man six years younger than him but with an animal power over women is clear. Liszt's playing, Andersen writes, 'interested me without moving me, he seemed like a demon chained to a rack,' and he notes with snide satisfaction that the bouquets thrown to the pianist were supplied by the hotel owner.)

I polished off my breakfast – including the kind of over-sized pretzel that would have George Dubya calling for a paramedic – as the train arrived, but panicked over what to do with the debris. The Germans are even more recycling-crazy than the Danes and I was faced with four bin choices: 'Waste', 'Paper', 'Packaging' and 'Glass'. In the end I decided that 'Waste' seemed like a nice umbrella term for my mound of plastic, paper and packaging, and stuffed it in the appropriate hole when nobody was looking.

This is precisely the kind of test devised by foreigners to make the British feel uneasy when we go abroad. The German system of train seat reservations is another. It was a good half-hour, including several hostile encounters with other passengers understandably perturbed to find a large rucksack with an Englishman beneath it in the seat they had reserved, before I found a place to which no one else had prior claim.

Andersen had left Hamburg by steamship, sailing up the Elbe. On the way he passed a ship of emigrants, sailing in the other direction for America. On board he had another poignant encounter with a female passenger, this time 'a tall and rather stout lady with a proud carriage not in harmony with her faded chintz gown'. She was an actress, past her prime but still clinging to her dignity ('What is your line?' I asked. 'The affecting parts,' she replied). He later saw her disembark, flinging her feather boa over her shoulder like Gloria Swanson in *Sunset Boulevard*: 'Our postillion played a merry tune, but I thought of *The Maid of Orleans*, the old actress on the cart . . . and I became sad from her smile . . .'

Our narrator is clearly feeling a little melancholy, but cheers up dramatically at the prospect of his first ride on a steam train, excitedly explaining the ins and outs of what was still a shockingly new form of transport.

The first steam train line had opened in England in 1825, but it took the Germans another decade before their first line – the very one Andersen was to travel on – opened.

Not that everyone was as excited by the prospect of steam travel as Andersen. The Romantics were not known for their love of technological progress, and seemed especially to loathe steam travel. The nimbyish Wordsworth campaigned against a railway line to Windemere, while the novelist Charles Lever wrote that the whistle of a train was 'the death note to all the romance of life'. In this regard at least, Andersen was no Romantic.

Influenced in part by his friend, the physicist H.C. Ørsted, he embraced new discoveries with an admirable open-mindedness (although Darwin's theory of evolution distressed him terribly), and as the day of his first train ride approaches he is quaking with nervous excitement.

'As many of my readers have not seen a railroad, I will first endeavour to give them an idea of such a thing,' he begins what is a priceless first-hand description of this most revolutionary of industrial inventions. 'We will take an ordinary road, it may run in a straight line, or it may be curved, that is indifferent, but it must be level – level as a parlour floor, and for that purpose we blow up every rock which stands in the way.' The carriages are, he says, like gondolas waiting by the side of a quay; the railway lines cross at a junction like 'magic ties invented by human skill'. He is in his element, reporting on the news story of the day, and revelling in the kudos this will give him back in Copenhagen (immediately after the trip, his first priority was to reel off several breathless descriptions of the journey in letters to friends in Denmark, letters which he knew would find their way in to the newspapers).

Oddly, Andersen never got this excited over steamships – probably because steam power didn't make all that much difference to sailing times, given a good wind – but he has been as giddy as a schoolgirl, in a state of 'railway fever', for days leading up to his train trip: 'When one is here for the first time, one thinks of overturnings, of breaking arms and legs, of being blown in the air or crushed to death by another train; but I think it is only the first time one thinks of all this.'

Andersen boarded the train at Magdeburg for a three-hour, seventy-mile ride to Leipzig, and soon they were on their way.

The first sensation is that of a very gentle motion in the carriages . . . the speed increases imperceptibly, but you read your book, look at your map, and as yet do not rightly know at what speed you are going. You look out of the window and discover that you are careering away as with horses at full gallop; it goes still quicker; you seem to fly, but here is no shaking, no suffocation, nothing of what you anticipated would be unpleasant . . . We have an idea of standing outside the globe, and seeing it turn round . . . We feel ourselves as powerful as the sorcerers of old! We put our magic horse to the carriage, and space disappears; we fly like the clouds in a storm – as the bird of passage flies! Our wild horse snorts and snuffs, and the dark steam rushes out of his nostrils. Mephistopheles could not fly quicker with Faust on his cloak!

What better way to put Copenhagen and all its miseries behind him?

At one point a fellow passenger offers him some snuff. 'I bowed, took a pinch, sneezed, and then asked: "How far are we through Köthen?" "Oh", replied the man, "we left it behind us while you were sneezing!"' You would need to be a chronic hay fever sufferer to miss Köthen these days. As with most of the towns and cities we passed through en route to Leipzig, it was heralded by miles of industrial dereliction. A sign of the economic woes brought about by German reunification, or simply indicative of a move towards a service-based economy? Hard to tell. Then again, who cares, as long as we are richer than them! Ha! (Sorry. Still can't quite forget those penalties.)

Actually, in his diaries, Andersen mentions that his train stopped in Köthen, and far from accepting the offer of snuff from his travelling companion he became irrationally concerned that the man might attack him: 'The thought occurred to me that he might be crazy and have a fit. I got all worked up about it.'

Leipzig station, our next stop, is a wonder, a cathedral to rail travel. Built in 1915, it is the largest railway station in Europe, but for all its majesty it is a welcoming place; it smells of baking bread, there are newsagents galore (I fell upon them like a current affairs-hungry locust) and its basement is full of takeaway food vendors selling high-cholesterol, deep-fried, butter-soaked indigestibles. I gorged on a plate of fried potato with cream, garlic and bacon, followed by a piece of chocolate cheesecake the size of a brick, before setting off on my whistle-stop tour of Andersen's Leipzig.

Trouble is, Andersen's Leipzig was thoroughly bombed during the Second World War and then rebuilt by the Communists, who seem to have had something against the nineteenth century. Still, it was nice to be in a city with shop windows you could walk past without blushing like a girl guide. Most seemed to be selling either very posh handbags or very posh chocolates. Or the dreaded Swarovski crystals (which suggest that the Germans are not quite the paragons of taste and discernment that their choice of music might lead us to believe. Can you imagine, for example, anyone in full possession of their faculties paying €400 for a small crystal duck on wheels?).

In 1840 Leipzig was the home of the composer and conductor Felix Mendelssohn and, never one to miss a chance to rub shoulders with a celebrity, Andersen was keen to meet him. As a twelve-year-old boy Mendelssohn had stayed for some weeks with Andersen's great hero Goethe (then aged seventy-two) and he had made a great impression on the writer. By 1840 he had already made his name as a Romantic composer, one often inspired by literary works, and so excited was Andersen to meet him that he interrupted a rehearsal of Beethoven's Seventh to introduce himself.

Mendelssohn was at the height of his powers, having ruled the Gewandhaus Orchestra and the *Singakademie* with a rod of iron since taking over, aged twenty-six, in 1835. He had been born into a wealthy, cultured Jewish family in 1809 and the comparisons with Mozart started at an early age when he showed a precocious talent for the piano. By the age of seventeen he had composed one of his most celebrated pieces, the overture to *A Midsummer Night's Dream Opus 21*. He founded the Leipzig Conservatory in 1843, but took the prodigy thing perhaps a little too far by also dying young, aged just thirty-eight.

In his autobiography Andersen describes their first meeting in the Gewandhaus (cloth exchange), his smug relish at the reception he received from this great man all too apparent: 'I did not send in my name, only that a traveller was very anxious to call on him . . . "I have but very little time, and I really cannot talk here with strangers!" said he. "You have invited me yourself," answered I. "You have told me that I must not pass through the city without seeing you!" – "Andersen!" cried he now, "Is it you?" and his whole countenance beamed.'

I spent a few hours wandering around the city, trying to find the original Gewandhaus and the grave of the poet Gellert, which Andersen had once visited and graffitied, but neither seems to exist any more. Back on the station platform, sitting with a plate of deep fried fat on my lap, I tried to think up my truthful tourist board slogan for Leipzig, something I often do in strange cities. I had developed the Truthful Slogan™ game after a conversation I had with a friend who worked for the Danish Tourist Board. I had suggested that in the absence of anything better they could always use: 'Visit Denmark, There's Parking'. I had meant it as a joke, but she had taken me seriously and there had very likely been numerous departmental meetings on the subject afterwards. The Gellert goose chase might well have coloured my mood, but the most fitting slogan I could come up with was: 'Leipzig: Don't all rush at once'.

From Leipzig the scenery grew more varied. I saw my first vines about forty minutes south: an encouraging sign that I was leaving northern Europe. I had tried hard to like Germany, but it had reminded me too much of Denmark and everything I wanted a break from. Bavaria brought the scent of the south, although the light sieving of snow on the hills gave a warning of just how freezing it would be in Nuremberg, my next stop.

By the time Andersen arrived in November 1840, Nuremberg's golden age had long since past, but this richly cultured town still had much to offer the Romantic aficionado. In fact, according to his account of his visit in *A Poet's Bazaar*, Andersen was so overcome by the city's medieval charms that he climbed the castle ramparts and declaimed: 'Thou art yet Bavaria's capital! It is true thou wert compelled to give thy crown to Munich; but thy royal dignity, thy peculiar greatness, thou bearest still!'

He lists all the great men to have come from the city, including the polymath printer Albrecht Dürer; Hans Sachs the so-called cobbler poet; and Peter Fischer, the renowned bronze caster.

I knew who Dürer was, but had to look up Sachs before I left on my trip. It turns out he was quite a card. He dabbled in humorous short stories and tales in verse (or *schwanke*, as the Germans call them). 'Dabbled' is perhaps an understatement as, even by Andersen's prolific standards, Sachs (1494–1576) was a writing machine. His quill must have quivered virtually non-stop from sunrise to sunset as he claimed that, by the age of sixty-seven, he had written '4,275 songs, 208 dramas, 1,558 comic stories, fables, histories, figures, comparisons, allegories, dreams, visions, lamentations, controversial dialogues, psalms and religious songs'. That works out at one piece of writing every three and a half days – he was virtually a one-man guild. Understandably, Andersen was keen to pay homage to a man who is still regarded as a bit of a wise old goat, despite his 'never mind the quality feel the width' approach to writing, but was crestfallen to find Sachs' house had been redeveloped.

The fair was in town and Nuremberg's main square was packed with shooting galleries, merry-go-rounds and crepe vendors. The smell of pop corn, doughnuts and hot dogs set my nostrils twitching as I walked in the twilight to the Schöner Brunnen (Beautiful Fountain). 'Could I paint, I would go into the market, force my way through the crowd, and sketch the fountain there, but I am not a painter, I am a poet,' Andersen writes in *A Poet's Bazaar*. I found the fountain – a kind of mini-Albert Memorial – engulfed by the funfair rides, blaring out old Whitney Houston numbers and excremental Europop. Later, on Ludwigsplatz, I passed a much more eye-catching piece of public art, the so-called Marriage Merry-Go-Round Fountain cast in bronze, and based on a poem by Sachs. This colossal, gothic-horror depiction of marital trauma features a naked man holding chains wrapped around his big-breasted fraulein;

the rotting carcass of a goat; the decaying corpse of a woman astride the similarly moribund body of a man with her hands around his throat – both riding a giant lizard-frog-fish-type creature – among other characters, all of which suggests that Nurembergers are desperately in need of a spot of marriage counselling. Either that or a weekend in Hamburg.

Today, as it was in 1840, one of the main highlights of the Nuremberg tourist trail is Dürer's house, a three-storey, half-timbered building, with windows made from bottle bottoms. Andersen was an obsessive sightseer, but only saw the house from the outside – it opened as a museum in 1876 – so I jumped at the chance to go inside. It was near closing time but I persuaded the ticket seller to let me in (she reduced the price, bless her).

Dürer (1471–1528) was the first great Protestant artist to emerge following Luther's church-door antics and he helped make Nuremberg *the* centre for printing in Europe at the end of the fifteenth century and early sixteenth century. He led a flowering of artistic and scientific exploration, and considered himself very much the fashionable art prince, as his self-portraits show. Like Andersen, he hobnobbed with the rich and famous of his era, painting Emperor Maximilian I and Denmark's Christian II, among others.

In his house I also learned that in 1527, for unspecified reasons of health, Dürer had a toilet installed in his kitchen. But in Germany rules is rules and he was promptly fined for a medieval building code violation. 'His secret cabinet shall not be treated differently from others' even though he is a famous painter,' wrote the town council at the time. My guidebook also drew my attention to what it claimed was Dürer's 'superb grasp of anatomical detail', and it is true he was a consummate draughtsman. We all have our off days, though, and Albrecht's definitely came the day he was commissioned to draw a rhino. His looks like it has leprosy.

From there I climbed the city ramparts. Squint, ignore the suburban sprawl, the obligatory communications tower and the distinct echo of *I Will Always Love You* from the funfair, and it is not too difficult to imagine the Nuremberg of the mid nine-teenth century. With its pink sandstone castle, turreted ramparts and narrow, winding cobbled streets it has more than a whiff of the fairy-tale citadel about it and I see why Andersen was so enamoured of the place.

As a chilly late-afternoon mist descended I left the city centre and headed out to the suburbs on another dead German hunt (following my failure earlier in the day to find the grave of the poet Gellert). Actually make that dead *Germans*. In his diary Andersen records the burial plot numbers of both Dürer (649) and Sachs (503) in St Johannes churchyard, but, by the time I arrived at this tiny, toy-like red and pink chapel, the gates were locked. I cursed Andersen's obsessive corpse-spotting. Why couldn't he hang out in bars and go shopping like everyone else does on holiday? But I was determined not to be defeated. After a quick recce of the perimeter wall to plan my best line of attack for an after-dark assault, I walked back into town for dinner.

As a child I promised myself that I would never eat sauer-kraut, unless forced to while undergoing an improbably sadistic interrogation, but though I would never actually *willingly* eat it again, the soggy pile of vinegary cabbage and wrinkly chipolatas laced with juniper berries that I ate at the Bratwursthäusle was an interesting experience (a glass of beer the size of a traffic bollard probably helped).

As I was psyching myself up to begin eating, a barrel-bellied local was shown to my table. With him was a small white dog to whom he fed sausages from a huge platter that had been brought swiftly to our table. He and the rat-dog were obviously regulars. We sat in an intimate, awkward silence, avoiding eye contact for a while, as the code of the solitary diners forced to share a table decrees. (Unless you greet the stranger immediately, whether at a restaurant table, in a train compartment or lift, the chance of any acknowledgement of the other party becomes exponentially less probable as the seconds tick; once past the minute mark contact is virtually unthinkable.) Heck, I thought to myself, I'm on holiday, to hell with the code!, and I asked him how often he came here. 'Once a week – he likes it,' he said, nodding to his dog, before returning to his demolition of the European Sausage Mountain. We exchanged not another word, the silence broken only by muted slurps and excited heavy breathing from beneath the table.

Darkness had now descended and, back at the cemetery, I gracelessly vaulted the wall at its lowest point by the front gate. I began my search for Sachs and Dürer, but the poor light defeated me. After about twenty minutes and repeated barking of knees, it was almost a relief when I spotted the policemen's hats above the wall. Some curtain-twitcher in one of the apartment blocks overlooking the cemetery must have summoned them. It was, undeniably, a fair cop.

Aware of the fact that the policemen were both armed and, recalling countless concentration camp movies, probably crack shots, I mimed that I needed to return to the gate on the other side of the cemetery in order to climb over (if this had been an episode of *What's My Line?*, the panel could well have surmised that I was one of those men who direct airplanes with table tennis bats). In order to assure them that I was not attempting an escape, I continued the performance at intervals as I walked.

As I began my explanation to the policemen – both moustachioed, which somehow made them slightly less intimidating, in a Village People kind of way – at a rate of about 200 words a minute, I was acutely aware of my beery breath. I'm not certain they bought the Andersen spiel; this wouldn't be the last time that I would embark on an explanation of what I was doing only for self-doubt to set in halfway through, so I could hardly expect others to take me seriously.

After taking my passport number and walking me round to a sign displaying the cemetery's opening hours, they let me go. As I walked back into town I looked back over my shoulder a few times but the policemen remained standing by their car, watching me until I slipped out of sight. I retreated to my ghastly guest house (why are all German *pensions* decorated from garage sales?) and bed.

I did return to the cemetery for a third time before catching my train to Munich the next morning, and among the Schmidts, the Funks and the Kochs I did eventually find both Sachs and Dürer. It was the first time that I felt I had literally trodden in Andersen's over-sized footprints. I might even go so far as to say it was worth the trouble.

On his way to Munich, Andersen stopped off for a quick visit to Augsburg, where he discovered a potent augury of the modern age: an exhibition of daguerreotypes by an artist called Iseuring – '. . . every feature was so exactly shown that even the eye had a clearness and expression. The most felicitous delineation was in the silk dresses of the ladies; it seemed as if one could hear them rustle.' The first daguerreotype had been created by Louis Daguerre in January 1839. It was the first successful photographic process – achieved by exposing copper plates to iodine. This so-called 'mirror with memory' had caused a sensation. One early photographer, Carl Dauthendey, recorded that: 'People were afraid at first to look for any length of time . . . They were embarrassed by the clarity of these figures and believed that the little, tiny faces of the people could see out at them.' As it turned out, the daguerreotype was a dead end – the images could not be reproduced, subjects had to sit still for half an hour and then there were the noxious chemicals involved.

On the train to Munich I went through the usual seat-number farrago before finally coming to rest beside a dishevelled man reading a broadsheet newspaper. Had I known he had flu and would spend the next thirty minutes snorting phlegm and noisily gulping it down, I would have carried on walking to another carriage. As it was, by the time I had shed my backpack and coat and sat down, it was too late. Of course, what I should have done was to tap him politely on the shoulder and say, in my best John le Mesurier:

'I'm awfully sorry, but would you mind terribly not making those dreadful snot-gargling noises? It is rather *distracting*, do you see?' Instead, I decided to communicate my displeasure by making equally loud phlegm noises back at him. He carried on regardless, too deeply engrossed in his paper to notice. We must have sounded like two rutting sows.

Andersen had an equally stressful journey to Munich: a woman took his umbrella mistaking it for her parasol. This flustered him greatly and he sent urgent instructions for its return. Nevertheless, the image of him waiting for its return, pacing anxiously carrying a parasol is a rather lovely one, I think.

My Munich expert, Dirk Heisserer, cheered me up immediately. I had found Dirk on the Internet, advertising his services as a literary guide to the city. He picked me up outside my guest house, waving his black beret through the sunroof of his car with gusto and, as we drove through the city on a whistle-stop, mid-nineteenth-century tour, it became apparent that Dirk was more than your average tour guide. I had struck Google gold.

'When Andersen was here Munich was having a massive expansion,' Dirk told me as he steered his dilapidated white Opel Astra with a blithe disregard for the rules of the road typical of all literary academics. 'The city was expanding in all directions and Ludwig I and Max II were great for artists.' Andersen likened Munich's expansion at that time to a budding rose bush with 'every branch a new road, every leaf a palace, church or monument' and he seemed drawn to the city's dynamic cultural life. Throughout his life, Munich would be one of the five or so cities that Andersen would gravitate towards – he later found King Max to be a particularly welcoming host. But on this, his second visit, Andersen was strangely out of sorts. From his diary entries he seems tetchy, and the reason why soon becomes clear.

He had arranged to hook up with his friend Hans Peter Holst, a Danish poet of little lasting consequence but who, at the time, and much to Andersen's chagrin, was considerably more highly thought of in their home country. In his autobiography Andersen makes clear his resentment concerning Holst's popularity among the Danish community in Munich: 'I had no great pleasure here, and among my countrymen were none who interested me; and I was no doubt judged as a poet much after the Copenhagen scale.' As with Liszt, it hardly helped that Holst was six years younger than Andersen; he referred to Holst with undisguised bitterness as 'the lucky poet of the moment'.

The plan was that he and Holst would travel on to Rome together, but they rowed – one all too easily imagines Andersen picking jealous fights – and in the end Andersen set off alone. Holst was having far too good a time in Munich, using the excuse that his portrait was not yet finished and promising to catch up with Andersen in Italy. Which he did. Eventually.

From *A Poet's Bazaar* you would think that Andersen spent his time in Munich moping around in miserable solitude, but his diary records the usual theatre visits and heavy socialising with diplomats, the philosopher Schelling and artists, including Cornelius and Stiegler (who, he notes in his diary with delight, was a big fan). He records with great excitement in a letter back home that one night he sat just one seat away from the famous pianist Sigismund Thalberg in the theatre and, before he leaves Munich, he is proud that this acquaintance has developed to the extent that they are on nodding terms when they pass on the street.

But still, by the ninth day he records that he is 'bored of being here', two days later he complains that there is 'nothing to see'. For lack of anything better to do, he grows a moustache. While writing to Jonas Collin, he bursts into tears. 'I felt a disquiet here, a desire to leave it again,' he wrote. 'Munich is a town like a hundred others in Germany. The post office, with its red-painted walls and hovering figures, is taken from Pompeii; the new Palace is a copy of the Duke of Tuscany's palace in Florence . . . The Au Church . . . reminds us of St Stephen's Church in Vienna. I found but one part in Munich that can be called great and characteristic, and that is Ludwig Street.'

Ludwigstrasse would have been an astonishing sight for any Dane, as it remains today. Copenhagen has nothing to match this monumental avenue, lined with the extravagant, Italianate palaces built by the seventeenth- and eighteenth-century Bavarocracy. Inside its main church, St Ludwig Kirke, Dirk took me to the east wall, which is entirely covered by one of Andersen's favourite Munich paintings, *The Day of Judgement* by Peter von Cornelius.

Cornelius (1783–1867) was one of the so-called Nazarene painters, a group of German artists who had come together in Rome in the 1830s. In *A Poet's Bazaar* Andersen recalls meeting him for the first time in Rome, six years earlier: 'No one had told me who it was I had been conversing with; I only heard that he was a painter, and of painters there are plenty in Rome. I therefore thanked the gentleman for his invitation [to his studio], but said that I regretted I could not accept it. "You will come!" said he with a smile, as he laid his hand on my shoulder, and went hastily away.'

Of course, as soon as Andersen learned who the man was he hot-footed it over to his atelier where he saw the cartoon for this very painting. Seeing the finished work in 1840, Andersen pronounced it 'one of the greatest that Munich may be proud of'. I am not so convinced. At 18 metres high and 11 metres wide (or 2,500 square feet) it is a whopper, but it's a bit 'fire and brimstone' for my taste and, in contrast, the colours are rather 'happy clappy' evangelical. The church itself is an oasis, however. 'You can feel the calm of the 1840s in here!' exclaimed Dirk, and he was right. Despite being located on a busy six-lane road, it was silent.

Andersen stayed in Karlsplatz on his first visit to Munich and, in fact, he drew a picture of it. I had brought a copy along to compare to the Karlsplatz of today, but nothing remained of what he had seen. As we stood looking at one of the present-day gates to the city, trying to reconcile it to the picture, the police came to move us on – Dirk had parked virtually at a right angle to the kerb, astride double yellow lines and in front of a no-parking sign. 'But he is writing a book about Hans Christian Andersen!'

he explained, with what I felt showed a heartening, if overly optimistic, enthusiasm for the importance of my project. We had just
enough time to turn around and realise that we had probably
been looking in the wrong direction and that Andersen had more
likely drawn the view behind us. (In fact, Dirk, who seemed to
be becoming as obsessed as I was with Andersen's journey, later
emailed to say, 'Great fortune!: I have found the address of HCA
at Karlsplatz, because A. writes in his "tale of my life" that he got
a chamber with "an honourious comb maker"'. The comb maker
was called Ehrl, Dirk told me, and his family lived at number 10
and 11 Karlsplatz, what's more, the funny thing sticking out of
the top of one of the buildings in his drawing was probably an
early telegraph aerial, which is kind of interesting.)

Andersen's Munich frustrations continued on a visit to its
booksellers where, as usual, he sought out copies of his own
books. He is delighted to find a German translation of his first
novel, *The Improvisatore*, published in 1835, but confused that it
consists only of the first half.

'But I wish to have the whole novel!' said I.

'That's the whole!' he replied. 'There are no more parts,
I have read it myself, sir!'

'Do you not find then,' I enquired, 'that it ends rather
abruptly; that we do not come to any conclusion?'

'O, yes!' said he. 'But it is in that as in the French novels!
The author points out a conclusion, and leaves it to the
reader to finish the picture for himself.'

'It is not the case here,' I exclaimed. 'This is only the
first part of the work.'

'I tell you,' said he, half angrily, 'I have read it!'

'But I have written it!' I replied.

The man looked at me from top to toe; he did not
contradict me, but I could see in his face that he did not
believe me.

After a quick visit to the city's collection of nineteenth-century art to hunt down some of the other paintings that Andersen had enthused about, Dirk dropped me in the centre of Munich at the end of a giddy afternoon in which I really felt my journey had begun. All that sleazing about in Hamburg and grave-dodging in Nuremberg seemed slightly amateurish and embarrassing now that I had spent some time with a proper, serious literary historian (albeit one who wears a beret).

And then I went and spoiled it all.

Just as he was about to drop me off, I had begun to tell Dirk about my visit to Sandra in Hamburg. He seemed confused.

'You see a prostitute there?' he asked, perplexed. 'I don't understand.'

'Well, you see, Andersen went to see prostitutes but says he didn't actually, you know, do anything and I wanted to . . .' I tailed off.

Dirk was still smiling, but the smile was fixed, the eyes betrayed a hint of panic. We said our polite goodbyes. Dirk refused to accept any fee for his services (he had given up an entire Sunday afternoon) – perhaps he didn't want to be categorised with Sandra as one of my paid researchers – and we parted.

As improbable as this sounds, Munich on a wet Sunday evening soon cheered me up. It was Carnival time and as I walked through Marienplatz, the square where Hitler had honed his rabble-rousing skills, I was accosted by the smell of sugared almonds and frying sausages. A band of drummers were competing against a German soft-metal group and an impressively loud oompah band for the attention of a downright surreal audience that included confetti-throwing witches, an elderly couple dressed as chickens, and nightmarish clowns. One of the chickens tried to engage me in a waltz. I pulled my head down into my jacket and scampered away.

After an Andersen-in-Munich tribute meal whose two principal ingredients were beer and radishes, I retired to my guest house near the station for what proved to be a troubled and explosive night.

★   ★   ★

I woke up the next morning to find heavy snow outside my window, with more predicted. This would have been fine, picturesque even, were it not for the fact that I would be swapping the train for a hire car in which I intended to traverse the Alps in a day.

Andersen's departure from Munich was, if anything, more miserable than his arrival. The marriage of Louise Collin had taken place in Copenhagen the previous night – he refers to it in *A Poet's Bazaar* only as a marriage 'in that house where I am regarded as a son and brother' – and he left Munich on his own, without Holst as originally planned, in a diligence heading for the Brenner Pass, and Italy.

At the car-hire office at Munich station I asked the man if he thought the Pass would be open: 'How should I know?' he said. 'I am just happy I am staying inside.'

Munich looked completely alien carpeted in snow and despite my keen sense of direction I soon found myself woefully misplaced in the city's suburbs. As usual in such circumstances I adhered to the Male Driver's Rules, which state that:

a) You must never admit, even to yourself, that you are lost.
b) You must never turn around, no matter how apparent it may be that you are heading, terminally, in the wrong direction.
c) You can never stop and ask for directions, sooner or later there will be a clue.
d) If you accidentally left the map in the boot, there it must stay.
e) If all else fails, follow the car in front of you.

Forty minutes later I found myself back at Munich station.

Newly furnished with map and directions I discovered that one is unlikely to see signs to Innsbruck if one has been travelling in completely the wrong direction. Soon, I was free from the gravitational pull of Munich's suburbs and entering a desolate snowscape of farmland and hills, and then mountains. Tragically, for what is one of the most scenic parts of Europe, I could see no further than the bonnet – and that only by virtue of a full-on Clint Eastwood squint with my nose pressed up to the windscreen Mr Magoo-style. The car careered like an errant supermarket trolley, at times the steering wheel seemingly serving no other purpose than to distract me from my doom, like the oxygen masks in a passenger jet.

I had visions of being trapped for days in this little tin box, with no food or water, and eventually no fuel or heat. When the St Bernard finally found me, having picked up the still pungent scent of cheap guest-house soap, I would be a meat-flavoured popsicle. The newspapers would interview the last man who had seen me alive: 'I told him not to go,' said Helmut Koch of the car-hire company's Munich office, 'but he laughed in my face. He said he lived in Scandinavia, and, "Do you call this snow?"'

After around three hours of this, and with nothing resembling Innsbruck looming out of the white shroud, my bladder was overflowing. I scrabbled to a halt, turned the engine off, pulled my fingernails out of the steering wheel and unclenched my buttocks. Outside was snowy silence – a 'deep, death-like stillness' is how Andersen described this frozen landscape. Had the Snow Queen appeared from out of the forest behind me, tethered me to her sleigh and whisked me off to her lair, I would not have been at all surprised.

'The Snow Queen' (1844) is regarded by many as Andersen's greatest tale. He wrote it in just a couple of days. 'It came out dancing across the page,' he later claimed. This menacing, magisterial story tells of a young boy named Kai, into whose heart falls a splinter from the devil's mirror, turning him into a mean-minded, cynical adolescent. As if that wasn't misfortune enough, he is then abducted by the Snow Queen, a terrifying yet rather sexy creature – '"Now you're not getting any more kisses," she said, "or else I'd kiss you to death!"' – who sets him the task of solving a jigsaw in order to win his freedom. In the end it is his childhood friend, Gerda, who rescues him after a lengthy and demanding quest in which we meet creepy old women, a feral robber girl with whom Gerda shares a bed, talking flowers and a friendly crow, and we learn about Hindu funeral rites. It is a truly extraordinary piece of writing and it cemented Andersen's reputation as the pre-eminent writer of literary fairy tales.

But as I stood beside the car the only sound was a torrent of steaming urine and the ticking of the engine as it cooled. The car was disappearing beneath snow drifts by the second. I jumped back in, tensed every muscle and sinew in my body, and set off at around 3 mph in the direction of Innsbruck.

At least the weather was fitting – Andersen had donned his Icelandic stockings in preparation for the journey by carriage through the night from Innsbruck over the Brenner, as there was deep snow all around then too. The windows of his carriage were covered with 'icy flowers' and he and his fellow passengers sat with their feet in hay to keep warm. Above, the stars in the clear night sky appeared, he writes, 'as if one were in a large cemetery for the whole race of Adam: the still-born child, the most wretched beggar, each had his monument.' It is a striking simile – that the night sky brings comfort in death to even the most wretched of people. Gloomy, depressive, yet with a hope of eternal redemption for even the most lost of souls – a fair pointer to his mood at the time.

Andersen had passed through Innsbruck before, on his way to Italy in 1834. 'It appeared to me as if but a few hours had passed since I was here,' Andersen writes in A Poet's Bazaar, 'and I became thoughtful, and with good reason. How many reminiscences slumber in our minds, how much that we would gladly have forgotten . . . ? I believe that the mind forgets nothing; everything can again be awakened, as fresh and living as in the moment it happened.' He echoes this sentiment a little later on in Mantua: 'They say that sorrow gets up behind a man and rides with him: I believe it; but memory does the same, and sits faster. Memory rode its hobby on my knee, and laid its head against my heart.'

Throughout his life he would travel to stay a step ahead of his sorrows, his memories bringing little comfort.

The tourists were gathered like weather-worn sheep in the colonnaded arcades – 'heavily-built' as Andersen describes them – in the centre of Innsbruck, inspecting the windows of the city's fancy cake shops and Swarovski outlets. Judging by the architecture, it would seem that, a couple of hundred years ago, Innsbruck's city council, for reasons lost to both time and taste, decided to hand over the design and construction of their major buildings, like the palace and most of the churches, to the city's confectioners. As with the local *sachertorte*, the effect is quite satisfying, in small doses.

At the top of the main pedestrian area I came across a film crew. As usual, their pantechnicons and paraphernalia had engulfed the surrounding area and so the few tourists who had ventured out were having to tread over dolly tracks, lighting rigs and cables. Location film crews are one of my pet hates. Having worked as a dogsbody (or Second Assistant Director, as I was misleadingly titled – the closest I came to assisting a director was fetching him sausage butties) on a number of them, I am well aware of their blithe disregard of 'civilians', as they like to call us. Capturing that crucial shot of Nigel Havers crossing the road takes priority over anything else, regardless of whether it will cause a tailback to Inverness, force mothers with prams to cross four-lane highways or delay life-saving organ transplant deliveries, and no matter how humble or crappy the show. I worked, briefly, on *The Bill*, so I know of what I speak and I regularly held up traffic with all the authority that a *The Bill* baseball cap carried, demanding that road menders suspend work and shepherding innocent bystanders out of the way, with no authority whatsoever.

This crew were filming a Citroen 2CV driving down a pedestrian passageway little wider than the car. They were Canadians, it turned out, making a film called *The Crazy Canucks* about some apparently legendary downhill skiers from the 1970s. Watch out for that one at the multiplexes!

Chapter Three

FLORENCE

After stuffing my face with *sachertorte*, I Yeti-ed back to the car through the abominable snow storm. As I drove onward to the Italian border the radio tuned itself, as if guided by a divine musical spirit, to some appropriately apocalyptic tunes: Nick Cave and Tom Waits back-to-back for over an hour.

Sadly, my arrival in Italy was heralded by the fuzzy fading of this unlikely daytime radio scheduling, to be replaced by a prattling DJ – an aural dead ringer for Terry Wogan, but Italian. The second sign that I had left Austria came when a Lancia loaded to the gunwales with nuns cut me up on the autostrada, forcing me to swerve violently. Nuns are, in my experience, the worst drivers in the world – they make Cairo taxi drivers look like Advanced Motorists – so you can imagine the terror evoked by the sight in my rear-view mirror of a cluster of black habits in a high-performance saloon.

As is usual in Italy, the road had been transformed into a Darwinian arcade game in which the players were either quick or dead. At least the snow abated at Trentino, to be replaced by a biblical deluge.

'Six years had elapsed since I had left Italy; I was now here again,' writes Andersen in *A Poet's Bazaar* as he crosses the Alps for the second time in his life – also to be greeted by torrential rain. 'In the first hostelry on Italian ground I had determined to empty the cup of welcome; but the diligence drove past the first, the second and the third, for the conductor slept.' As it turned out, the conductor might have done better to keep sleeping until

Naples. Andersen's second visit to Italy would be a troubled one.

Holiday destinations are rarely as good on the second visit (except for Margate, which, if you downgrade your expectations, is fantastic every time), and this was very much the case for Andersen as he arrived in Italy in December 1840. This time round he would find that everything, from the weather to his health, to his financial and professional fortunes, and even his fellow passengers, would sour the mood of this leg of his journey.

In contrast, he always recalled his first stay in Italy – in the winter of 1833–34 – through peachy lenses. 'If France is the country of reason,' he wrote at the time, 'then Italy is the country of the imagination . . . Here is all you could wish for in a land-scape . . . Everything was like a painting.' His first visit was nothing less than a spiritual awakening; it was, he wrote, 'as if the snow melted away from my eyes and a new world of art rose before me.' He fell for Italy with all his heart – the art of the Renaissance (much of which he was seeing for the first time); the scenery; the sun; the chaotic vibrancy of the place; and even the women. 'Here at last are beautiful women to be found,' he wrote to a friend.

But as he crosses the snow-covered Alps second time round his mood is downbeat. He is sharing a carriage with a Professor Becker who talks incessantly (and, worse, has paid less than him); his hotel room on his first night in Verona is cold and charm-less; in Mantua he is anxious about losing his passport, 'dejected' that his room costs 18 Zwansiger and, it seems, more than a touch paranoid: 'I walked in the arcades and felt unfamiliar and that the people didn't know me or took offence to me,' he wrote in his diary that night.

He spent his morning in Verona trawling the tourist sights – the churches, the castle and the Roman arena, which, he reports, was newly restored. These days the arena looks like it is made from well-worn pumice, but the acoustics are still magnificent. I could hear a complaining English child on the far side virtu-ally whinge for whinge. ('When can we go? Can I have an ice cream? Oh, pleeease.') It is dimly lit and shoddy, which I rather liked. If this was a Scandinavian tourist sight, it would have been restored to within an inch of its life, panelled with blond wood and loaded with interactive visitor centres. As it was, much of it was boarded up, sections of railings were left lying around as if a riot had recently occurred, and a large part of the outside wall was draped with an advert for shoes.

From there I walked on through medieval streets to the star of Verona's tourist firmament, Casa di Giulietta, and the famous balcony where Juliet stood and enquired where for art Romeo was. Or didn't, as the case is.

Of course, virtually nothing is known of the sixteenth-century lovers from rival Montecchi and Capuleti families but this doesn't stop the Veronese from stretching the credulity of visitors to extraordinary lengths with this particular attraction. Juliet's house does have one genuinely remarkable feature though. The stone walls of the vaulted hallway that connects the courtyard to the street, as well as the walls of the courtyard itself, are plastered in love messages, written on tiny scraps of paper and stuck to unfeasible heights with chewing gum. It looks like a million razor cuts stemmed with tissue paper. I spent some time reading the messages, mostly mundane but oddly touching – 'David Kemp and Sophie Hunt, 23/3/03 First holiday together, love always X'; 'Bob and Annette, heart to heart, July 1999'; 'I love you Justin Timberlake', and so on.

Inside, as you would expect of the fictional abode of a fictional character, the house is largely bereft of exhibits – aside from 'Juliet's Desk', an interactive display 'designed expressly for the Casa di Giulietta to give the visitor the possibility to communicate with the Shakespearean heroine by way of computer technology!' which was out of order. And you can actually stand on the non-actual balcony – imagine the hilarity that must ensue.

I went back outside clutching my photocopy of the drawing Andersen had made of Juliet's house. Strangely, the modern-day Palazzo Capuleti bore absolutely no relation to his picture. I walked around the city centre for a couple of hours, grasping my increasingly bedraggled piece of A4 and holding it up to every building I saw, but none matched. It suddenly occurred to me that perhaps I had hot new evidence as to the location of the *real* pretend Juliet's house, which, following my presentation to the mayor, would see me given my own weight in pistachio ice cream. I tried to find the tourist board in order to set this chain of events in motion, but instead chanced upon something that sounded even more promising: the Centro Storico.

After a good deal of arm waving and a heated debate among the Centro's librarians, they admitted that none recognised the building Andersen had drawn. One launched a futile Internet search, another picked up the phone and then, realising he had no one to ring, quietly hung up again. In the end one of the female staff broke ranks and confessed: 'Is not real, forty years old.'

The only thing to do in such circumstances as these, I find, is to have lunch. In a side-street trattoria I dithered between various unfathomable menu options. My eventual choice turned out to be oily, heavily herbed minced horsemeat, served on a bed of unusually thick spaghetti. I had never tasted horsemeat before and was oddly gratified to discover that it does actually taste of horse – which tastes slightly like damp beef. This is not as nice as it sounds, but was still preferable to the pizza topped with chips (a local delicacy) that a Roberto Benigni-lookalike was wolfing down on the table next to me.

From here I walked to Verona cathedral, which is where I first became aware of my trousers.

I had bought the trousers especially for this trip; a serendipitously smart buy I thought at the time. The shop did not have my size and as I am physically incapable of passing a patisserie while abroad, I thought it was sensible to buy a size too large rather than a size too small. And as well as being a bit baggy (or 'street', as I felt at the time) they were also made from an unusually tough corduroy. Good, I thought, they would take longer to wear out those embarrassing smooth patches just below the crotch that signal the premature demise of all men's corduroys. Better still, they boasted a total of ten pockets.

The theory behind this was that the Artful Dodgers I felt certain I would encounter, particularly on the Italian leg of my journey, would be so befuddled by the sheer choice of pockets to pick that they would run screaming back into the crowd and leave my necessaries untouched. There would be no need for me to sew money into my jacket lining as that old neurotic Andersen did when travelling. The downside, I later realised, was that, should anything happen to me, my corpse could well remain unidentified for some months while they tried to find my passport (which I kept in the pocket by my right ankle – this is not neurotic, by the way, merely a sensible precaution). After I had bought the trousers, Lissen helpfully pointed out that, actually, due to the wealth of opportunity I represented, I might well attract thieves like stray cats to a fishmonger's rubbish bin. Later still, it began to dawn on me that the suspicious looks I occasionally received from shopkeepers were probably down to the fact that the trousers would be absolutely perfect if I were intent on a spot of shoplifting.

So, I had already begun to rue my purchase long before the door to Verona cathedral closed behind me with an echoing thud and I found myself in the middle of a Mass. Then, as I began to walk across the church amid the silence of communion, the extra tough corduroy came into its own, rubbing between my thighs and making a noise akin to a fistful of thimbles on a washboard. I was a walking, one-man skiffle group, with my squeaky, wet trainers adding to the chorus.

Thankfully only half the congregation turned to stare at this sodden, sorry backpacker with his musical garb, but it was enough to make me feel like the worst kind of lumbering, insensitive tourist – what Henry James termed the 'trooping barbarians'. I backed out slowly, legs bowed John Wayne-style in an attempt to minimise the thigh-friction.

Back in the car I drowned my embarrassment in a bag full of pastries – sumptuous ricotta-filled cannoli, rich yellow custard tarts and exploding croissants. At the end of my feast, as I sat back with Tony Wogan on the wireless, encrusted in a carapace of pastry flakes, icing sugar and chocolate chips, I looked like I'd been tarred and feathered by the Mr Kipling posse.

Outside Verona I became lost almost instantaneously; so lost in fact that after about an hour of steep, first-gear hairpins snaking upward through olive groves and ever deepening snow, I actually *turned back*. This meant that my visits to Mantua, Modena and Bologna – all of which Andersen had passed through – were somewhat curtailed. In fact, I skipped Modena altogether. Andersen had only stopped for a pre-dawn coffee there anyway and, hardly surprising given the time of day, pronounced it 'completely dead and deserted'. He stayed the night in Bologna, but doesn't seem to have done much else there than have a nice dinner and write a letter home. Nevertheless, I battled my way into Bologna city centre, parked the car, and walked to the tourist information office where I discovered that private cars are banned from the city centre and that I had in fact chosen to leave my car outside the police station.

I raced back, fighting alarming chest pains, to find two female traffic wardens, their freshly licked biros poised to issue a financially crippling chit. I threw myself prostrate on the ground before them in a mock mercy-beg, managing also to muster some genuine tears, which I hoped would help my case (I swear to God, the irony of this has only just struck me). Their expressions did not change; but, as I reflected later, with Italian males such masters of the histrionic gesture, short of setting fire to myself or eating my trousers, there would have been little I could do to distract them from issuing a ticket.

The fine was something of a downer, though my mood was nothing compared to Andersen's on this stretch of the journey. That night as he sits writing in his room in the hillside town of Lojano – the next stop on the way to Florence – his loneliness is palpable: 'The solitude of the valley imparted – I will not say a stamp of melancholy, no, I think it must be called quietude ... [I] felt no more alone that I am in my little room in Denmark. He who has a home at home, can feel homesickness; but he who has none feels himself equally at home everywhere.'

You can't blame him for trying. Though he often claimed to suffer instead from 'out-sickness' (i.e., his travel urge) in truth, he was as vulnerable to homesickness as the rest of us. He had complained of a variation of it in a letter to Jonas Collin a few weeks earlier in Munich: 'By "home" I only think of your house; that is the place which can give me homesickness, otherwise I never want to see Denmark again.'

According to Andersen's account of his night in Lojano in *A Poet's Bazaar*, his inn has a dark, Bronte-esque secret. He hears a flute repeating two notes over and over, and follows the sound through a small door in his room, down a narrow passage. He comes to a door, which flies open to reveal an old peasant man with long, white hair, half undressed – he discovers later that it is the owner's insane uncle. 'When the old man is dead,' Andersen pontificates, 'the inmates of the house will, in the stillness of the night, think that they hear, like ghost tones, what I now heard in reality.' In fact, according to his diary, the night passed without incident. I suspect that the whole story was inspired by Conrad Rantzau's mentally deranged brother.

As I approached Florence some hours later a crack of sunlight appeared ahead. This lifted my spirits, which soon began to soar as, through olive groves bathed in an electric apricot sunset, I caught tantalising glimpses of the city. There are no squalid suburbs on the northern side of Florence to spoil your arrival in this bewitching city; my appalling sense of direction did that all by itself.

I dropped off my hire car. Sounds simple, doesn't it? But this oh-so-innocuous phrase in reality encompasses what was one of the most torrid experiences of my adult life. And I doubt it was much more pleasurable for the poor woman in the car-hire office who dealt patiently but helplessly with my progressively more hysterical phone calls over the course of the next hour and a half.

At first, all was going smoothly as I circled the city centre, at times coming encouragingly close to the drop-off point, before finding myself being swept out of town towards the airport on a tide of rush-hour traffic. Florence city centre is a blizzard of one-ways, whose directions were, I am convinced, being altered literally as I was driving along them.

With four minutes to go before the office closed (and I would incur another day's fee) I seriously contemplated giving up and abandoning the damn thing by the roadside, when, on my fifth call (in which I insisted the car-hire woman stayed on the line with me until we made visual contact), by complete fluke, I arrived at the office exhausted, pathetically grateful and utterly humiliated.

Florence soon cheered me up. Even after having gorged on palazzos, piazzas, churches and ancient stadia over the previous few days, the beauty of this city still rendered me dumbstruck at every turn. From the peach, ivory, emerald and ebony jewellery box Duomo, to the Baptistery's fabled bronze doors, to the Ponte Vecchio, Florence is possessed of innumerable architectural glories, each of which, if placed in virtually any other city in the world, would be its prime tourist destination.

Andersen loved the city too; it had opened his eyes to the art of the Renaissance on his first visit. The three nights he spent in Florence in 1840, meanwhile, are best remembered for the story he wrote about one of the city's less well-known but more charismatic statues. The story, 'The Bronze Hog' (or 'Bronze Boar') is a jolly picaresque that Andersen cleverly contrives to work as a fairly good sightseeing guide to the city. It was first published as the Florence chapter of *A Poet's Bazaar*, and is one of the book's highlights.

The story tells of a 'pretty, half-naked boy . . . the image of

Italy – so pretty, so laughing, and yet so suffering' who, one night, while he is out begging, drinks from the snout of a bronze fountain in the shape of a wild boar. As he drinks, the boar awakes (he can only come to life with an innocent child on his back), and carries the boy off for a whistle-stop tour of the sights of Florence. The next morning the boy returns to his mother – who is a prostitute – empty handed and she attacks him with a cauldron. He runs away and is adopted by a glovemaker's wife whose neighbour, a young artist, inspires him to start drawing. One of his subjects is the small dog belonging to the glovemaker's wife whose legs he ties together (the dog's, that is, not the wife's) to make it stand still. When the owner sees this she is ready to throw the boy out onto the streets once more, until the young painter intervenes and agrees to take him under his wing. The story ends with a visit Andersen claims to have made to an exhibition at the Acadamia della Arte in 1934 (though there is no reference to it in his diary from that time) where he sees two paintings by the young boy, who has gone on to become a great artist. One is of the scene with the dog as artist's model; the other is of the bronze hog.

The story does not end happily, however, as, at the very last moment, the boy/artist fulfils one of Andersen's own oft-repeated desires: to die at the height of his artistic achievement. The character's death is believed to have been inspired by the demise, aged twenty-eight, of the Odense painter Wilhelm Bendz in Vicenza in 1832.

It was a magnificent picture; a large gilt frame encircled it, and on the corner of the frame hung a laurel wreath, but between the green leaves, a black ribbon entwined itself, from which a long crepe veil hung down.
The young artist was just then dead!

The statue of the wild boar still stands beneath the loggia of Mercato Nuovo (new market), close to the Piazza della Signoria.

It is a lucky mascot for visitors who rub its nose, and toss a coin through the grate below (the money goes to children's charities) to assure their return to the city. The locals love Andersen's statue too; they have nicknamed the market *il Porcellino*, or piglet, in its honour.

At least I *assumed* it was Andersen's statue but as I began to explore Florence's art collections an incredible story of intrigue, deceit and mystery in the murky world of international art and drug dealing began to unfold.

Okay, I admit I am trying to jazz this up a bit (the bit about drug dealing is a complete lie, for instance), but I am still rather proud to be the first Andersen fan to have unearthed the true story behind the bronze hog, or rather *hogs* . . .

Seeing as Andersen meant the story to double up as a kind of guide to Florence I thought I would use it for my day's sight-seeing, and so in the watery early-morning light I walked from my hotel – a former home of Rossini (the composer lived there from 1851 to 1855, and I chose to stay there because Andersen later met him in Paris, in 1866, pronouncing him 'rather grubby' and declining an invitation to a concert as his guest) – to the gardens of the Palazzo Pitti, where the boy in the story begins his evening's adventure.

The city was emerging to face the day, with fishmongers laying out their shimmering stock and greengrocers arranging oranges in gravity-defying pyramids. Despite being comparatively traffic free (unique for an Italian city), the centre of Florence is still terribly noisy. Give or take the odd generator and the bicycle bells, the sounds of hammers on stone, saws cutting wood and the other miscellaneous bangings of hairy-arsed artisans would have been the background music to Andersen's visit too. The smells can't be so different either: baking bread, freshly made coffee and leather (as it was in 1840, leather-making is still a major industry here).

In a narrow side street I was engulfed by a crocodile of kids on their way to school and, soon after, the torrential rains began again. I hugged the walls but soon began to feel like Eric Morecambe in the *Singing in the Rain* sketch as various decrepit drains, dripping balconies and other pedestrians' umbrellas conspired to give me a good soaking.

At that stage I was unaware that the Pitti was to play a pivotal role in my hunt for the 'real' pig, and only spent a few moments marvelling at its monumental Flintstones' architecture, replete with gigantic iron rings on the walls – presumably for tethering your dinosaur – before making my way towards the Ponte Vecchio.

Just before the bridge was a glove shop, housed in a building that was certainly old enough to be contemporary with Andersen's story – who knows, perhaps this was the very glove-maker that inspired him. The owner turned out to be an English woman. I asked her how long it had been a glove shop. 'Oh, it's always been a glove shop,' she said. Now I was excited. 'Oh yes, always since 1966.' Sadly, though 1966 may have been a fairly monumental year for the Charlton family, I don't think it quite qualifies as the beginning of time.

As in December 1840, the Arno was swollen and fast flowing; it looked like angry tea. I followed Andersen's directions to the Piazza del Mercato Nuovo where the stallholders were ready with open mouths waiting for the day's tourist plankton to fall upon their handbags and gloves, fake Versace scarves and, in the case of one optimistic stallholder, curtains of blubbery, grey tripe. The gloves were made in Yeovil. I gave up on the glove thing.

The first time Andersen saw the statue, he noted it in passing in his diary as an 'exuberant wild pig made from metal, water streaming out from its mouth and looks comical that people look like they are kissing the pig when they drink, it is completely worn on the snout and ears.' (7 April 1834.) It still stands today on the south side of the market, a handsome beast captured in a majestic, life-size reclining pose like a Roman emperor. I could quite imagine him springing up and flying off around the city.

Water dribbles, rather than streams, from his snout, which has been rubbed to a shine by a million visitors' fingers and, on this occasion, I was upset to see, was covered with fake snow from an aerosol (I wiped it off with my sleeve). Around the statue's base were frogs, crabs, newts, snails, turtles and snakes, also cast in bronze.

According to the footnotes to the most recent edition of *A Poet's Bazaar*, the original statue is in the Uffizi, which, by a happy coincidence, is where the story takes us next.

The boy and his steed arrive at the world's pre-eminent collection of Renaissance art via the Piazza del Granduca, today the Piazza della Signora. 'The bronze horse which bore the statue of the Duke neighed aloud; the variegated arms on the old council Hall shone like transparent paintings; and Michelangelo's *David* swung his sling. It was a strange life that moved! The bronze groups with *Perseus* and the *Rape of the Sabines* were living too: a death shriek from them passed over that magnificent but solitary place,' Andersen writes. As is the case every morning, there was a lengthy queue of Japanese tourists outside the Uffizi. Reader, I jumped it.

The boar carries the boy up the stairs (the Uffizi might do well to consider employing a fleet of pigs for just this purpose, as it is quite a climb) to 'a beautiful naked female, as beautiful as nature and marble's greatest master alone could make her. She moved her fine limbs. Dolphins played around her feet, immortality shone from her eyes': it is the *Medici Venus*. Andersen visited the Uffizi often during his first stay in Florence, on one occasion spending an entire hour spellbound in front of this iconic statue, which had been unearthed from the ruins of Hadrian's villa 180 years earlier (begging the question, how on earth does something like that get buried?) Try and sit for even a few minutes before the Venus today, as I did, and you will find yourself dragged up by your elbows like some festering vagrant and ushered round the outer edge of the Tribuna (the octagonal room in which she is exhibited), with the rest of the non-stop crowd.

Also mentioned in the story, and still exhibited alongside the Venus, are the 'naked well-formed men', Arrotino – the knife-grinder – and the wrestling gladiators. Health and safety would have a field day with the grinder, as he has decided to carry out his grinding duties stark naked and isn't paying the slightest attention to what he is doing, which seems beyond reckless to me.

I found the original Roman *Il Porcinello*, rendered in marble and stuck, forgotten, at the end of the Third Corridor. It was stationed by the toilets, behind a group of tragically under-endowed male figures, and was actually slightly inferior to the bronze copy I had seen earlier.

Back to the story: the bronze boar flies, with the boy still clinging to his back, to Santa Croce. Here he sees the monuments to Michelangelo, Alfieri, Machiavelli and Dante. I entered the church past the statue of a very cross-looking Dante and four equally angry – yet at the same time slightly camp – lions outside on the square and, whaddaya know, there as described were the monuments, along with the tomb of Galileo, which, according to his diary, Andersen had knelt before six years earlier. The boy loses consciousness at this point, waking to find himself back in the market square where the flight had begun, the boar a statue once more.

The story has, in the past, been interpreted as a depiction of the transition from childhood to adolescence – the drinking of the water from the hog's snout representing a kind of loss of virginity, or at the very least an awakening of his sexuality. One critic took this further, believing that Andersen's reference to the *Rape of the Sabines* and *Perseus* was a subconscious – or perhaps even deliberate – reference to his struggle with his own sexuality, while Freudians interpret the various flights of stairs that appear as symbols of sexual intercourse. As is often the case with Andersen's short stories, their simplicity and our extensive knowledge of the author's life does tend to invite these readings, but for me this one at least had worked well enough as a substitute city guide.

My own porcine odyssey didn't end there, however. The next afternoon, I returned to the Pitti to try to track down some of the other Florentine masterpieces that had taken Andersen's fancy. Leaving the gallery, deep in thought about a picture I had just seen of Cleopatra's cleavage (which Andersen mentions in his diary), I very nearly missed something really rather extraordinary in the *Sala delle Nicchie*. It caused me to do a perfect double take: it was another statue of the wild boar, the third I had seen so far in Florence, also in bronze. As I approached I could see its snout was so worn it was almost falling off. Its back, too, was burnished to a golden shine by children riding it. It required but a fraction of my nascent skills as a literary detective to deduce that this pig had obviously stood outside for a long time. Might this be the original – the boar Andersen had described in the story – and the current occupant of the Mercato Nuovo a replica?

I bustled to find out more in the administrative offices of the museum. Initially the man in charge there denied all knowledge of the statue then, following some classic arm-waving, a small, round, bald man came forward with a catalogue detailing the statue's full history. It turned out that Cosimo Medici commissioned the original – which was indeed the one I had just spotted – in 1642 from his bronze specialist, Pietro Tacca (1577–1644), who used the stone boar in the Uffizi as his model. This in turn is a Roman marble copy of a Greek original depicting the Erymanthian boar, which Hercules captured as the fourth of his twelve labours. The *third* boar statue, the one now standing in the square, was cast in 1999, while the original that I had just found in the Pitti was due to be returned indefinitely to storage.

I couldn't help thinking this was something of a scandal when you consider that, unlike the wretched statue of the Little Mermaid on Copenhagen's harbour, this was a piece of art that Andersen had not only seen but which had inspired one of his stories and a uniquely imaginative piece of travel writing. When I explained all this to the museum staff they immediately set about finding a permanent pride-of-place position for the statue, thanking me profusely for my timely intervention and offering me an executive post on the museum board. Or, did they just shrug and make meaningful glances towards the door?

Anyway, I was sufficiently encouraged by my porky Sherlockery that the next day I set out to track down the hotel Andersen had stayed in during his visit to the city in 1840. I was determined to pin down the location of at least one of his residences on this trip and had a hunch that in a city as well preserved and documented as Florence I stood a decent chance.

I realise that this is beginning to sound like a fixation verging on the demented and, I have to admit, I had started to be a bit furtive in conversations with Lissen over the phone in case she found out just how obsessed I had become, but Andersen had by now utterly possessed me. By tracking down the exact locations of the places he stayed, standing where he stood and seeing the things he looked at – whether they were views, artworks, a social type, or, as would later transpire, cacti – I really did feel I was drawing closer to him.

The very fact that I wanted to get closer to Andersen was telling too. When all this had started, back in Copenhagen, I had been amused and enchanted by his stories and fascinated by *A Poet's Bazaar*, but as for the man, well, I had formed a fairly unpalatable picture of him as a self-obsessed, prissy neurotic – a pathological narcissist, utterly consumed with his own reputation. I imagined that, had I met him, he would have irritated me immensely, not least, as I have said, because he served as a mirror for some of my less endearing qualities.

There was his colossal vanity for a start. Nothing delighted Andersen more than public recognition, however trivial. He apparently felt no embarrassment, for instance, in approaching people to whom he had not yet been introduced and saying: 'They write in the paper that I have such thoughtful eyes; do you think my eyes are thoughtful?' When his career began to take off, he monitored his success like a politician scrutinising the opinion polls, and sought praise with a childlike neediness to his dying breath, feeling each criticism with a raw keenness: 'I could be made wretched for a whole day, if I met with a sour countenance where I expected a friendly one,' he once admitted.

Henrik Ibsen recalled visiting Andersen towards the end of his life. He refused to come down from his room so Ibsen went up to get him. When asked how he had persuaded Andersen to join the soirée, he said: 'I embraced him and paid him a casual compliment. He was moved, and returning my embrace he asked me, "So you really like me then?"' (His reluctance to join the party may have had something to do with his jealousy of a young rival. After the publication of Ibsen's first work Andersen was asked by a dinner partner one evening if he had read it. 'Have you never heard, madam, of a Danish poet named Hans Christian Andersen?' he replied, grossly offended.)

He was also an unconscionable snob who fawned over the nobility and, later in life, would cross Europe at the drop of a hat if he suspected there was a royal audience in the offing. His autobiography frequently labours under its author's craven toadying and is full of passages of extravagant praise for Count this and Duke that: 'I had the happiness of visiting the Princess of Prussia many times . . . Prince Pückler-Muskau also was present'; 'I received still one more proof of my favour and kindness of the King of Prussia towards me, on the evening before my departure from the city. The order of the Red Eagle, of the third class, was conferred upon me . . . I confess candidly that I felt myself honoured in a high degree.'

The names fall like napalm: Dickens, Mendelssohn, Henry James, Balzac, Browning, the brothers Grimm, Victor Hugo, Alexandre Dumas among them. At one point he simply resorts to listing the notable people he has met.

Then there was the hypochondria. He was forever fretting

about draughts, headaches, toothache and his own self-inflicted penile contusions, all of which he assumed – as most hypho-chondriacs tend to do – would be equally compelling topics for his friends. One wrote after his death: 'He had no power of enduring physical pain, or any notion that it was undignified to bemoan himself. He would talk to his friends of every ailment and sensation with quite pathetic earnestness [and] rub his stomach slowly and heavily, while he explained, "I was bad all night, and when the pain came I asked the good God to take me away, but when it went I thought I should like to live."'

Here is a random selection of health worries recorded in his diary on this trip alone:

Hamburg:	'Sore penis and worried about it.'
Rome:	'My big toe is swollen and painful . . . my big toe is one big blister'; then the next day, 'My foot is better, but my sore throat is still with me.'
Boat to Greece:	'Pain in my throat.'
Athens:	'My penis is giving me trouble, and heaven knows it isn't my fault.'; 'Penis still bad, I do hope I haven't caught anything in the ship's loo!'; 'I had a stomach ache and had to go to a chemists in Piraeus and drink bitter schnapps'; 'Pain in knee and testicle [both recurring].' 'I am in a kind of fever state; shall I travel to Constantinople or not?'

And if he was unable to summon physical ills, there was always his 'passport angst':

Malta:	'A little worried that my passport might not be on board; after lunch it was given to me.'

Constantinople: 'Anxious that something might be wrong with my passport. Oh how good I am at finding things to worry about!'; 'Passport anxiety – that it hasn't been stamped with the proper visas.'

Or his fear of dogs:

Athens: 'Big Greek dogs were watching me.'

Or in the absence of all of the above, simply a vague unease, as when he sets sail into the Black Sea and notes: 'I'm suffering from a strange apprehension.'

He must have been awfully tiring to be around. He seems to have spent his life on the verge of neurotic hysteria. On one occasion, having fled up three flights of stairs to escape his land-lady's dog, he turned and screeched: 'Did he bite me? Did he bite me?' During his later years he became more and more para-noid. He once received a box of preserves from a far-flung Danish colony, but became convinced they had been poisoned, so gave them to a friend to try first. He called on her a week later and asked: 'Did you eat the preserves I sent you?' She had. 'Oh, how glad I am!' he replied. 'I was a little afraid they might be poisoned, so I said to myself, "My dear friend is the most courageous of women. I am going to send her a sample." I am delighted to learn, as I hoped, that there is no danger.'

Hoped!

Despite all this, my affection for him continued to grow, thrusting up through the paving slabs like a determined daisy, excusing or at least obscuring many of his frailties.

There is that remarkable childhood, for a start. Few writers' life stories are as fantastical as their fiction (and if this is the case, there is usually something amiss with the fiction), but Hans Christian Andersen gripped life by the lapels, pushed it up against a wall and demanded that it empty its pockets. He was the ultimate self-starter, systematically dismantling the seemingly insurmountable obstacles that lay between the poverty of his childhood and the glittering prize of global fame, at a time when such a thing was the sole preserve of admirals and kings.

The man had guts. He was no fragile orchid, despite the picture many have painted. Can you conceive of the courage it must have taken for this goofy, introspective child, who had led a comparatively cosseted life obsessing over his puppet theatre and dolls, to venture out in to the world, alone, at the age of fourteen? He set out for the big city with the equivalent of £100, a worthless letter of introduction and wearing his dead father's hastily altered clothes. I don't know about you, but when I was fourteen it took all the courage I could muster to go to the hairdresser's.

This explains, and to a certain extent excuses, much of Andersen's paranoia and snobbery later in life. He spent his teen years desperately trying to adapt to a social class whose rules and conventions he had little knowledge of, yet upon whom he was entirely dependent for his survival. They, in turn, treated him fairly condescendingly at times. The Collin family never accorded him the respect as a writer that he deserved or craved, while the Danish critics, though not quite as negative about him as Andersen made them out to be, mocked him mercilessly. They could never quite appreciate him for the revolutionary artist the rest of the world knew him to be, at least not in his lifetime (once he was safely dead and gone, that was another matter). And, as I mentioned earlier, such was the insular nature of Copenhagen's literary clique, that Andersen was personally known to most of its prime movers, which can't have helped.

However, the more I read about him the more I realised that the public persona of the foppish, self-regarding artist was markedly softened when he was among friends with whom he felt secure. Here, another Andersen emerges – eccentric, yes; self-regarding, always, but humble, doubting and desperate for approval. As the renowned Andersen academic Elias Bredsdorff wrote, 'Everybody could see his vanity, but only those who knew him were aware of his humility.' Within his intimate circle of friends – of which, it is worth noting, he accumulated a great many – he felt able to let his guard down and laugh at himself. He would often set himself up for ridicule: 'Andersen's sense of humour and fun might get the better of his egocentricity to such an extent that when he saw himself being placed in a funny light he might find it amusing,' wrote Edvard in his memoir of Andersen, published after the poet's death. 'This was especially obvious with Ingeborg [Collin – the eldest sister], for instance when she caught him in a little white lie . . . Then he would scream with delight at having been caught out.'

While a grown man who squeals with delight at being exposed as a fraudster is not an immediately appealing type, it does at least demonstrate a capacity for self-mockery that helps explain why so many otherwise sane, serious people – like H.C. Ørsted, Admiral Wulff, Bertel Thorvaldsen and, later in life, well-to-do families like the Melchiors and Henriques – tolerated Andersen's vanities. They indulged these quirks as the harmless by-product of a damaged yet fundamentally charming, loyal and decent man.

He was able to laugh at himself in his fiction too. As early as 1829 he had written a short poem describing himself as, 'a lanky person . . . His nose as mighty as a cannon . . . His eyes are tiny, like green peas,' concluding with the line: 'He's either mad, a lover or a poet.' In 'The Beetle', he is the eponymous, petulant, delusionary insect who goes on a long quest to seek his fortune having been denied the golden shoes he felt were rightfully his: 'If I had received golden shoes, I should have become an orna-ment to the stable. Now the stable has lost me, and the world has lost me. It is all over!' (This was written at a time when he was angling for a knighthood.)

He seems to have been a genuinely open, accepting man; affectionate and quick to forgive his enemies. He was as happy in the company of men as with women and, of course, he exerted a powerful magnetism over children. He once wrote: 'I feel myself everywhere at home, attach myself to people, and they give me in return confidence and cordiality.' It is an admirable approach to life, but one that only really works if you have the hide of a rhino. For someone with gossamer-thin skin, like Andersen, it leaves you wide open to the most bitter disappointments, but despite this his personality remained fundamentally unaltered throughout his life.

That's not to say he wasn't aware of his childlike qualities and nor was he immune to exaggerating them when it suited his ends. 'One of my later friends has told me that he saw me for the first time . . . in the drawing room of a rich tradesman, where people were making themselves very merry with me,' Andersen wrote of an incident in his youth. 'They desired me to repeat one of my poems, and, as I did this with great feeling, the merriment was changed into sympathy with me.' From an early age he understood the power he had over an audience in thrall to the romantic myth of innocent youth, and who can blame him for exploiting it? (The English, in particular, fell completely for his apparent innocence.)

He was by all accounts the most entertaining dinner guest, in demand at the grandest houses in town every night of the week. It is true that no one else would get a word in edgeways when he was around, but with a man possessed of a Wildean wit, a catalogue of improbable stories and a keen eye for the absurdities of social pretence, no one seems to have minded much.

After dinner he would often read his stories aloud. He was a great loss to the stage after all, it seems. George Griffin, an American diplomat who heard both Andersen and his rival for oratorical prowess, Charles Dickens, read from their works on different occasions, gave the points decision to the Dane. 'Dickens was in truth a superb reader,' wrote Griffin, 'but I am inclined to think that Andersen's manner is far more impressive and eloquent . . . Dickens' voice was, perhaps, better suited for the stage than the reading desk. It was stronger and louder than Andersen's, but nothing like as mellow and musical. I heard

Dickens read the death-bed scene of Little Nell in New York, and I was moved to tears, but I knew that the author himself was reading the story; but when I heard Andersen read the story of the Little Girl with the Matches, I did not think of the author at all, but wept like a child, unconscious of everything around me.'

Another eyewitness wrote: 'He held one spell-bound, seeing, hearing nothing but him, and his story-telling was even more charming. General conversation he had none; he brought every topic back to himself . . .'

Another of Andersen's great party tricks was to create elaborate paper cuts. His hands would be a blur for a few minutes as he wielded a pair of unfeasibly large scissors (virtually shears), and a scene of fabulous intricacy would unfold – often accompanied by a story. One witness described how his 'great, ugly, ape-like hands, which looked as if nothing that they touched could escape sullying or destruction, deftly cut out the quaintest designs in paper, with wonderful rapidity and delicacy as he spoke. Fairy-scenes, dances, lovers seated under trees, groups of flowers and plants; these things and countless other objects, would drop from his curling, twisting, snipping scissors . . .' You can see many of these paper cuts in the Andersen museum in Odense. They often feature grotesque monsters and animals – an echo of the creatures his mad grandfather would whittle from wood for the local children of Odense. And still today you find paper cuts everywhere in Denmark – in living rooms, hanging from the ceilings of dentists' waiting rooms, in classrooms – they are regarded as an art form in their own right, mostly because of Andersen.

Above all, I was beginning to feel immense pity for the man. Pity at his childhood, his appearance, his tortured sexuality, his sensitivity, and his lifelong isolation. Though he was adept at making friends, after the death of his mother he had no living relatives (other than his illegitimate half-sister, and the rather seedy aunt, neither of whom he wanted anything to do with).

He longed to have a partner with whom he could share his life, but never found one. These were lonely footsteps I was treading in. I hoped he would welcome the company.

In my search for Andersen's Florentine hotel I tried first the Danish Consulate, assuming they would welcome my investigations and fling open their archive for me. Unfortunately, the secretary didn't speak Danish and her English was little better than my Italian. She had never heard of Andersen, and somehow – and I am not sure at what point our wires became quite this crossed – I ended up leaving with the phone number of a cheap student hostel on the outskirts of town, and an apple.

I fared even worse at the National Library where I was literally thrown out of the door – having tried to saunter nonchalantly through security without a pass – by a woman who resembled, both physically and in temperament, Jabba the Hutt. Meanwhile, the records of the Associazione de Hoteliers had been lost in a flood in 1966, which left me one hope: a Danish academic who I knew was working at the city university. But when I gave his name to the receptionist there I was rewarded with the most spectacular eye-rolling and arm-waving display thus far. The receptionist then scrunched his face up as if struck by a sudden sharp pain, and asked his assistant to repeat the name (which she did, pronouncing it exactly as I had done). 'He not here. Copenhagen.'

I was on my own, with only my unflinching resolve to fall back on.

I gave up.

But then, by a miraculous stroke of luck, on my way to never actually finding the city museum, I saw a sign saying Archivo Storico. Here my database angels were Maria and Barbara who, despite being in the midst of building work and massive reorganisation of the archives, gave up an hour of their time to help me track down the location of Andersen's Hotel d'Europe. They soon found that in 1840 the owner was a Madam Hombert and that the building was the former Palazzo Feroni. The problem was that there was no exact address, and there were *two* Palazzi Feroni in Florence, one in Piazza Santa Trinita, the other on the far side of town.

I adopted a facial expression intended to convey that this was important additional news that I was at that very moment cross referencing with the masses of historical data in my memory banks. Maria and Barbara were actually doing just that. As it turned out all three of us realised simultaneously that the Santa Trinita Feroni was now the head-quarters of the fashion brand Ferragamo. By coincidence I had been there the previous day to see a column that stands in the middle of the square.

The column is one of the first things that the boy from the Bronze Hog story draws with his new-found artistic skills. In 1834 Andersen had also sketched it, along with the house behind it in the mistaken belief that that had once belonged to Michelangelo. (The house is actually the Palazzo Bartolini-Salimbeni.)

I knew from his diary that Andersen had stayed in a hotel near by on his previous visit to Florence, so it seemed likely that, staying just three days in the city in 1840, he would have kept close to the city centre in an area he was familiar with. I was convinced this was the Hotel d'Europe.

I thanked Maria and Barbara profusely and scuttled back across town to the thirteenth-century Palazzo Spini poi Feroni on Piazza Trinita, today home to the Salvatore Ferragamo Museum. The piazza lies at the Arno end of one of Florence's grandest boutique streets, not far from the Palazzo Strozzi (another monolith from the Flintstone School). The Palazzo Feroni takes up most of the southern side of the square (which is more of a triangle actually), and on its ground floor is the flagship Ferragamo shop. I took a lift to the museum above.

As his beloved father was a shoemaker, I like to think Andersen would have approved of Ferragamo, a Neapolitan cobbler turned shoemaker to the stars (Monroe, Garbo and Hepburn among them). That said, being strictly a black leather walking boots man himself, he might have raised an eyebrow at some of his saucier stiletto-heeled creations.

Andersen's father was an enduring influence on his life and work. The son always held his father's trade in high esteem and shoes are a recurring motif in his stories – from 'The Red Shoes', to 'The Girl Who Trod on the Loaf', to the fantastical 'Galoshes of Fortune', and, you could even argue, 'The Little Mermaid', whose greatest dream is a pair of feet with which to stalk her prince.

After Andersen's death they found a curious ode to the Danish shoemakers' guild – 'Which Guild is the Most Famous?' – among his papers. Almost sixty years after his father's death he had written: 'I maintain that the shoemakers' guild is the most famous, for I am the son of a shoemaker.'

His father was a frustrated, depressive man. 'He very seldom associated with his equals,' recalled Andersen. 'He went out into the woods on Sundays, when he took me with him; he did not talk much when he was out, but would sit silently, sunk in deep thought, whilst I ran about and collected strawberries, or bound garlands.' In many ways Hans Christian lived to be the things his father had dreamed of becoming – educated in Latin and well read. As well as a desire to learn and a love of his father's favourite stories – the writings of Voltaire and the Danish playwright Ludwig Holberg, La Fontaine's Fables and the *Arabian Nights* – Andersen also inherited his father's scepticism about organised religion, his openness to developments in science, and, of course, his morose introspection. Hans' only real joy, it seems, was reading to his son, 'it was only in such moments that I can remember to have seen him really cheerful, for he never felt himself happy in his life . . .'

Hans allowed his son an unusual amount of freedom. As Andersen's most recent Danish biographer, Jens Andersen, points out, Hans allowed his son to be himself, rather than trying to mould him to fit society. He built him a puppet theatre to indulge his dramatic fantasies and explore his imagination. He also instilled in him the importance and wonder of travel, telling him: 'It would do you good to travel! God knows if you would get very far, but you must!'

I can't help thinking that if Andersen's father had lived longer he would have been a very different man. I don't necessarily mean that his genius would have failed to blossom – on the contrary, given Hans' love of literature it might have flourished sooner – but perhaps he might have turned out, well, a little less 'hung up' about the workings of his nether regions. As it was, without a male role model and following a series of unfortunate incidents in which Andersen was exposed to various uniformly unpalatable aspects of female sexuality, it seems almost inevitable that he turned out the way he did.

There was, for instance, the time when he was visiting the local lunatic asylum with his beloved grandmother who worked there tending the gardens. 'On one occasion, when the attendants were out of the way, I lay down upon the floor, and peeped through the crack of the door into one of these cells,' he recalled in *The True Story of My Life*. 'I saw within a lady almost naked, lying on her straw bed, and she sang with a very beautiful voice. All at once she sprang up, and threw herself against the door where I lay; the little valve through which she received her food burst open; she stared down upon me, and stretched out her long arm towards me. I screamed for terror – I felt the tips of her fingers touching my clothes – I was half dead when the attendant came; and even in later years that sight and that feeling remained within my soul.'

Then there was the time Inger Cathrine Meisling, the sluttish wife of Andersen's feared headteacher, tried to seduce him in his room in Helsingør: 'One evening she came into my room, told me that she was starting to lose weight and that her dress was hanging rather loosely on her body, asked me to feel it . . . I was on tenterhooks, I might be wrong but she made me think badly of her, and I rushed away as soon as I could.' One can only imagine the decrepit condition this woman must have been in, with her ginger wig and considerable girth, not to mention how desperate she must have been to want to get off with Andersen.

And then there was the time he fell into a pond and had to wear a girl's skirt while his clothes dried. 'I felt a strange loathing for grown-up girls, or for girls of more than about twelve years; they really made me shudder, I even used the term about anything which I did not like that it was so "girlish",' he wrote in one of his autobiographies.

Decades later, while travelling in southern France with Jonas Collin jnr, Andersen told of another traumatic incident that occurred when he was four. His mother had sat him on a table in their house when a neighbour, a boy called Christian Kögaard (you'll realise why Andersen remembered his name so vividly before the end of this sentence), wandered in, lifted his clothing and bit him, very hard, on the penis. Andersen screamed, the doctor was called and he didn't urinate for a day. He vividly remembered his mother imploring him: 'Pee, my sweet boy, pee!' Ten years later Andersen discovered that he could not retract his foreskin and became convinced it was as a result of Christian's ill-advised chomp.

Poor Hans Christian. No wonder he developed such a kaleidoscope of complexes.

On my way out of the Ferragamo Museum, I couldn't resist telling the museum assistant about my discovery. He seemed underwhelmed by the news that a famous Danish writer he had never heard of had stayed in the building 164 years earlier when it was a hotel. He showed me a book about the palazzo's history. There was no mention of Andersen, but Oscar Wilde (who stayed as a guest of Lord Alfred Douglas), George Eliot and Prince von Metternich, the Austrian statesman, among other notables, also stayed in Fanny Hombert's Hotel d'Europe, after it opened in 1834.

I left Florence the next day on the same road Andersen had taken, driving through hills so preposterously picturesque they could have been arranged by da Vinci; each cypress a wrist-flicked brush stroke.

It was on this road to Rome that Andersen encountered one of his more memorable travelling companions, a man whose ego, temper and selfishness are so monstrous that, when I first read the description in *A Poet's Bazaar*, I assumed he must be fictional. Andersen's diaries, however, attest to the fact that the unnamed man, who I am ashamed to say was English (and recognisably so), was every bit as insufferable as he appears in the book.

Andersen elects to take the pretty route, via the waterfalls at Terni instead of the quick way via Sienna, and travels by *vettura*. This Italian equivalent of the horse-drawn hackney carriage was by far the cheapest way to travel through Italy, but passengers were very much at the mercy of the driver, or *vetturino*. Food and lodging were included in the fare but if the *vetturino* found higher paying customers along the way, passengers ran the risk of being dumped by the roadside with only a small financial compensation. What's more, on this route the passengers incurred an additional charge for protection from bandits by soldiers.

The other catch was that the *vettura* invariably left early. As always, Andersen rose an hour before he was due to leave, taking his bags downstairs to Piazza S. Trinita at 2 a.m. so that the other passengers wouldn't have to wait for him. Several carriages pass as he sits there, but his ride doesn't arrive until 6 a.m. He records with some annoyance that the delay had been caused by a stout Englishman, also travelling in the carriage, who had been asleep when the *vetturino* had called for him.

Also aboard are an elderly married couple – the 'Signora' and her husband – and a young Camaldolese monk, also English, who joins the carriage soon after they leave Florence. The monk proves to be something of a conversational non-starter, intent as he is on reading his prayer book and smoting his breast 'as if he would have nothing to do with either trees, mountains, or sun, much less with such a heretic as myself'.

Fortunately, the stout Englishman is a much more rewarding

subject. He is wearing, we are told, 'women's fur boots, a large blue cape and a thick woollen neckerchief about his thin red whiskers', and he turns out to be as accomplished a name dropper as his Danish travelling companion. He regales his fellow passengers with stories from the royal salons he has visited and boasts of how two princes had recently held a bedside vigil during his illness in Florence. That he is travelling unaccompanied with the *vetturino* is, he says, a mark of his modesty, 'for one is not in Italy for one's servants' pleasure!' Despite boasting that he has paid less than the rest of them, his luggage fills the carriage. At dinner he lunges for the best cuts of meat; he hogs the fire in the inn's guest room, forming a screen around it with his sheets; and in the carriage at night demands that Andersen nudge him awake if they pass anything worth seeing. When Andersen and he share a bedroom the Englishman gets there first and nabs Andersen's pillows and counterpane. 'I took them [back] from him. He looked amazed. He was an insupportable sleeping companion; he wanted so much waiting on that at last I was obliged to go to bed to get rid of him. I pretended to sleep . . .' writes Andersen.

In Castiglione the Englishman launches into the first of many tantrums. He is dissatisfied with the food, and rants to such an extent that the staff in the inn believe him to be royalty. He gets a brief comeuppance the next day though: 'Our buttoned up and overcoated Englishman trod on something – I know not what – and rolled from the topmost step very gracefully down the whole stairs, step for step, but this did not put him in better humour,' writes Andersen. (In fact, according to his diary, it was he who took the tumble, not the Englishman, noting at the time that it has given him an idea for a comic novel set in Italy.)

The Englishman's behaviour grows even more abominable as they journey south. In Assisi the Signora admonishes him for failing to tip the monks after a guided tour – 'These fellows have nothing else to do!' he replies. That night Andersen refuses to share a room with him and another confrontation ensues: '"Will you leave me alone in this robber hole?" said he . . . "Am I to lie, and be murdered alone! . . . I shall not speak to you during the whole journey!" I thanked him for it.'

The journey ends in a crescendo of abuse in which the Englishman announces that the Signora talks too much and that her husband is stupid. Her husband produces his educational certificates, to which the Englishman responds by standing up and flapping his arms around in impersonation of a turkey (which, you have to admit, is a fairly effective rejoinder). The owner of the inn settles things by emptying a bowl of cauliflower over the Englishman's head, and the rest of the journey is completed in silence.

In a letter to Henriette Wulff at the time Andersen wrote: 'I had an Englishman who was so boorish and unbearable that I feel salt in my blood at the mere thought of him, but he was also so original that in a novel he would be just as amusing for the reader as he was a plague in reality . . . For the first two days I was friendly towards him, but since I have shown him the winter way.' (Ironically, later in life Andersen began to adopt some of the very habits he had deplored in the Englishman, as one acquaintance recalled: 'Like many men of genius, Andersen . . . likes to be served first; and such is the respect in which he is held in his own country, that in private life all give way to this fancy and even the ladies humour him, at the expense of their own time-honoured rights.' Apparently, he would sulk and refuse to eat if this didn't happen.)

As I drove onward to Rome, just past a sign for something called the Titty Twister Disco Bar, I spotted the turning for Pasignano. I was intrigued by the fact that, in his diary, Andersen points out that this is the town he describes in his time-and-space travel fantasy, 'The Galoshes of Fortune'. Rather suspiciously, he uses the same phrase – 'a robber's hole' – as the Englishman to describe it.

In one passage from the story, a travel-hungry clerk, who puts on the eponymous wish-fulfilment boots finds the reality quite different to his fantasy of the open road: 'He had a headache and a crick in his neck, his legs were swollen from sitting so long, and his boots pinched him. He was half asleep and half awake. He had a letter of credit in his right hand pocket, and his passport in the left, and a little leather purse with some Louis-d'ors sewn up in it in his breast-pocket. Every time he dropped off, he dreamed that one or other of these was lost, and he started up in a feverish haste; the first movement of his hand was a triangle from right to left, and up to his breast, to feel if they were still there. Umbrellas, sticks and hats swayed about in the net above their heads and considerably impaired the view, which was grand in the extreme.' The clerk goes on to bemoan the 'poisonous gnats, crippled beggars' and 'water soup flavoured with pepper and rancid oil', in tones that almost certainly reflect Andersen's own ambivalence about travelling in Italy.

In fact, this modern lake-side resort was merely ghostly out of season with the rain lashing down. These days if you are looking for an authentic robber hole, I recommend you take a detour towards Assisi, which shone like a giant marble bathroom across the murky valley, and pay 15 euro for a manky slice of pizza in one of its restaurants.

From Assisi I drove on past the kind of picturesque hill-top towns that are the English middle classes' enduring property fantasy. One town, Bastardo, seemed a nice enough place but it must be hell for the locals when it comes to ordering things over the phone. I pressed on as I was especially keen to see the famed waterfall at Terni – an important stop on the Grand Tour at the time – which the Englishman, against his travelling companions' wishes, had demanded to see.

Whatever happened to waterfalls? It seems to me that, looking back at my childhood, not a weekend went by without my mum, dad, brother, sister and I squeezing into our Austin 1100 for a five-hour drive to see water cascading down a hillside. But these days, you just don't seem to see them so much. Or at least I don't, but on reflection, this is perhaps simply because I am no longer a small child easily amused by gallons of water descending at high speed, followed by a Cornish Mivvi and a badge saying 'I love Cheddar'. Am I rambling? Sorry. Let's get on.

It took me an hour or so in the car to reach Terni from the road to Rome, so heaven knows how long it would have taken Andersen and his motley gang. According to his diary, they arrived after dark, but the Englishman insisted they climb the falls by torchlight, eventually concluding that it was 'a poor affair'. I am inclined to agree. The falls are high, but despite all the rain and snow of the recent days, they were more reminiscent of an old man with prostate trouble than Niagara.

Meanwhile, that evening, 18 December, back in Copenhagen Andersen's new play *The Moorish Girl* had its first night. He had been relying on the income from the box office to pay for the next part of his journey, from Naples to Greece and hopefully even Turkey. In *A Poet's Bazaar* he refers somewhat disingenuously to the premiere, comparing his discomfort that evening with the audience's experiences back in Copenhagen: 'The public were, certainly, much better satisfied that evening than the author.' But the truth was the audience was not better satisfied. The play was a disastrous flop and ran for only three performances. Andersen knew nothing of this as he endured one more night on the road to Rome, but *The Moorish Girl* time bomb was now ticking. Just how great a disaster it had been, he would not hear for another three weeks, in the midst of a miserable, lonely Roman winter.

Chapter Four

ROME

The journey has been arduous for Andersen and his delight at seeing his beloved Rome for the first time in six years is palpable: 'I discerned the cupola of St Peter's. O! How my heart beat at the thought of seeing Rome again . . .'

He rents three large, cold rooms from the 'good natured' Signor and Signora Margaretha on Via Purificazione – just off the lower part of Via Veneto – for five scudo per month. Virtually the moment he dumps his bags he hurries off to check that the Forum, the Capitol and St Maria Maggiore are still there, afterwards lunching with his old Rome friend, Albert Küchler, and recommencing his familiar Rome routine of a twilight walk up Monte Pincio – the hill beside the Spanish Steps – with its time-less view to St Peter's and gangs of pimps and hookers. He ends the day 'sitting like the father of the house in my room with the doors well bolted'. It is as if the last six years haven't happened.

'Rome has opened my eyes to beauty,' he wrote during his first visit to the city in the winter of 1833–34, aged an impres-sionable twenty-eight. 'It is the city of cities, where soon [after arriving] I was to feel as if I had been born.' During the four months he spent there he made new friends, devoured its great art galleries, soaked up the arcane rituals of the Catholic Church and was inspired to write his first novel. And then, of course, there had been the torrid encounters with prostitutes that had sent his sexual urges ricocheting like a pinball.

Rome was a fraction of the size it is today and not yet the Italian capital. The Pope was still top *doge* and in fact Rome wouldn't officially become part of the kingdom of Italy until 1870. The city was bounded by the Emperor Aurelius' city walls, beyond which were fields, but it had been Grand Tourist Central for over a century and, by 1840, you could hardly move for crinolined Helena Bonham Carters and floppy haired Byron-wannabees moping around the ruins clutching their collected works of Keats, their noses in their well-thumbed Baedekers.

In 1833 Andersen had been just another one of these cultural locusts, hanging out with a band of Scandinavian émigrés and tourists who visited each other's ateliers and the city sights by day, and caroused together late into the night, telling bawdy stories, playing lotto and, if Küchler's later reminiscences are anything to go by, ribbing Andersen about his lack of sexual experience.

Once a victim always a victim: just as he was in Odense, in the factories as a teenager, and at school in Slagelse, Andersen remained a sitting duckling for the ribald joshing of his male peers. You have to feel sorry for him; who hasn't, at one time or another, found themselves exposed as a hopeless virgin in the company of those more sexually experienced? (Except me, obviously.)

Lording it over this Bohemian crowd was the towering figure – both physically and by reputation – of Bertel Thorvaldsen, one of Europe's foremost neoclassical sculptors, and a resident of the city since 1797. Thorvaldsen, nicknamed Thor, looked every inch the Nordic god, with his wild, grey Beethoven hair and friendly, fleshy face. He and Andersen became firm friends during his first visit to the city. It was Thorvaldsen's shoulder Andersen had cried on when the poem he had sent home from Rome in 1833 – 'Agnete and the Merman' – was rejected by his publisher and lambasted by the Collin family. 'I know the people,' he told Andersen. 'It would not have gone any better with me if I had remained there . . . Thank God that I did not need them, for they know how to torment and to annoy.'

By 1840, however, Thorvaldsen had returned home to a hero's welcome, and the Nordic clique that had surrounded him had largely dispersed. With Holst still larging it and incommunicado in Munich – much to Andersen's intense annoyance – he was left to rattle around his cavernous, cold apartment in Via Purificazione, alone.

'The wind whistled and screeched through the crevices in the doors,' he writes in *A Poet's Bazaar*, 'the few sticks in the chimney blazed up, but they did not throw any warmth into the room; the cold stone floor, the raw walls and the high ceiling, seemed only adapted for the summer season.' In order to keep warm he sat with his fur-lined boots; a surtout, or frock coat; a cloak; and a fur cap, turning 'like a sunflower' to keep both sides warm by the paltry flame.

It was the kind of weather that had done for poor, pale John Keats in Rome twenty years earlier and matters weren't helped by the return of the toothache that harried Andersen throughout his adult life.

'My teeth began to give some nervous concerts ... A real Danish toothache is not to be compared to an Italian one. Pain played on the keys of the teeth as if it were Liszt or Thalberg,' he writes. Near delirious with pain, in *A Poet's Bazaar* he claims to see his pen jump up and begin writing down a story dictated by his boots. It is their autobiography, telling the story of the journey so far from their perspective – highlights include new soles in Munich, and meeting other footwear in a hotel. Tragically, when Andersen wakes the next morning, he tells us that his boots have shrivelled in the heat from the fire while the paper is covered only with ink spots because the pen has written their story on blotting paper.

He is desperate for news of *The Moorish Girl*, and visits the post office daily – experiencing anxious palpitations on the way – but there are no letters from the Collins. On 21 December he hears an unwelcome titbit from a friend: that the play did not open on 5 December as planned. In his diary that evening he notes that he has written to the king; his almanac confirms that this is his application for another travel grant, which suggests that he already holds little hope the play will be a success.

So far he has spent 266 *rixdaler* on the journey, but his spirit remains strong: 'It is like a dream for me to be here again, I feel so at home.'

After the Florence debacle, I had allowed myself what I thought was a generous two hours to find the car-hire office in central Rome but, yet again, found myself lost, frightened and be-wildered amid a seething sea of Fiats.

To this day, I have a strong suspicion that the Florence office had warned Giorgio – the man who answered the phone when I rang the car-hire company's Rome office for directions – about me because, as soon as I began to explain my predicament, he simply hung up. I rang back, assuming his hand had slipped on the receiver.

'Hi, I was just talking to you, I am outside the—' I began again.

'I am sorry, sir, but no I can't help.' Giorgio hung up again.

Rage and desperation boiled within me as I punched in the number again. When Giorgio answered for a third time I let fly with a torrent of abuse – I believe at one point I may even have uttered the immortal: 'Do you know who I am? I am going to have your job for this!' I also think I said the 'f' word, though I am not sure. This time, *I* hung up before *he* had a chance to answer. Ha! That will teach him, I thought, as I put the car into gear and drove off in completely the wrong direction once again.

I assumed grovelled apologies would greet me – the customer – when I finally arrived in the underground car park where I was supposed to deposit the car but instead, despite an hour having elapsed, Giorgio's anger was every bit as raw as mine. There ensued an ugly showdown, replete with full-on *Sopranos*-style hand gestures (he even did the one where they make a 'V' with their index and middle finger and prod them at your eyeballs), and curses on my family. As men often do in such situations, we both implied, through highly choreographed arm flapping and chin-jutting, that we were about to erupt into a display of deadly and masterful violence, while at the same time having absolutely no intention of doing so (the car park was deserted, so bearing in mind that Giorgio was several stone larger than me, and a good deal hairier, I was very grateful for this).

In the end, realising that it was the only way I could persuade this raging ape to sign my release form and so be sure that he wouldn't immediately go and kick in every panel of the car's bodywork, wrench out the stereo and then send me the bill – I apologised.

'I am sorry I said "fuck",' I said, as it seemed this was what had got him so het up in the first place.

'Oh, you say sorry, you say sorry,' he said, jerking his chin and looking down his nose sceptically.

'Yes', I said, 'I am sorry I said that, it really wasn't on. I was just a bit upset, you see, because you wouldn't tell me where you were.'

Miraculously, this completely took the wind out of Giorgio's sails. He didn't seem to know quite how to react. In fact, I do not believe that anyone had every said sorry to him before. Down there in his subterranean lair, bereft of daylight, fresh air and company, all he had really needed was a little understanding. He signed my form with a triumphant, Mussolini-esque flourish and I fled his cave for ever.

I emerged into my first Roman evening beside Harry's Bar, at the top of Via Veneto. This broad avenue, which snakes down to Piazza Barberini, will forever be associated with men in cool sunglasses fleeing paparazzi aboard Lambrettas together with laughing girls in headscarves, but these days it is a desolate place lined with costly American hotels. I loitered briefly by the window of Harry's Bar, displaying photos of its international showbiz regulars: Stallone, Caine and my close personal friend, Roger Moore. Peering into this glittering, glamorous world I felt like the Little Matchgirl on Christmas Eve (only more dishevelled). I could see from the clientele's dress code – double-breasted navy-blue blazers with gold buttons over heavily starched denim and tasselled loafers, for the men; and shoulder pads for the women – that a bedraggled backpacking oik was unlikely to be welcomed with open arms, a gaudy cocktail thrust into his hand by a grinning maître'd. So I straightened my back, adjusted my rucksack and set off across the centre of Rome to my hotel, passing – oblivious in my self-pity – virtually every Andersen site that I would then spend the next two weeks trying to relocate.

The profound rubbishiness of my first hours in Rome were compounded not only by the Hammer Horror hotel I had booked into, but also by my first experience of dining out in the Italian capital. At the appropriately named Restaurant Grotte I ordered what turned out to be a slither of wet cardboard with a solitary anchovy draped across the top of some black bits, which could have been olives but might equally have been the detritus harvested from between the chef's toes. While picking at this my eye was caught by the chilled cabinet beside me – firstly by the thermometer, which was registering a worrying 15 degrees, and secondly by a large black lobster, which I had assumed was frozen, but which now began to twitch its antennae exhaustedly. It was dying.

I could, of course, have eaten somewhere more salubrious – Andersen either dined with friends at a local restaurant or alone in his rooms – but as a lone traveller my criteria for choosing a restaurant of an evening ruled out the decent, popular, groovy places where the beautiful people go. That would only make me feel even more of a Billy No Mates. My restaurants had to be places that weren't completely empty, but weren't very full either. There is nothing worse than being the only diner, the centre of attention for the entire waiting staff and the restaurant's only source of income for the evening. The waiters will whisk your plate away as you spear the final forkful and cajole you into having dessert; and there will be insupportable pressure to express gratitude and pleasure throughout the meal. The only thing worse than being a lone diner is to sit alone in a restaurant full of couples and groups having a whale of a time, all

regarding you as if you were a venereal leper with a cloud of
flies buzzing around your head. So I prefer to skulk in a dark
corner of a sparsely populated dining room, behind a pillar if
possible, where I will pretend to read or make important notes
and watch the crustacea die.

Back in my hotel, I struggled to sleep against a background
noise of the other residents' toilet trumpets (which meant that,
even more disturbingly, they could hear mine), and screams of
an indeterminate seriousness. I checked out the next morning,
swallowed hard, and checked in to the nearby, and grand-beyond-
my-means, Hotel Locarno. Soggy pizza would be a staple here-
after; no more horsemeat and cannoli for me.

Rome and I had not got off to the best of starts, and I was
conscious that all of this would sound like the annoying whining
of someone too consumed by the process of disappearing up
his own self-pitying fundament to appreciate that he was off
the leash in one of the world's greatest cities (and I know what
that's like from Andersen's diaries). To give my stay a kick start
I headed off to Caffè Greco on Via Condotti, just down from
the Spanish Steps. This had been Andersen's regular haunt during
all five of his visits to Rome – he even rented rooms there
during one stay – so it seemed an appropriate place in which
to do something I had never, ever done before: have a cup of
coffee.

One of my more cherished theories is that everyone has a
secret something they have never experienced, something that
most of the rest of the world takes for granted. One friend of
mine has never tasted Coca Cola, for instance; another, who in
most other regards is fairly normal, has never seen a live band
in concert. Lissen has never, ever seen an episode of *Baywatch*.
Some people never have problems returning their hire cars. You
get the gist.

Of course, I had a fair notion of what coffee tastes like from
the smell, and from my experiences playing Revels Roulette (the
orange- and coffee-flavour chocolates look identical, but, oh,

the horror when you get a coffee one!), but I had now reached the stage in life where I cherished my abstinence as – and I know how feeble this sounds – one of the very few things that made me special.

A small cup promptly arrived at my table with two sugar sachets in the saucer. I was heartened to see it was no more than a quarter full with a viscous and not entirely unappetising choco-laty brown liquid. Eschewing the sugar – I'm an all-or-nothing kind of guy, me – I took a deep snort of its heady aroma, with its whiff of adult sophistication and danger, and downed it in two gulps.

Well, I won't be doing that again in a hurry. It tasted of burnt toast, with a foul, lingering aftertaste of soil. I made a face that, looking up into the mirror opposite me, I immediately recog-nised as the one our dog had made when he pounced on a tumbler of whisky that my Uncle Brian spilled on the carpet one Christmas and had begun slurping enthusiastically in the mistaken belief that it was orange squash.

What *are* you people thinking of? Never again, not even in the interests of medical science.

As it happens, Andersen preferred the coffee elsewhere, as he advises in a footnote in *A Poet's Bazaar.* 'Coffee in Greece and the Orient is quite excellent – indeed so good that the traveller who comes from these countries can at first find no taste in coffee made in the ordinary European way. One drinks it "thick" – the coffee is quite smooth, but it is not ground, it is pounded to a powder, just like chocolate.' Now he tells me.

Other than a name change to Antico Caffè Greco, I suspect little has changed in Andersen's favourite hang-out over the years. With its red flock wallpaper, dusty oil paintings and waiters in tails and bow ties scuttling between the marble-topped tables it isn't hard to imagine a mid-nineteenth-century traveller lingering here. To complete the cultured coffee salon *mise-en-scène*, there was even a Toulouse Lautrec double sitting in one corner putting the finishing touches to an oil painting of the Forum.

Over the next few days I spent a large proportion of my time roaming the streets around the café – the Tridente district, now a Gucci-Prada-Versace ghetto. Andersen stayed within this area, with the Spanish Steps at its heart, each time he visited Rome, the first time renting rooms at 104 Via Sistina (then called Via Felice), then for this second trip in 1840, staying on Via Purificazione. This part of Rome also features as the starting point for Andersen's first and finest novel, *The Improvisatore*, which he had begun writing on that first visit in 1834, completing it in Copenhagen the following autumn.

The Improvisatore was an astonishingly successful debut; pacey, original, dramatic and packed with vivid descriptions of Italian life. Readers in Denmark, and elsewhere in northern Europe, lapped it up. Though *The Dying Child* and his first German travel memoir had brought Andersen some fame, this would be his first, significant literary breakthrough prior to the first volume of fairy stories published later the same year.

As is usually the case with Andersen's novels, *The Improvisatore* is a thinly disguised autobiography about an artistically gifted, though socially disadvantaged and sexually naive, young boy – in this instance, named Antonio. He is born into Odense-style poverty in a house on Piazza Barberini with a doting mother but no father, and a mad uncle, called Peppo (based on a beggar of the same name whom Andersen encountered daily on the Spanish Steps). Antonio is the 'Improviser' of the title – his gift being that he can improvise songs, an art form that was treasured at that time, but virtually killed off by Richard Stilgoe in the 1970s. Antonio's mother is tragically killed but the Borghese family funds his education at a school ruled by a tyrannical headmaster (sound familiar?). Later Antonio falls in love with an opera singer, Annunziata, but believes – wrongly as it turns out – that she is in love with his friend Bernardo. Meanwhile, he and Bernardo develop a friendship with obvious homo-erotic parallels to the one Andersen yearned for at the time with Edvard Collin, and a married woman attempts to seduce him (using the same chat-up lines as Mrs Meisling some years earlier). He befriends another girl, Flaminia, who is more like a sister to him (Henriette Wulff?), and ends up marrying a girl called Maria – which, of course, is where the life-as-art theory begins to disintegrate.

'Every single character is taken from real life . . . I know and have known all of them,' Andersen said of *The Improvisatore*, and this first-hand experience undoubtedly helped give the novel its uncommon vitality. 'It is one of those books which are full of Italy so that as you read it in Connecticut, or wherever you may be, you are transported to that far country,' wrote the American magazine *Harpers Monthly* when it was published there in 1875 (it wasn't published in Italy until 1959 – although I guess they had slightly less need for vivid depictions of Italian life).

I had brought a copy with me to read while I was in Rome. Andersen's novels are largely forgotten outside Denmark but this one at least deserves a second look. The plot rambles a bit, there are some absurd coincidences, and the characters are either flimsy cut-outs or transparently autobiographical, but its pace and obser- vations of Italy still hold your attention.

It is, then, fitting that today the only material evidence that Andersen ever visited Rome is a plaque commemorating 'Scrittore Danese Hans Christian Andersen's' first stay in the city and the writing of *The Improvisatore*. (Actually, this isn't strictly true; I did spot a small plaque outside the Capuchin monastery that mentions him along with the Marquis de Sade, as being among the 'famous personalities who have mentioned the monastery in their writings' – surely the only instance of these two men appearing together in print).

It is mounted high up on the front wall of number 104 Via Sistina, which is these days a private apartment block. Finding the door ajar as I was passing one day, I entered and climbed the narrow marble stairway, much altered since Andersen's day and now bereft of any period charm. My initial excitement at gaining access was further tempered as, one by one, I knocked on all of the doors only to find no one at home. I have no idea what I would have said had anyone been at home; it just would have been nice to look out onto the streets that had made such an impression on Andersen during his first stay in the city, from the same spot he had looked out onto them (I do realise that, if I were describing this to you at a party, you would be beginning now to back away from me nervously). I left a note with my phone number and a brief explanation of my mission by the mail boxes in the entrance hall, but no one rang.

I walked a little further on to Via Purificazione, where Andersen stayed on his second visit to Rome. Before I had left Copenhagen I had tried to find out the exact address he stayed at. In the published version of his almanac the address appears as three dots, as if whoever transcribed them couldn't make out the figure. Rather bumptiously, I thought I could do better and so went down to the Royal Library and asked to see the almanac for myself. Turning the actual pages across which Andersen had scrawled in his scratchy, unfathomable hand was a unique thrill but when I came to the relevant page I was deflated to find that he had himself only noted three dots for the address on Purificazione, as if he had planned to add the number later on.

As Christmas 1840 approached Andersen was more and more isolated in his echoing attic garret here (wherever it was). In *A Poet's Bazaar* he writes: 'No one had thought of any arrangement for Christmas. Every one sat at home. It was cold weather; the fire in the stove would not warm my chamber. Thought flew far away, towards the North. Now, it whispered, there is the Yule-tree lighted up with a hundred parti-coloured lights; the children exult in sweetest happiness! . . . O, Christmas is a merry time in the North.'

The truth, revealed by his diary, is that he had argued with friends who wanted to use his apartment for their celebrations; his lonely Christmas dinner was cheese, bread, grapes and wine. Of course, though painful for the Andersen fan to admit, one can't rule out the possibility that the rest of the Scandinavians in Rome were having a merry time elsewhere, without having told him.

Perhaps this explains why, by 28 December, just a week after arriving in Rome, his thoughts were already on the next part of his journey: 'Have a great desire to see Greece and Constantinople.' And things had not improved come New Year's Eve. That night, as the city partied, he retired to bed at midnight with a sore throat.

The next morning he visits St Peter's and, as he stands under the colossal dome, he offers up the following prayer: 'God give me an immortal poet name, give me health and give me your peace.' The order is telling, but all three wishes were to seem more remote than ever when, with the River Tiber bursting its banks, and his own emotions having reached a rolling boil of anxiety, he finally received news from Copenhagen of the failure of *The Moorish Girl*. It was a personal and professional disaster that scarred him for life.

'If you think that the unfavourable criticism of *The Moorish Girl* has left any lasting impression in your disfavour, then you are wrong, for it has already been forgotten,' wrote Edvard Collin with his usual tact a couple of weeks later. 'Another important literary *Erscheinung* has taken its place, namely Heiberg's *New Poems*, of its kind and by its brilliant form a most remarkable product.'

It was 'Agnete and the Merman' all over again, except this time the humiliation was public.

The Moorish Girl had been written in a fit of pique in the wake of accusations of plagiarism surrounding Andersen's previous play, *The Mulatto*. He had wanted to prove that he could create something wholly original but, just as Heiberg's wife Johanne Luise had turned down the leading role, so had the public rejected the play as a whole. Not only that, but now it seemed her husband was basking in the acclaim Andersen felt was rightfully his *and* he had taken a pop at Andersen in his *New Poems,* joking in one that *The Moorish Girl* was performed as punishment for the damned. Andersen had been relying on the proceeds from the play to fund the next leg of his journey. Now it seemed as if he would not only have to return home early, but that public humiliation and financial ruin would be waiting for him on the quayside.

Years later in his autobiography Andersen set aside two pages in which to harp on about the critical response to the play, writing: 'My new piece did not please Heiberg . . . from this hour Heiberg became my opponent.' But it is hard to know who to side with in this dispute. Andersen had acted like a truculent child when Johanne Luise had turned down the role, but her husband had kicked him when he was down, which was hardly sporting. Heiberg was everything Andersen wasn't: a pillar of the literary and theatrical establishment, good looking, sophisticated, learned, and married to one of the country's leading actresses. To make matters even worse, the Heibergs were regular guests of the Collin family and it was Johan, not Andersen, who was their favourite writer. Just before Andersen left on his *Poet's Bazaar* journey he had noted with fury in his almanac the presence of these magpies in his nest:

Sept 3: Yesterday the Heibergs were to dinner with the Collins. For them there *was* merriment . . . Despair. (His italics.)

Sept 4: Sick. One has no friends. [Did not go] to the Collin's.[+]

The truth is that Heiberg – once described as the 'dictator of literary taste in intellectual circles in Copenhagen' – had long resented Andersen's lust for fame and constant self-promotion. Though initially he had championed the younger man's poetry, like many in Copenhagen he had come to resent this toadying fop with his outsized ego. On one occasion he told Andersen that he was only reviewed in Germany because his publisher paid the reviewers. Andersen could not help replying: 'Oh really, you are aware we have the same publisher?' – the implication being that the publisher, Reitzel, didn't think Heiberg's work worth the expenditure.

Meanwhile, in the spring of 1840, Andersen had enjoyed a

hero's welcome at a university in Sweden. When he returned to Copenhagen Heiberg had commented sarcastically that the next time he went to Sweden he wanted Andersen to accompany him so that he, too, might be 'paid homage'.

'You should take your wife with you,' Andersen replied with a Dorothy Parker flourish. 'You will get it much more easily.'

Andersen took a kind of revenge – albeit childish – on Heiberg's criticism of *The Moorish Girl* in *A Poet's Bazaar*: 'I dreamed that I was imprisoned in a Heibergian inferno and sure enough it was just as he had recounted – only my pieces were performed and this pleased me very much . . . Incidentally, I also heard down there that it had one evening been decided that in addition to my two plays Heiberg's *Fata Morgana* would be given as the concluding piece – but the damned had protested; even Hell can be made too hot and there must be moderation in all things!'

In Rome, the result of all this terrible news was that Andersen's hopeful New Year's prayer soon gave way to overwhelming nihilism. His post-*Moorish Girl* diary is nothing less than a martyr's manifesto:

> Fri 8 Jan: The Moorish Girl has not been a success and gone only two times [it actually ran for three performances]. The other Danes asked me what the letter said, and I had to tell them. All day throat and teeth pain. Wrote letter to the father [Jonas] . . . Have given up journey to Constantinople and Greece! Home and sick; read Ingemann's 'Prince Otto'.

And then the illnesses begin in earnest: sore throat, headaches and the inevitable toothache. He develops a fever and takes a foot bath with salt and vinegar before he goes to bed. For toothache he tries rubbing mustard behind his ears but for some reason this doesn't seem to relieve the pain. His mood is hardly lifted by the fact that Holst *still* hasn't written and neither (at that time) has his beloved Edvard. His solitude is almost overwhelming.

Friday 15 Jan: Looked out of the window for half an hour
at the lonely street where nearly all lights were off, except
in a poor trattoria.

By the next day he has hit rock bottom:

Sat 16 Jan: I am not afraid to be attacked; sometimes I even
think that it would be a good thing if I were killed; I know
well enough that I have nothing left to live for. Art itself
is something unknown to me, desire to be talked about is
so great, that I find it interesting to suddenly die, yes, I
appreciate my weaknesses, and see my mistakes! O God
soon give me a great thought, or a great happiness, or death!'

In his increasing desperation for news – either from home or
from Holst – he visits the post office seven times in one day and
tries to distract himself by working on his ambitious epic poem
'Ahasverus'. When that doesn't work, he shaves off his moustache. A few days later he encounters a funeral procession for a
small boy who has died of typhus, an enviable fate: 'I want to
die; nothing to live for.'

Holst finally arrives on 7 February, suddenly appearing before
Andersen in the street and greeting him with a kiss. Andersen's
reaction is frosty but Holst explains that he took a two-week
detour to Venice en route from Munich and all is soon forgiven.
Holst and his travelling companion, the theologian Conrad Rothe
(who comes across as an especially comforting presence in the
diaries), do their best to cheer Andersen as he hears more news
of just how disastrous *The Moorish Girl* has been – the audience
had apparently hissed – and that no decision has been taken on
his application for a royal travel grant. But Holst spoils it all by
saying something supportive of Heiberg. They row: 'We began
mildly but ended with him saying that I have been hard and
strange towards him since he arrived.' Andersen promises to be
milder and that night Holst disappears – 'for a fuck', Andersen

notes in his diary – leaving him 'happy in my solitude' in his chambers on Via Purificazione.

Purificazione ends in Piazza Barberini where I stood, clutching another of my soggy photocopies, trying to figure out where Andersen had stood to draw his vibrant sketch of Bernini's Triton fountain in its centre. 'Splendid white oxen, with horns an ell long, lie here detached from the wagons,' he writes of the square; 'groups of peasants with variegated ribbons around their pointed hats, stand and play *mora*; girls so healthy looking and handsome, with golden combs in their glistening black hair are looking at a couple of dancers. The tambourine sounds – it is merry to see and hear.'

The piazza is today a ceaselessly busy roundabout, and virtually all of the buildings from Andersen's time are gone. It does, however, boast a resident village idiot from the old school.

I know one should not mock mental illness, but this was one Olympic fruitcake of a kind that is all too rare these days. The care-in-the-community cases you encounter now, on the streets of Britain at least, evoke pity and fear in equal measure, while in Denmark, needless to say, homeless or mentally ill people are, like the ugly or obese, nowhere to be seen. But the bonkers Barberinian had really made an effort, tucking his trousers into his socks, donning a red cummerbund and strapping fake headphones made from cigarette packets to his ears. He appeared to have a set routine in which he would approach a car stuck in traffic, put his face to the driver's or passenger's window and either blow a long and hearty raspberry or make loud chicken noises while thumbing his nose. All good, clean, wholesome fun; the kind of thing, in fact, that they used to fill the children's TV schedules with for hours on end when I was a kid.

The Romans have a tradition of this kind of liberated public display, at least if Andersen's description of the Carnival of 1841 is anything to go by. Unlike the low-key way they celebrate the Carnival now, in Andersen's day it was a week-long public spectacle (oddly, while the supposedly pious Popes ran Rome the carnival was a lusty, carnal riot, but it died out as a public event after the revolutions of 1849), as he describes vividly in *A Poet's Bazaar*. 'Any lady may freely venture out in man's clothing . . . The poorer classes contrive to procure a carnival dress: they sew salad leaves all over their clothes . . . husband and wife, and sometimes children too, are quite clothed in lettuce. Orange peel is cut out and worn as spectacles.' He also sees, 'coachmen, old fellows with genuine Italian physiognomies, dressed out like ladies, whilst a pug dog sits by their side dressed like an infant in long clothes, or as a young miss.' There is a man who has made an improbable musical instrument out of cats stuck in tubes with rope tied around their tails, 'the cats protest when he pulls the rope and he is, somehow, able to construct a tune.' (So *that's* how they did Radiohead's last album.)

There were riderless horse races along Il Corso; events in which elderly Jews were force-fed cakes and made to run down the street; and everyone, even mooning poets, was clown for a day. Andersen rents a *polichinel* costume – a three-cornered white hat with a gold and black plume and a red silk mask – and is delighted at the attention it generates: 'I received many bouquets from women in carriages, they said it was a delightful mask. One lady waved and asked if I was English, French or Spanish, and I said yes to all, she crowned me with a big cake, which the other two *polichinels* stole from me . . . What hilarity!' His mood at last seemed to be lifting.

As I explored Andersen's Rome – excited to find so much as he had described it – I soon discovered that the city is built upon a criss-crossing pattern of extremely powerful magnetic fault lines. This is the only explanation I can come up with for the fact that, throughout my time there, I would become muddled virtually every few yards, finding myself constantly, irredeemably lost. Guidebooks and maps seemed to transform themselves into Escher-esque illusions before my eyes. My usually infallible sense of direction deserted me completely, which meant that my challenge of

trying to beat Andersen's 'most churches visited in one day' tally
(seven on 26 December) would prove trickier than expected.

As a Danish Lutheran more used to places of worship so puri-
tanically spartan they could double as art spaces, Rome's glittering, action-packed churches must have been quite shocking
to Andersen on his first visit, and he ticked off a great many of
the city's 328 churches in his time there. But his insatiable desire
to visit them all over again was just as strong on his second visit
in 1840, which struck me as slightly curious.

I know that, led by their new guidebooks, visiting churches
is one of the things that the cultural tourists of the day did
without really questioning it, but few did it with the fervour
and dedication of Andersen. What is particularly strange about
this is that, back home, he was not usually a regular churchgoer.
Andersen was a deeply spiritual man, it is true, and his religious
faith is a constantly recurring theme in his work to the point
where his lesser stories can sometimes labour under the weight
of their author's piety (a trait that particularly annoyed W.H.
Auden, for one), but, like his father, he tended to shy away from
the restrictive dogma of organised religion.

In fact, he was notably progressive – New Age, you might
even say – in his interpretation of the church's ideology to the
point that he occasionally fell out with some of the more devout
members of the Danish aristocracy. One redoubtable dowager
was appalled when Andersen claimed not to believe in the
immaculate conception, for instance, and neither did he hold
much truck with notions of the devil, miracles or the resurrec-
tion. I suspect he only really began to incorporate the Lutheran
church into his life while at school where, with characteristic
pragmatism, he realised that if he wanted to progress in Danish
society he had to join the God squad.

A more revealing insight into his belief system comes earlier
in *A Poet's Bazaar*, when he is travelling with the *vetturino*. Here,
when confronted with the bible-bashing monk, Andersen claims
that *his* bible is nature. It is a sentiment he repeats later in the

book while travelling up the Danube on the way home: as his fellow passengers are observing the Sabbath – singing mass, reading the Bible, etc. – Andersen's thoughts fly 'out to nature – and there we are always near the Almighty!'

In his belief in the divinity of nature he had more in common with pantheists than Lutherans, while animism is also, obviously, a strong presence in his fairy stories – what with their talking animals and objects. A respect for other beliefs is another tenet he shares with the pantheists. 'I am in as solemn a mood in the synagogues of Jews and the mosques of Turks as I am in our Christian churches,' he once told Ørsted. After a hostile reception in a mosque in Constantinople, he writes: 'Look not so angrily at us, thou old priest; thy God is also our God! Nature's temple is the joint house of God for us; you kneel towards Mecca; we towards the East! "God is the light of heaven and earth!" He enlightens every mind and every heart!'

As for his relationship with the Almighty, He seems to have been more of a fairy godfather, granting wishes, looking over Andersen and ensuring that, in the long run, everything would turn out for the best. He often addressed God directly in his diaries. One of the earliest excerpts dates from his time at school, where he pleads for assistance: 'My God! My God! Are you really there? . . . Praised be thy name! . . . O Lord, oh! Let me not lose hope that you govern everything . . . God! I could become great, respected by other people, create happiness . . . O Lord, you are the only one who can decide the fate of this person in despair!' He never really grew out of this kind of thing.

So, for a Dane of his background he was unusually open-minded and inclusive as far other faiths were concerned but, *still*, this does not really explain his insatiable appetite for visiting Catholic churches.

As I visited many of the churches he mentions in his writings on Rome, and saw many of the religious paintings and sculptures that he had described, it began to dawn on me that something other than religious curiosity might have been driving

Andersen's exhaustive ecclesiastical tour. I began to wonder if it was a sensual rather than a mystical yearning that fuelled his interest in Catholicism. Was it a bodily rather than a spiritual desire that lured him to these places? To get to the point, was it, in other words, at least in part, if you will forgive the crudeness, and I am speculating wildly here, an interest in the male form?

Now, I realise I am not the first writer to identify the sensual, homoerotic undertones in a great many of the religious artworks created since the Renaissance, but when you see as many as I did in such a short space of time, the undertones begin, eventually, to drown out the melody.

In short, I have never been exposed to quite so many flaccid fellows in one place as I was in Rome (they had been far from flaccid in Hamburg). Every other painting, fresco, has relief or sculpture features a male nude; if not Christ, then bottom-baring cherubs, skimpily dressed saints and all manner of heretical, doomed, tortured and redeemed bystanders. The martyrs are the most overtly homoerotic and sadomasochistic of the lot.

By the end of my first couple of days' sightseeing I was left punch drunk by the sheer volume of meat and two veg that passed before my eyes. In Rome, not a park, piazza, church or museum is without a porcelain or plaster Percy, all of them, without exception, no larger than a cocktail sausage. (And if this is in any way an authentic representation of the Italian male member, it is all the explanation we need for those huge pepper mills, big red sports cars and the fact that they have to pinch girls' bums all the time.)

Now I appreciate a good penis as much as the next man (yes, ladies, the horrible truth is even men have a sneaking fascination for the things), but there is a difference between having your idle, comparative curiosity sated and encountering them at every turn. Critical mass came for me in, of all places, the Vatican Museum where the profusion of pricks actually began to overwhelm me. Here, right in the Pope's backyard, are literally hundreds of naked members dangling left, right and, mostly (though with scant regard for statistical accuracy) centre, all for the edification of bishops, priests, nuns and visiting church groups. Is it me or, in one panel of the Sistine Chapel ceiling, is Eve actually depicted as if she has turned away having just given, or is about to give, Adam oral gratification?

And they wonder why Catholic priests are so deviant.

Not to hark on about this, but despite the fact that pretty much all of these depictions are of the kind of wieners you wouldn't bother to bait a hook with (stand up Michelangelo's *David*, oh sorry, you are standing up), they still would have been something of an eye-opener to a man who had led as sheltered a life as Andersen. What's more, the majority of classical and neo-classical depictions of nudity are often asexual or androgynous. I don't want to sound like my gran passing judgement on Boy George on *Top of the Pops* circa 1984 here, but, genitalia aside, in many instances it is impossible to tell the girls from the boys. For a man clearly terrified of his own sexual urges and appalled by others' animal habits, this soft-core, wholly unthreatening depiction of the human body would, I suspect, have held great appeal. And what more respectable venue can there be in which to view the naked form than a church? It's certainly a whole lot more socially acceptable than a visit to a mucky book store.

Could it be that the frequent bouts of 'sensuality' Andersen records in his Italian diaries have as much to do with the art he was devouring day in, day out, as the tempting *bella donnas* he was offered on his evening perambulations around Italy's red-light districts? One thing is for certain, if Andersen was gay – as many have posited – then he had definitely come to the right place for eye candy.

But was he really gay? Actually, I had hoped we could avoid this delicate subject, but if you absolutely insist on bringing it up, I suppose we had better get to the bottom of it.

Many believe Andersen was a homosexual but many – predominantly older, male Danish Andersen scholars, it has to be said – have argued with equal conviction that he wasn't.

This is a bold statement, I realise, but I think I can solve the knotty puzzle of Andersen's sexuality once and for all. But before I draw an end to a century and a half's fevered speculation, let's just have a quick run through of the sexual [non-] adventures of one very mixed-up poet.

Having been roundly rebuffed by Riborg Voigt in 1830, Andersen moved on to her brother, Christian, claiming he was 'the one I feel most attached to of all . . . It is as if he has cast a spell over me, I do not know how I can be so fond of him.' They appear to have had an unusually close, though certainly not sexual, relationship, and remained in contact throughout their lives (Andersen was later godfather to Christian's eldest son).

He then made a play for Edvard Collin, the son of his bene-factor Jonas, writing numerous letters scarcely concealing his desire, only to find his love missives fall like seeds on stone. With that avenue looking distinctly unpromising, he fell in love with a theology student, a pretty, wavy-haired thirty-two-year-old named Ludwig Müller, whom he met during one of his regular visits to country houses.

'You will probably laugh at me, but I miss you so dreadfully,' Andersen wrote after they first parted. 'I am as fond of you, as if you were my brother . . . How empty it was at home in my little room last night! I went in to look at your bed, walked around alone, fell into a miserable mood and hardly slept at all – Oh, do come, come my dear, dear Ludwig, and I will – I will not be loving to you at all, that is what you like best! Then you will come, won't you? . . . If you find this strange, then remember, as you say, I am an original.'

You can almost hear Müller trying to brush away Andersen's puppyish nuzzling with the backhanded: 'You original, *you*!' But then something miraculous happened – Müller wrote back: 'How dear you are to my heart . . . I think of you so often and look forward as a child to our meeting soon.'

Andersen was giddy with joy, replying: 'Oh how can I tell you how much, how unutterably much I care for you . . . ? You are so close to me, so unutterably close . . . If there was a chance, which there isn't, I would come to you for a couple of hours, I long for you so much.' But just as he was about to send this reply he discovered that the letter was a hoax written by a female friend. Astonishingly, he sent the reply anyway, with a copy of the hoax and another letter asking, 'Would you have written it?'

The real answer was a firm no.

On the rebound from Riborg, Ludwig and Edvard, Andersen turned, like a heat-seeking love missile, towards Edvard's youngest sister, the eighteen-year-old Louise. Again, hers was a love he knew he could not have – her family would never allow it for a start. It is likely that Andersen refers to this in *The Ugly Duckling* when he writes: '"How ugly you are!" said the wild ducks. "But it makes no difference to us as long as you don't marry into our family!" Poor thing! He certainly wasn't thinking about marriage. All he wanted was to be allowed to lie in the rushes and to drink a little water from the marsh.'

In 1837, he had also enjoyed what he called a 'minor infatuation' with Ørsted's daughter. Sophie Ørsted was only sixteen at the time and not the slightest bit interested, but Andersen was never one to pass up an opportunity to moon over what was always destined to be another doomed love. Hearing of Sophie's engagement, he wrote: 'Now I'll never be married! There are no young girls around for me any more!' So he turned once more to boys.

He first met Henrik Stampe, at that time half his age, a year later while visiting Thorvaldsen who had by then moved into a studio in the country home of Henrik's father, Baron Stampe, at Nysø. Henrik was rugged, pretty and a bit of a bounder. The two became close over the following years, but it seems Henrik was only really interested in using Andersen to get to a girl called Jonna Drewsen. That Jonna was a granddaughter of Jonas Collin must have really rubbed things in for Andersen, although judging by the crosses in his almanac and his regular complaints of a 'sore penis', Andersen did a fair bit of rubbing himself during this period.

Around the same time as he was falling, in private, for Henrik, Andersen was openly wooing the nineteen-year-old Lady Mathilda Barck. But she was certainly no 'beard'; he genuinely seems to have been besotted by her. Before he left on his *Poet's Bazaar* journey in 1840, he wrote Mathilda a wonderfully melodramatic love letter: 'I am leaving in a sad mood. The South with all its warmth and splendour will not breathe sunshine into my spirit . . . My heart's prayer is to die abroad, or to return home in order to produce a work which will bring honour to me and to Denmark.' He ended it: 'If you write at the beginning of November and address it Munich "poste restante", then I shall get it before I cross the Alps.' In a turn of events that would be comic if the rest of his love life weren't quite so tragic, Mathilda's actually fairly encouraging reply was delivered to Andersen three years late, having been mislaid by a friend. By then both parties had moved on to other suitors – Andersen to Jenny Lind, and Mathilda to the Belgian ambassador.

The *Poet's Bazaar* journey imposed a hiatus on his courting activities for a while but, upon his return, his love life, like his writing, exploded with a new energy and confidence. In the years immediately following his journey to the Orient, Andersen experienced two of his greatest infatuations – one the very public attachment to the Swedish singer, Jenny Lind; the other, a far deeper and more mutually rewarding relationship with the Hereditary Grand Duke Carl Alexander von Sachsen-Weimar-Eisenach.

The Duke was possibly Andersen's most 'successful' relationship; were it not for the peculiarities of the protagonists, one might almost call it conventional. Soon after meeting him for the first time, Andersen wrote of Carl Alexander, 'I quite love the young duke, he is the first of all princes that I really find attractive, and that I wish was not a prince, or that I was one myself.'

Though the Duke had recently married, the two soon forged a bond. Andersen had at last found a match for his own particularly theatrical brand of emotional display. Carl Alexander was only twenty-six, but he had drunk from the fountain of Romantic excess from an early age and, like Andersen, seemed to live in a permanent state of heightened emotion. In him Andersen found a soul mate with whom he could sit holding hands; write gushing, sentimental letters; and make lifelong declarations of love. It was, by any standards, an intense, intimate and unusual relationship. In his diary Andersen almost makes it sound as if he is the heroine who finally gets her prince in one of his stories: 'The Hereditary Grand Duke walked arm in arm with me across the courtyard of the castle to my room, kissed me lovingly, asked me always to love him though he was just an ordinary person, asked me to stay with him this winter . . . Fell asleep with the melancholy, happy feeling that I was the guest of this strange prince at his castle and loved by him . . . It is like a fairy tale.'

Never before had Andersen had his love reciprocated in such a way; for a blue blood to write him letters proclaiming 'your letter now lies among my most sacred treasures' must have been like manna from heaven for this died-in-the-wool royalist.

On a return visit to Weimar in 1846 Carl Alexander and Hans Christian cemented their love. 'He said we must always remain friends, and that one day I should come to live with him for ever in Weimar . . . He clasped [my hand] so firmly in his, told me he loved me and pressed his cheek to mine.' The intimacy extended to the bedroom, though not the bed, as Andersen recounted in his diary: 'Went to see the Hereditary Grand Duke at eight o'clock in the morning, he received me in his shirt with only a gown around himself; "I can do that, we know each other." He pressed me to his breast, we kissed each other. "Think of this hour," he said, "as being yesterday. We are friends for life." We both wept.'

Of course the love was doomed and, if it hadn't been, Andersen would probably have contrived a way to make it so. Despite the Grand Duke's entreaties to stay in Weimar and 'always to love him' the wars between Prussia and Denmark over the territories of Schleswig and Holstein that smouldered on from 1848 to 1864 (prompting Lord Palmerston's famous comment, which can bear endless repetition as far as I am concerned: 'Only three men understand the Schleswig Holstein issue, one was Prince Albert, who is dead, the second was a German professor who went mad. I am the third and I have forgotten it'), and which Denmark eventually lost, made the relationship untenable. Andersen did return to Weimar after things had settled down but, though Carl was as friendly as ever, his court was openly hostile to the Danish literary lion. Andersen never quite felt the same about him again.

Meanwhile, there was Jenny, feted across Europe as the most adored singer of her age. Andersen reports in his autobiography that people camped outside the theatres where she was playing in order to get tickets to hear her fabled voice. He met her first, briefly, in 1840, just before leaving for the Orient, but formed no great impression of her. She had seemed, he later wrote, 'of a very ordinary character which soon passed from my mind'. But Lind returned to Copenhagen in 1843, and this time he decided he was in love.

There were striking similarities between Andersen and Lind. Both were conceived out of wedlock and had clawed their way up from poverty-stricken childhoods. Andersen's oft-repeated 'motto' that 'God gave us the nuts but he doesn't crack them for us' could equally have applied to Lind's single-minded determination to make something of her talent. Andersen even described himself as a male version of her, which can't have been very flattering for Lind, but was fairly close to the mark.

Sadly for Andersen, Lind preferred to think of him as brother material. She made clear her feelings were platonic only after she had toyed with Andersen's affections at a time when she needed the emotional support. (She strikes me as a sanctimonious prick tease, but what do I know? Perhaps my feelings towards her are tainted because it was Lind who inspired Andersen to write the story that inspired the musical that brought me to Denmark.)

After Jenny, Andersen's bipolar sexuality swung for the last time back towards safer territory: boys. He fell head over his size-14 heels for a sexy young ballet dancer, Harald Scharff, whom he first met in Paris in 1857. Andersen was in his early fifties, Scharff in his early twenties.

Andersen's diaries reveal that Scharff revitalised his sexuality and, following the recent death of Jonas Collin, he seemed to become more open about such relationships – the two of them were publicly demonstrative of their love to the extent that friends warned him that tongues were wagging. 'I long for him daily,' Andersen wrote at the height of their whirlwind romance. But still, as biographer Jackie Wullschlager points out, 'we can only guess at the physical details of [their] relationship'. It is hard to imagine the lusty young Scharff being physically stimulated by Andersen, but they were theatrical creatures and, though the dancer eventually moved on to younger meat, their relationship lasted a good few years. I like to think, though, that Andersen achieved some kind of emotional satisfaction with Scharff, who was his last great crush. (Sadly, the dancer ended his days an alcoholic, having been forced to retire early through an injury which, ironically, was incurred during a rehearsal of a ballet based on an Andersen story. He died in a mental asylum in 1912.)

So, Andersen's 'partners' were what you might call a mixed bag. Statistically there is a slight bias towards men but Danish scholars have tended to respond to this by mounting a stern, backs-against-the-wall-boys! defence of his heterosexuality. One can understand why; back in those days, homosexuality was hardly a respectable orientation and anyone who had raised their head above the parapet and outed their most sacred literary cow would have been sent to Iceland. The Danes are Vikings, let's not forget, and the Vikings didn't exactly mince their way across Europe. It would hardly be fitting for their national poet to be a 'lavender aunt', would it?

'There seems to be little mystery as to why Andersen did not marry,' the early Andersen archivist and Hollywood actor Jean

Hersholt, claimed. 'His bony facial structure often exaggerated his homeliness, and he was quite without the means to make a good marriage risk in his early days.' In a similar vein, another Andersen expert wrote: 'His unhappy lot as a lover has given occasion to more ingenious explanations than are really necessary, since his three abortive wooings may without difficulty be attributed to his notorious uncomliness.' The academic Wilhelm von Rosen, who wrote a long and influential dissertation on Andersen's sexuality, concluded: 'Andersen was not a homosexual: he only fell in love with men – and with women too, possibly – and most of all with Edvard Collin.'

The best euphemism I have read regarding Andersen's sexuality was that he was a 'restless old bachelor' (which is uncannily similar to a description in the *Radio Times* of a prominent, closeted comedy actor I once worked with as 'a vigorous, squash-playing bachelor'), although I also love the comment in the March 1851 edition of *Eclectic* magazine: 'He has never married and according to Copenhagen gossip, he never will.'

Reading between the lines, the implication of the older literary critics' harrumphing on the subject is that being gay is a negative thing, a character flaw that a man of Andersen's genius could never be guilty of. The first suggestion – in print at least – that Andersen *was* gay came as early as a 1901 thesis written by Carl Albert Hansen Fahlberg (who was himself homosexual and suffered considerable persecution for it), but even the latest doctoral thesis on Andersen quotes an early-twentieth-century Danish psychologist, Professor Hjalmar Helweg – who claimed Andersen was heterosexual through and through – as the definitive diagnosis. Meanwhile HCA 2005 – the organisation charged with organising the bicentenary celebrations – has airbrushed any hint of male friendships from his biography.

So what about all those love letters Andersen wrote to men? Hmm, bit tricky to explain those away, surely? One noted biographer of the 'old school', Elias Bredsdorff, concedes that 'some of Andersen's letters are *almost* declarations of love' (they're my italics). He also admits that a letter Andersen wrote to Edvard Collin in 1835 in which he writes that he longs for him as if he were 'a lovely Calabrian girl', is in fact 'a love letter'. Bredsdorff concedes that Andersen 'was physically attracted to the opposite sex' but ultimately defers to Helweg, who wrote: 'If under favourable circumstances he had met a homosexual young man whom he liked it is not easy to say what this might have led to. Maybe he then in practice might have become a homosexual.'

The truth is, of course, that he did meet many homosexual young men.

Another common line of defence – and not without merit – is that Andersen's displays of affection for other men can be explained by the context of the Romantic fashion of the day. As with middle-class white boys who like to pretend to be black rap stars today, in the first half of the nineteenth century a certain type of heterosexual young man enjoyed emulating the protagonists of his favourite novels, who often tended to be 'a bit poofy' – Goethe's Werther being the most famous example. Parents, and teachers who might otherwise have intervened, dismissed this kind of boy-to-boy effusiveness as a phase.

The 1926 introduction to the English edition of Andersen's autobiography chastises him for just this kind of thing: 'Andersen's many weepings – fashionable for men in those days – and his overwhelming share of what was then called "sensibility" are apt to put a reader out of patience.' But the truth is, there is more to his letters to men friends than fashionable weepings.

'Ah, but,' say the oh-no-he-wasn't camp, 'you cannot use modern labels like "homosexual" when talking about historical figures.'

'It has been discussed whether Andersen was a homosexual,' writes von Rosen. 'This, however, is an un-historical way of presenting the problem. The word, the concept and the phenomenon of "homosexual" did not exist in Andersen's day.' It is true, the term 'homosexual' was not invented until 1868 (by Karl Kertbeny, the Hungarian writer and proto-gay rights activist). The argument – propagated by Michel Foucault, among others

– goes that it is therefore technically impossible for anyone to have been a homosexual prior to that date.

This isn't really my field, and I have no wish to tread on anyone's white Patrick Cox loafers, but while it is true that homosexuality did not become a topic for discussion until the latter part of the century – when it resulted in the kind of witch hunt that led to Oscar Wilde's trial – to claim that Kertbeny invented gay sex is clearly preposterous. As the respected biographer (of Victor Hugo, Balzac and Rimbaud) Graham Robb illustrates in his book on this subject, *Strangers: Homosexual Love in the Nineteenth Century*, the early part of that century was actually a fairly tolerant time in which to be gay and there was, as they say, a lot of it about. (Although, equally, there was an instance in Denmark in which a contemporary and acquaintance of Andersen's, Laurids Kruse, was drummed out of the country by rumours of his homosexuality – he died in Paris.)

But still, as final, conclusive evidence that Andersen wasn't gay, the older Danish academics point out that, if he were that way inclined, the Collin family – who were closer to him than anyone else – would, a) have known all about it and, then, b) would never have allowed Andersen to go travelling with the various Collin grandsons, as he did towards the end of his life.

'If there had been even the slightest suspicion that Andersen was homosexual it is quite unthinkable that [Edvard] Collin would have allowed his young son to travel round Europe as Andersen's sole companion,' writes Helweg. This hopeless argument, still wheeled out today, seems to imply that if Andersen was gay then he must also be intent on ravishing anything with a penis. The reality, of course, is that gay men have preferences just like everyone else and maybe, by that stage in his life, these men weren't his type. As it so happens, the boys *were* very much Andersen's type and, though he was by then old enough to know better (he was in his sixties, they in their early twenties), there is a strong undercurrent of yearning – jealousy even – in his relationships with these young men, particularly where Edvard's son Jonas jnr is concerned.

Unfortunately, Andersen knew the Collin boys were as straight as Warren Beatty (Ingeborg's son Einar, for example, took a far more hands-on approach to the produce in the Parisian brothels he and Andersen visited); he was aware also that, while they were travelling in Europe, they were his responsibility and he was nothing if not trustworthy. He was never likely to queer his pitch – so to speak – with the Collins.

And, *crucially*, the Collin family *were* very much aware that Andersen formed unusually strong, emotional attachments to men. Theodor Collin warned Andersen to be more discreet with Harald Scharff, as Andersen noted tetchily in his diary at the time: 'Theodor put me in a very bad mood . . . he emphasised how strongly I showed my love for S., which people noticed and found ridiculous.' Edvard, himself a long-term target of Andersen's unwanted ardour, warned him that his affair with Carl Alexander was inappropriately intimate. After Andersen's death Edvard returned his letters to former male 'lovers' so that they could destroy them if they wished. And, as we have already heard, Theodor was among several of Andersen's friends who tried to persuade Andersen to visit prostitutes, in the hope perhaps of diverting his desires to more conventional targets.

Those who deny Andersen had homosexual tendencies are on stronger ground when citing his courtships of women. There was no question that he could be aroused by women, but these romances were of a very different nature to his dalliances with men. The women he set his sights on were, almost without exception, beyond his reach – the relationships were pre-doomed, if you like. Either the women in question already had more suitable suitors lined up (as was the case with Voigt, Louise Collin and Jenny Lind) or their families would never have allowed things to progress beyond the histrionic letter-writing stage (as was probably the case with Sophie Ørsted and Louise). With Sophie, Louise and Lotte Oehlenschläger (the daughter of Denmark's leading poet of the time), you also have to ask yourself if it was the fathers', rather then the daughters', affections Andersen ultimately sought.

His courtships of women – Lind especially – were very public affairs; he revelled in the heightened emotion of the chase, and wallowed in the aftermath of their disintegration. These rejections brought him the attention and sympathy that were pure oxygen for his ego, as well as the kind of real-life experiences that were useful for the development of a Romantic writer. After all, you could hardly write love stories if you had never plumbed the depths of romantic despair. I am not suggesting that Andersen contrived his relationship with women out of a cynical need for material, but they definitely had the air of a pose about them. He was, as Bredsdorff pointed out, 'In love with being in love.'

Ultimately, as a profoundly self-obsessed man – one who often referred to his 'womanly' ways and once identified his 'semi-womanliness' in a letter to Edvard – he seemed resigned to, and even comforted by, the prospect of never finding a woman to share his life with: 'I shall never be engaged,' he wrote after he lost Sophie to the son of the local chemist, 'and it would be a great misfortune if it were ever to take place . . . Now I am at home, alone – alone as I shall always be.' After attending Louise Collin's silver wedding celebrations he wrote: 'I thank God that I did not become Louise's husband, then quite a different kind of poetic activity – God knows which one – would have been mine.'

In contrast to his public posturing with women, Andersen's relationships with men seem to be more keenly felt, somehow more *authentic* than those he had with women. Long after Henrik Stampe jilted him for a woman, Andersen was harping on about it in his diary, for instance, while his obsession with Edvard took decades to dissipate.

The reason for this, I think, is that, though he enjoyed tormenting himself with the idea of one day forming a lifelong partnership with a woman, deep down – as his relief at not becoming Louise's husband implies – he knew that his monstrous ego would prohibit such a bond. Andersen was impossible marriage material, a fact he was well aware of. He knew the kind of drive and dedication required by his art would inevitably preclude a lasting, intimate, sharing love of the kind Edvard enjoyed with his wife Henriette.

As Georg Brandes put it, 'The women who attracted him in his youth gave him no affection in return . . . But there was one, the most beautiful of all, an Immortal, whom he loved longer and more passionately than any earthy creature. Her name was Glory.'

This was the one area of his life that could bring him an alternative immortality to that sought by most people in bearing children. The approval and love he earned for his writing was not dependent on someone finding him physically attractive, but on his talent. As he grew older and his success spread across Europe, the warm welcome he received in the homes of the aristocracy and among his fellow writers in France, England and Germany was some compensation at least for his appalling romantic record.

So he chose women he knew he could never possess as a form of pre-emptive sabotage. On the rare occasions when friends began to suggest that marriage might be on the cards, Andersen would usually invoke his financial situation as an excuse not to propose. He was too poor to marry Sophie Ørsted, he told his friend Henriette Hanck, because, really, he needed an income of two thousand *rigsdaler* a year to make an honest woman of her; to the poet B.S. Ingemann he used the excuse of being too old. 'Beloved Sophie, you will never know how happy I could have been with you, if only I had the money!' he wrote shortly after the 'affair' ended. Then, as his wealth grew, he simply raised the bar on the figure he felt was needed to marry until he became so wealthy he could no longer use it as an excuse, by which time he was able to protest that he was too old to propose, or too ugly.

Like the eponymous hero of his story 'The Butterfly', 'He had been too long on the lookout, and that one should not be. The butterfly became an old bachelor, as it is called.'

With his male friends there was no risk to either his ego or his art; social convention was unlikely to pressurise him into a proposal to the likes of Henrik Stampe or Harald Scharff, and so he was free to delve deeper, expose his true emotions and fall, truly, in love.

I have heard people use the Michael Jackson 'He is not like other men' defence when discussing Andersen; he is neither a homosexual nor a heterosexual, they say, but 'special' – a creative genius whose sexual preferences are beyond categorisation. I don't buy this. The Danish biographer Jens Andersen comes closer to the truth when he writes, with characteristic elegance: 'Andersen was a rare blend of impulses. By putting him in a box labelled "homosexual", "heterosexual", "bisexual" or "asexual", we fail to see his exhuberant nature or the era's more nuanced and expansive perception of what a man's role in life actually could be.'

But I am going to stick my neck out. I think Andersen's sexual diagnosis is a fairly straightforward one: he was a latent bisexual with voyeuristic tendencies. It is as simple – or as complex – as that. He was aroused by both men and women, but made do with fleeting encounters with prostitutes, flirtatious romances with effeminate men and a lifelong, unrequited yearning for Edvard Collin. And though we will probably never know what lies behind the mysterious almanac references to 'MD' I am convinced that, had he lived in these more liberated times, he would have been the screamingest queen in town, and probably a great deal happier.

Returning to my mission, I did manage to ring up what I thought was a quite impressive nine churches in one day, beating Andersen's highest tally by two. That said, in the interests of fairness I should point out that, while Andersen treated a church as something to be savoured, its artworks to be pored over for hours, my visits mostly consisted of me stumbling over the requisite, hunched old beggar woman in the doorway as my eyes adjusted to the half light, followed by a lap of the side chapels – doing that kind of solemn, heel-first walking one automatically does in churches (with washboard accompaniment) – before stifling a disrespectful snigger at some detail or other I found funny (a statue of St Sebastian with dozens of arrows sticking out of him at all angles, like a magic trick gone wrong, for instance), and then a guilty sprint for the door, trying to avoid eye contact with anyone. In the interests of honest reporting I should also add that on the same day I rang up at least as many visits to ice-cream parlours.

But enough of monuments and marble, several of my Andersen-related tasks in Rome also involved the living. Prior to leaving on the trip I had made contact with the modern-day heirs to the Scandinavian Society, of which Andersen was an early member; arranged to meet Italy's leading Andersen academic and translator; and booked time for some Andersen-style social climbing at the Danish embassy. As well as this I had some more speculative plans involving the Pope and a cactus (and I would like to add that the last five words of that sentence have almost certainly never appeared in print together before in that order).

The cactus first. On his first visit to Rome Andersen had taken a fancy to a very large cactus he had found in the Quirinale gardens. He drew it, and mentioned it in his diary. It must have been quite an impressive plant and I was keen to see if it was still there – if it was, it would be a unique, living link to 1840.

The Quirinale was built to house the Popes but is today the presidential palace. As with every other public building in the city, it is packed with stupefying artistic riches. I didn't have the heart to ask one of the extraordinarily tall *carabinieri* for directions to a plant, so spent some time wandering around the sumptuous formal gardens with their immaculate box hedges, lemon groves, palms and marble statues. At the time I didn't even know whether a cactus can live 160 years (actually, they have been known to pass the 200 mark), but at the far end of the garden

I did indeed find two truly monumental cacti, one of which was a prickly pear strikingly similar to the one Andersen had drawn.

This was obviously one very old cactus, and it was growing against a wall in the Quirinale gardens. Andersen had seen and drawn a very old cactus, which had been growing against a wall in the Quirinale gardens. As far as I was concerned, this *was* Andersen's Cactus and I was able to overlook – with a steely self-delusion that I find comes in very useful at such times – the fact that the walls were totally different. Satisfied, I took a picture and left.

The Quirinale is only open on Sundays, which, of course, is when one of the city's star turns makes his once-weekly appearance, so I skedaddled across town, to the accompaniment of peeling church bells, to St Peter's.

No building can ever quite prepare you for St Peter's blend of monumental kitsch and overpowering majesty. Judging by the *Poet's Bazaar* chapter on it, entitled 'Fairy Tale Palaces in Reality', Andersen felt the same way: '. . . the Vatican and St Peter's Church in Rome present a vastness, a pomp, and an appearance similar and equal to those palaces which fancy has raised in the old oriental book, *A Thousand and One Nights*.' The crowd, he writes, are reduced to 'pigmies' by the building's scale; while the church's galleries house 'the richest and most glorious treasures in the world'.

I was raised a Catholic, but these days I am so lapsed I almost don't feel guilty about it any more, which made what happened next all the more surprising. I had just passed the famous statue of St Peter and was standing at the back of the congregation, when I began to feel a tidal wave of emotion building in my solar plexus. I had been thinking about my parents – about my father who converted to Catholicism in the 1950s, about my mother who also converted after a visit to Rome in the 1960s. I thought about all the arguments I had had with them about churchgoing, the Pope's evil ways, the riches of the Church and its destructive dogma. I weighed up whether to go outside and call my mother – my father is no longer alive – to tell her where I was; I knew she would be thrilled. But, equally, I knew she would begin to cry and that, when I heard her, I, too, would begin to cry.

And that's when it started. I began to cry. I tried fighting it, biting my lip and tightening my stomach as if straining to open a stubborn jar lid, but the emotion continued to swamp me in waves of . . . what was it? Grief? Existential angst? Andersen-style epic self-pity?

Unlike our poet, who burst into tears at the slightest provocation (a review that was only 99 per cent favourable; a dog barking; some artfully arranged flowers), I am not usually prone to bouts of lachrimosity. Admittedly I have been known to blub at certain select sporting events – that bit where they play the stirring music before the Grand National; the various occasions when Jimmy White lost the World Snooker Championship Final – but never about things that really warrant open displays of emotion like family, faith or feelings. So this was all very odd.

I concluded that, as with Michael Corleone's relationship with the Mafia in *The Godfather III*, just when you think you are free of the Catholic Church, it *drags* you back in. No matter how many times you protest your atheism, the nuns are going to get you in the end.

I walked out into St Peter's Square. The tidal waves subsided. A few minutes later there came a crackle of static from the loud-speakers stationed around the square. A roar erupted from the crowd, signalling that the Pope had come to his window. Stupidly, I had been looking up at the balcony above the entrance to St Peter's, while, in fact, all the time he had been planning to sneak up on me from a window in a building high up on my right-hand side. I turned round to see the entire piazza filled with people staring up, *Life of Brian*-style. There were banners and TV cameras and a lone seagull circled above the throng. All fell silent apart from the noise of a helicopter high above and the gush of the fountains. Kids sat on dads' shoulders; grannies strained their eyes; and thousands of mobile phones were held aloft like lighters at a U2 concert. A group of excited teenage American girls beside me let out an involuntary 'Oh my *gawd*!'

A familiar nasal growl began to emanate from the distant figure, dressed in white and visible from the chest up only, like a Jim Henson creation (disappointingly, this Pope was not 'shaded by peacock feathers' as he was when Andersen saw him). The Pope's voice grew stronger, as if energised by the crowd. He was speaking Italian, of course, so I turned to the couple next to me and asked if they spoke English. They did, but being Hindus visiting from New Delhi, their Italian was as poor as mine.

At the end of his fifteen-minute oration John Paul took time out to greet some of the various coach parties in the crowd, in the manner of a nightclub comic ('Is there anyone here from Wichita?'), to which the greeted responded with whoops of joy. 'Viva Mexico,' said the Pope at the end of one such greeting, and a mariachi band raised a fanfare in response. It reminded me of the time I saw Sinatra in concert just before he died. It was the same kind of hysteria – muted by reverence – that attends the public appearances of many great cultural icons in their twilight, usually tinged with an unspoken thought: will this be his last ever appearance?

Finally, the Pope waved goodbye, we all waved back, the white curtain billowed and he was gone.

In the Vatican Museum I surfed on a wave of Japanese tourists to the Sistine Chapel, where Andersen had lain on his back on the steps to the papal throne to observe the prophets. Writing about an artwork as iconic as the Sistine Chapel fits firmly into the 'dancing about architecture' category of futile expositional exercises, but I do have two observations. The first is that there are, again, masses of willies on display here, but I won't dwell on that for fear that you might begin to think me obsessed; the second is that, actually, the floor has a very pretty mosaic pattern, although I doubt that anyone has looked down upon entering this room in the five centuries since Michelangelo lay back and thought of Rome.

Standing in the midst of a crowd straining their necks upwards like tulips towards the sun, I was confronted with more nostrils than I would ever wish to see again. In the unlikely event that it would ever need more money, the Vatican could make a useful supplementary income by having a team of osteopaths on hand to administer back and neck rubs – they could even train the bolshie guards who roam the room 'shush-ing' everyone and removing baseball caps from the heads of disrespectful teenagers (it is still the Pope's private chapel, after all).

Andersen was overwhelmed by the richness of the Vatican's artworks, which he says 'produce an effect like the coloured patterns in a kaleidoscope'. Of the paintings he saw he singles out Domenichino's dying St Jerome; and Raphael's mesmeric *Transfiguration* and *Madonna di Foligno* (1511), which shows the Madonna and infant Christ sitting on a cloud above an old hippie bloke with a 'What's all this about then?' kind of expression on his face. My eye was drawn, however, to an unfinished, tea-stained da Vinci. Did this man ever finish anything? I mean, it is all very well doodling a helicopter in a margin, but it is quite another building one and actually going for a flight . . .

What has changed, or at least has become even more transparent, is the Vatican's rapacious greed. The entrance fee is twice that of any other museum in Rome, while every fifty yards or so there is a kiosk selling souvenirs – all a bit rich considering that the vast majority of its treasures were donated for the glory of God, and most of the rest were nicked by one devious pontiff after another.

From the Vatican I headed across town to the Colosseum and the Forum. On Christmas Eve 1840 Andersen had visited these great classical sites with the painter Carl Løffler who was, it seems, a man of limited vocabulary. Andersen wrote in exasperation to a friend: 'Everything he saw, Maria Maggiore, the Lateran, fountains – he would say "Oh isn't it dainty!" – in the end, he also said of the Colosseum "It is dainty!" by which time I was almost crazy!'

When Marvin Gaye sang that the world was 'just a great big onion', few had any idea what he was talking about and, who knows, perhaps close friends considered having him admitted for psychiatric evaluation, but standing surveying the sprawling field of history that is the Roman Forum from the Tabularium across to the familiar half-eaten cup-cake silhouette of the Colosseum, I suddenly realised what he had been going on about. Here, in George Eliot's 'vast wreck of ambitious ideals' are revealed more layers of the history of western civilisation than any other site in Europe, and the effect, particularly at twilight, is stupefying. I struggled to comprehend this shattered marble and brick land-scape, dotted with Corinthian columns, sculptures and ruined temples, with fragments of bas relief, other shards of sculpture, massive stone-paved roads and naked plinths scattered, crumbling all around. It looks like a gigantic Airfix kit and at the far end is the most remarkable ruin of them all, the Colosseum, which, though depleted over the years (the locals were still carting away its stone in Andersen's day), is one of the few sightseeing clichés that still possesses the power to astound.

Andersen likened the Colosseum to the Pyramids and the rock temples of India (neither of which he ever saw), and, more strik-ingly, to a mammoth's carcass, 'a stone skeleton that proclaims the departed greatness of Rome better than books can do'. Verona's stadium is, he writes, 'dwarfish' in comparison, continuing: 'The Colosseum preaches to us about the system of the world, about the greatness and the impotence of the human race, so that the mind becomes at once elevated and humbled.'

As with every ancient site in Italy, there is scaffolding every-where (the Colosseum appears now to be sponsored by Nike), and, to my great annoyance, the upper tiers of the stadium were closed. I asked an attendant why this was so.

'No, can't go up,' he snarled.

'Yes,' I replied, smiling, 'but why not?'

'Is closed,' he replied and stormed off to berate some small children for breathing.

As every visitor to the Colosseum does, I tried to conjure images of the carnal brutality – everything from lions snacking on elephants and women fighting dwarves, to the crucifixion of dogs – staged here to placate the masses. If such shows were staged today, would 2,000 years of civilisation temper our enthusiasm? Would we turn away in morally appalled unison? The place would be packed to its non-existent rafters with boxing, Formula 1 and Ridley Scott fans. Andersen would not have approved. He was mostly repelled by bloodsports, and was actually something of an animal lover, as he recounts in *A Poet's Bazaar* when he rescues a small tortoise 'no larger than a watch' from the road, and plans to take it home with him, 'but, as it afterward occurred to me that it would suffer hunger and thirst the further I travelled, I took it into a wood of Oleander-trees, where the rays of the sun played freely and it was right glad of its liberty!' (Many years later while travelling in Spain he was disgusted by the spectacle of a bullfight, calling it a 'brutal, horrible form of entertainment'.)

From the Colosseum I walked down Via dei Fori Imperiali to the Palazzo Venezia, which was pretty much as Andersen had drawn it. By my reckoning, he must have stood sketching in what is now Benetton's doorway. It is not exactly the quietest spot, and was probably a busy junction in his time too. It is a wonder he wasn't moved on. Then again, he was often mistaken for a priest while travelling (he is listed as 'Padre Andersen' on the passenger list of the boat he took from Naples, for instance), so perhaps no one dared interrupt him. This was because he typically dressed all in black and with his solemn, pale, equine face, and a weird beard arrangement in which the hairs clung to the underside of his chin like iron filings to a magnet – popular in the States and England, and called a Newgate frill, and perhaps all he could muster, having not even begun to sprout facial hair until the age of twenty-five – you can see how the mistake was made.

In Copenhagen they were used to Andersen, but his peculiar physiognomy often caused a stir abroad. In Spain people laughed openly at him on the street, which can't have been pleasant: 'I saw a couple of young soldiers and also some ladies on the balcony notice my long figure and laugh,' he wrote in his diary from that journey in 1863. 'I felt humiliated and embarrassed, went into a side street.'

Judging from the countless pictures and portraits of him, and the great care he took with his appearance (he was quite a dandy in fact), Andersen was, nevertheless, a vain man. Edvard Collin claimed he was incapable of passing a mirror, but if you saw him on a bus you would likely think twice about sitting next to him. He was, according to his friend and later travelling companion, William Bloch, 'strange and bizarre in his movement and carriage. His arms and legs were long and thin out of all proportion, his hands were broad and flat, and his feet of such gigantic proportions that it seemed reasonable that no one would ever have thought of stealing his boots. His nose was in the so-called Roman style, but so disproportionately large that it seemed to dominate his whole face. After one had left him it was definitely his nose that one remembered most clearly, whereas his eyes, which were small and pale and well-hidden in their sockets behind a couple of huge eyelids half covering them, did not leave any impression . . .'

Bloch was kind enough to add: 'On the other hand there was both soul and beauty in his tall, open forehead and round his unusually well-shaped mouth', but that hardly softens the impression one often forms of Andersen from contemporary descriptions. I always feel terribly sorry for him when I read about his looks. It can't have been easy having to walk into a room full of people looking like something that fell from the ramparts of Notre Dame. Unfortunately, though many of these descriptions refer to Andersen's peculiar charisma and personal charm, such qualities are rarely communicated via photography and portraiture.

★　★　★

I set off for my evening's visit to the Scandinavian Society – Rome's oldest cultural society – where I was to meet the twenty-first-century heirs to the Nordic Grand Tourists of the nineteenth century. To get there, I walked past the ruins on the Palatine Hill, ancient Rome's Beverly Hills, and then the Circus Maximus – around which modern Romans still race to the death – until finally, in a quiet suburb, in an anonymous modern apartment block, I found a small note beside an intercom buzzer which read 'Circolo Scandinavo: Open Night'.

The Scandinavian Society was founded in 1833 as a library (it grew, in fact, from the Danish Library, which Edvard Collin had founded in Rome) and gathering place for artists, architects, writers, scientists and painters from the north. Countless illustrious names have signed the visitors' book, including Edvard Grieg, the Danish painters Marstrand and Lundbye, and Henrik Ibsen, who campaigned to open the doors to women. It moved from Via Garibaldi to its current address in the Aventino district a year ago.

I was hoping to find the kind of artistic soirée where louche, wild-haired painters behaved disgracefully with their nubile young models, and bra-less Bohemian poetesses openly trawled the room in search of carnal pleasure. I had hopes of engaging in deep, philosophical debates with existentially troubled Norwegians long into the night over a bottle of vodka, before dancing until dawn to hardcore Finnish thrash metal with Swedish sex-succubi. But as it turned out, I was the only visitor (never mind, Swedish sex-succubi are overrated. Probably.)

The society's secretary, Helene, who actually was a Swede, welcomed me into the apartment, and showed me around. Much of the original furniture and art from the early nineteenth century is still in use by the society, including the small portrait of Andersen by Albert Küchler, painted in Rome in 1834. Having just likened Andersen to a gargoyle, I have to say that in this portrait he looks unusually suave, with pursed lips, a high fur collar and a vast expanse of forehead – every inch the Romantic hero.

Helene pointed out an entire shelf of the Society's library taken up with priceless first editions of Andersen's works that he had donated. She had also gathered some books from their library that she thought might be of interest to me. These included the minutes from the first meeting, on 28 January 1833, with a list of atten-dees' signatures below. There was Thorvaldsen's at the top, followed by Küchler, Eckersburg, Constantin Hansen, Conrad Rothe and others. I spotted a familiar autograph further down the list: Andersen's. This took me by surprise because he wasn't even in Rome when the document was drawn up, but Helene explained he had added it upon his arrival. Never one to be left out, Andersen.

The sound of a cork being pulled from a bottle of Frascati summoned the current residents – Tomas, a Norwegian photo-grapher with a plaited beard indicative of a tofu-heavy diet and regular outdoor music festival attendance; Ole, a short, Hobbit-like composer, also from Norway; Christina, a dark and slightly witch-like (in a nice way) Finnish writer; and Magde, a Finnish interior designer. Initially shy, the group soon warmed up as the first bottle was drained, and we passed a convivial, albeit Finnish thrash metal free evening, talking about Andersen and their ex-periences in Rome.

I was curious to know why they had come to Rome, which struck me as a place so rooted in the past as to be of little interest to contemporary artists. Surely they should all be pushing the artistic envelope in Tallinn or somewhere? Ole was the first to pipe up, shyly telling me that, actually, the city had inspired him to start composing that very day. 'I am interested in the layers of the past,' he said mysteriously. (Later, Helene told me that earlier that day while she was working in her office, she had heard Ole's door open, he had walked to the piano, played one note, and then retreated to his room. It was the only time she had seen him all day.) Tomas had found inspiration photographing 'details' at a recent Lazio vs. AC Roma derby match, but had initially come to stay at the Society simply because he wanted to be part of a community. Christina, meanwhile, was working on a play about Rome set 5,000 years ago and Magde, who struck me as fairly eccentric, talked about hairbrushes for ten minutes without taking breath.

At the end of a night that, though pleasant, had not quite lived up to my expectations, I walked back to my hotel, gazing up at the Colosseum, which was encircled by stray cats and, even at that late hour, floodlit by camera flashes.

The Hotel Locarno was a palace compared to the places I had stayed at so far on my trip. I had chosen it because in my guidebook it said that the film director Peter Greenaway stays there sometimes (perhaps, on reflection, not such a great recommendation given the content of some of his films.) I can understand his fondness for the place, with its art deco details, opulent wood panelling, open courtyard with vines and citrus trees and, best of all, the bar, replete with open fire and a barman who mixes a mean whisky sour.

Actually, the bar was its second best feature. The Locarno had one more celebrity secret up its sleeve, which I discovered the next night when I rang down to reception to ask how much longer they thought the rather noisy party in the next room would continue.

'Is photo shoot for actress,' the receptionist told me.

'Oh, who?' I asked.

'Italian actress, Greta Scacchi,' he replied. 'She interview for new film.'

That Scacchi was Italian was news to me. I was sure I had read in Hello! – in the dentist's waiting room, you understand – that she lived in mid-Sussex, and I can't say I had ever detected an Italian accent in her performances in such films as, um, you know, that one with Harrison Ford, but I was in too much of a hurry to get to my keyhole to question him further. (Actually, I looked it up when I got home; she was born in Milan to an Italian father and English mother, which shows I am not to be trusted on such matters.)

After a few tantalising glimpses of photographers, stylists and make-up people flitting between two rooms – one of which was obviously Scacchi's dressing room, the other a makeshift studio – I came up with A Plan.

Andersen never missed an opportunity to introduce himself to famous writers, composers, painters and actors. I realised this was probably the only chance I would have on the trip to do likewise. I changed into my last remaining clean shirt, a stripy Marks and Spencer number I had been saving for my meeting with the ambassador, popped a breath mint, and returned to my keyhole vigil. The next time the dressing-room door opened, ten rather uncomfortable minutes later, I scrambled to open my door to engineer a 'chance' encounter.

Unfortunately, as is my habit when staying alone in hotels, I had not only locked the door but put the chain on. In my attempted frenzy I had forgotten this and so, rather than a nonchalant saunter out into Greta's path, followed by a brief exchange of pleasantries, a discovery of our common link with the mid-Sussex area (I was born there), and then a dinner invitation (either from her to me or vice versa, I wasn't bothered), there was a noisy clatter of key in lock, followed by a frustrated rattling of the door handle and the tense jangle of metal chain on wood, before, finally, I lurched, like an angry drunk, out into the corridor just in time see the back of Greta's magnificently coiffed head disappearing into the next room.

One of the showbiz lackeys trailing in her wake witnessed the entire sorry affair and flashed me a look of such withering disdain that I was left with no option but to continue along the corridor and down the stairs to the bar in order to demonstrate that I wasn't some kind of crazed stalker. I missed Scacchi entirely; she never passed through the bar that evening and I can only assume she left by a back entrance to avoid the stripy-shirted, heavy breather in room 14.

My failure was compounded by the fact that the next day my shirt looked like a soiled dishcloth, and had developed mysterious whisky-type stains down its front. This was particularly regrettable as I had to wear it for my next round of attempted social climbing, the first stage of which was a meeting at the German Institute, housed in a delightful pink stucco villa in a park in Gianicolo.

This was my appointment with Bruno Berni, a short, dapper Italian literary scholar, in a houndstooth sports jacket, chinos and mirror-polished brogues. Berni has translated Andersen's fairy tales, as well as *A Poet's Bazaar*, into Italian, a feat akin, it transpired, to turning schnapps into Chianti. 'It took me a year to translate the fairy tales,' he told me in his airy, spacious office on the first floor of the palazzo. 'Danish is a very "short" language, if you know what I mean, but of course Italian is very "big", very expressive. This took a long time.'

If only the Victorian translators had taken so much trouble. From the 1840s onwards opportunists like Mary Howitt and Charles Boner undertook contemporary translations in an unseemly haste to be the first on the market with Andersen's, by then, wildly popular stories. Many early English editions of Andersen's works were made from German translations, while others were interpreted via a Danish–English dictionary – a bit like trying to figure out the sheet music to Beethoven's Ninth using Bert Weedon's *Teach Yourself Guitar, Part I*. The mistakes and omissions of one translation were amplified by the second, and through this linguistic prism were distorted even the most fundamental elements of Andersen's stories.

In one instance a German version of '*Den Grimme ÆLing*' ('The Ugly Duckling') was renamed 'The Green Duckling' ('*Grimme*' having been mistaken for '*Grün*'). This error was then faithfully carried over to the English version, thus missing the entire point of the story. Another German translation (and the concomitant English translation) placed three peas under the princess's bed instead of one in order to make her discomfort seem more realistic. One American version of 'The Little Matchgirl' even has her surviving the bitter cold Christmas Eve night.

In the translators' defence I should say that many of the Danish language's common phrases and colloquialisms – the nervous tics of the language, if you like – are almost impossible to translate directly. There are loads of Danish words and phrases that have no direct equivalent in English. The Danish concept of '*hygge*' – a special kind of convivial atmosphere, kind of like 'cosy' but so much more – is a good example. But there are many other more subtle 'untranslatables', the prepositions and adverbial modifiers that are particularly present in the spoken form of Danish which Andersen used to such striking effect in his stories: words like *jo* and *vel* and *dog*, which, as far as I can make out, mean 'hmm?' 'eh?' and 'huh!' (although I am sure I am almost entirely wrong, so make sure you have adult supervision if you intend using them when talking to your Danish friends). As the Danish critic, Erik Dal, wrote, Andersen's Danish used 'the most intimate shades of meaning our language has to offer, shades so fine that even the best translators have given up trying to grasp, or at all events reproduce, the full combination of overtones in the unmistakable soughing of the conch-shell'. (There's an example right there, I mean, what the bloody hell does 'soughing of the conch shell' mean?)

Further damage was caused by the prissy Victorian censoriousness (they often skirted the sexual subtext of Andersen's writing), and their almost complete failure to appreciate Andersen's humour and satire. Above all, Andersen was a funny writer – his comedy works on several levels, none of which the Victorians seemed to spot.

Bruno and I spoke Danish, which he had studied at university in Rome. This had brought him to Denmark in his twenties and he had lived there for some years. He thought of Denmark as a second home, he said. 'I could live there now if the weather wasn't so bad!'

I was curious to know what the Italians made of Andersen. I knew that his writings had taken longer to reach Italy than the rest of Europe (the first translation came in 1865), and wondered if he was as well known here as in Britain.

'No, Italians all know the *fiabe de Andersen*, everyone knows "The Ugly Duckling", "The Little Mermaid" and so on. In fact, I am writing a book on his influence in Italy and I have found that just as with every other country in Europe, this has been great. He wrote about things that were deep within most societies – "The Emperor's New Clothes" – for example. We all know about this kind of thing.' Italy's most beloved children's writer, Gianni Rodari, was heavily influenced by Andersen, Bruno told me.

I asked what he thought of Andersen's writing on Italy in *A Poet's Bazaar*. After all, he is a bit rough on the Italians at times. '*A Poet's Bazaar* is a funny, peculiar book. The name is quite right, his journey, all his journeys were, for him, like visiting a bazaar where he took the things he could use for his writing. He went shopping for material. There is great variety in it and some of it is less interesting than the rest. I think that, because he had been to Italy before, he did not have so much new material, he had used all of it in *The Improvisatore* and it was not new to him like Greece and the rest. The best part for me is Istanbul; you can really sense he works harder on that chapter.'

Finally, I asked Bruno if he actually liked Andersen. 'He had courage,' Bruno replied, with the careful diplomacy of a man about to receive that year's 60,000 kroner (£6,000) Hans Christian Andersen prize (Queen Margrethe II was the other recipient). 'He was an outsider and he was an egoist, but who isn't? I think the picture we often get of him is quite wrong. He was not naive, even though that is the picture he liked to give of himself too. He was very ambitious and strong. He felt badly treated by the Danish mentality, this thing they call Jante's Law today, so he had to leave Denmark to really challenge himself, to see what he could achieve.'

Excuse the regional TV presenter link, but someone who has done just that is Poul Skytte Christoffersen, with whom I had my last appointment in Rome. Poul is Denmark's ambassador in Rome and he also happens to be the uncle of a friend of mine back in Copenhagen, who had kindly set up the meeting. At the time it had seemed like a wizard idea – another opportunity for some Andersen-style social climbing – but as I crossed the Villa Borghese and walked down to Piazza Thorvaldsen on my way to the embassy I began to have serious concerns about what on earth we were going to talk about, the ambassador and I. I had never met an ambassador before; what little I knew about their lives I had gleaned mostly from adverts.

In the end the Danish Ambassador and I talked about waste disposal.

The Danish embassy in Rome is housed in an imposing red stucco palazzo in posh Parioli. After waiting for some minutes in the grand entrance hall (so far, so *Ferrero Rocher*), I was shown into the ambassador's office, a large, light room on the first floor, filled with Danish art.

Poul was a quiet, slight, grey-haired man, not what I was expecting at all. I had a vague notion that an ambassador should be a stout, imposing man, perhaps wearing some kind of sash. I felt like I had ventured behind the Wizard of Oz's curtain as Poul welcomed me in a business-like manner, which immediately threw me into a panic. I had nothing remotely business-like to question him about. Frankly, I had not thought this thing through, at least not beyond my social-climbing ambitions – and they went no further than meeting him and shaking his hand.

I sat down opposite Poul's desk. Somewhere behind me a clock ticked loudly. Beads of sweat began to form on my forehead. After a few minutes' nervous rustling with my notepad, I asked my first question, hastily improvised, and, consequently, desperately lame: 'So, what does an ambassador actually do?'

'Well, I travel a lot,' he told me, patiently. 'I promote trade interests, and one area we are getting into is waste treatment. I have been arranging for representatives from Italian cities to visit

Denmark to see how we do it and they may then use Danish companies. Italians are very interested in that kind of thing; and in our windmills too.'

He paused, as if suddenly conscious that he was wasting his precious time without actually knowing why. 'So why is it you wanted to see me exactly?'

Things pretty much went downhill from there. I had a few questions about the embassy's plans to mark Andersen's bicentenary, but I soon found myself back out on the street. Though my ejection had been handled with the smooth tact of a true diplomat, Poul had effectively grabbed the back of my trousers and the scruff of my neck and thrown me through the swing doors out into the dirt. It was nothing less than I deserved. Social climbing only really works in a social context, anywhere else and it is just misguided stalking. The reason Andersen was such a master at it was that he had something to offer – a spot of artful paper cutting, a story or a song. With me and the ambassador it had been strictly a one-way transaction.

On my last evening in Rome I crossed the river again to track down two things Andersen mentions in *A Poet's Bazaar*. The first was a rotating wooden barrel, which Andersen describes as being set into a wall behind a metal grille at the hospital of Santo Spirito. It is still there. Up until the 1950s unwanted babies would be placed through a square hole on one side of the barrel, and the mother would spin the barrel round so that the hole would appear inside the hospital. She would ring a bell to alert the nuns, and leave her child for ever – a kind of baby tombola.

My final duty in Rome was to light a candle in St Knud's (Canute's) chapel in Santa Maria in Transpontina, a short walk away towards St Peter's. Andersen also visited the chapel out of a sense of duty, on 19 January, St Knud's feast day. He was dismayed that only 'two small candles burned so dimly and looked so sordid' and summoned a monk from the adjacent cloister to explain why this Danish saint was not accorded a proper celebration. '"Alas, sir," said the monk, "our cloister is one of the poorest in all Rome! We can only afford to celebrate one great festival a year . . . St Knud is from the North, and therefore our cloister never receives anything!"

'I stood alone before the altar of my childhood's saint [Andersen was christened and confirmed in St Knud's in Odense], in whose church I had wept over my father's coffin, in whose church I was confirmed . . . The greatest festival thou has is that thy countryman stands by thy tomb and sketches this sorrowful picture in remembrance of thee, St Knud.'

I decided to pay my respects to the famous tide-turner and one-time conqueror and king of England (and, oh, don't my Danish friends *love* reminding me of that meaningless little historical anomaly). Mass was in progress when I entered and so I crept, knees apart, over to the second chapel on the right, which was hidden behind some information about Congolese nuns.

Capella di San Canuto dates from 1686 and is dedicated to *e primo martine della Danimarca*. It was every bit as neglected as it was when Andersen visited in 1841. They hadn't even bothered to use proper candles on the votive altar. Instead there was a row of fake candles with small electric lightbulbs on top, like the score board for a 1950s quiz show. I dropped a few euros into the box and lit all nineteen of the bulbs – probably a gravely sacrilegious act – said a kind of prayer (to Andersen, that he would forgive all that prying into his sex life) and left.

Outside on Via della Conciliazione I looked back to St Peters, backlit by a preposterously beautiful, blue neon, early-evening sky. Despite this belated attempt by the city to win my affections, in a defiant snub to all the rude waiters and bar staff I had encountered in Rome over the last couple of weeks, I ate that night in a Spanish restaurant where I was treated like an old friend.

I left on the train to Naples the next morning, highly ambivalent about Rome. On the one hand I had experienced nothing but grumpy, passive-aggressive hostility – and some not so passive

– from its residents, despite virtually grovelling for forgiveness for my very existence every time I went into a café, bar or shop.

Still on the same hand, I had found Rome to be terrorised by rabid motorists and, even in winter, gridlocked with tourists. It was a city stuck in a long since glorious past, but where they charged up-to-the-minute prices; the locals' transparent, grasping duplicity where financial transactions were concerned belied a deep-seated loathing of all visitors. Beside the Spanish Steps is a shop called, with an honesty uncharacteristic of the Italian retail trade, 'Expensive'. If only the rest of the city's shopkeepers were so candid they would have fronts with 'Fleeced', 'How Do We Get Away With It?' and 'Right This Way, Suckers!' on every corner.

If you require further evidence of their treachery, consider *proscuitto*. Here is a nation that has harnessed the white heat of technology, not to seek alternative fuels, nor to contribute to the quest for life on other planets, but to slice their already prohibitively expensive ham even thinner.

On one occasion – and I promise you this is true – I was sitting at a café table having just drained my glass of Coke, when I opened my map to check the route to my next destination. At that moment the waiter took the chair opposite me to give to some new arrivals. He might have asked, I thought to myself, but I wasn't that bothered. But then *he took my table away*, leaving me sitting in the middle of the room like some piece of installation art. When I finally gathered myself to protest, he simply shrugged and handed me the bill. They may not be entirely *au fait* with the arcane etiquette of English manners, but at least the Danes are civil. This would never have happened in Copenhagen, and for the first time I began to miss the place. (Incidentally, you might like to know that this was the Al Sipario bar at 140 Via Sistina – just up from Andersen's old house. If you go, I urge you to urinate against the bar – it is a tradition there, I have heard.)

Andersen complained of the 'eternal cheatings at the inns' in

Italy, but he doesn't mention anything like this. I can only assume the Romans' staggering rudeness is a recent development as, usually, it took only the slightest hint of hostility to send his fragile confidence plunging. As Violet Jacobs wrote of him in her 1926 preface to his autobiography: 'It is only too plain that he looked for slights as apprehensively as any old lady looks under her bed for a burglar and that he could scarcely bear a dissentient voice ... unequipped as he was with the serviceable hide that becomes many of us so well.' He wouldn't have lasted five minutes in modern-day Rome, and I was relieved to be heading off.

There is no other hand.

Chapter Five

NAPLES

If evidence were needed that Italians really ought to switch to decaff, it is Naples – a city so chaotic and squalid that it makes New Delhi look like Guildford. Neapolitans must be the most hyperactive people in the world. They do everything – drive, eat, talk and quite probably make love – at warp speed and, arriving by train from Rome, the frenetic energy of the place hit me like a roundhouse punch.

The sensation of having arrived in the capital of a banana republic on the brink of revolution intensified as I walked into the Centro Storico to try to find my hotel. With my rucksack now equivalent in weight to a wheelie bin full of phone books, I felt about as agile as one of those great lumbering, vegetarian dinosaurs. Any minute now, I thought to myself, a gang of thieves will descend on me like a pack of razor-clawed veloceraptors. Confused and unable to move at anything more than tortoise pace, they would pick this *straniero* clean within seconds and spit out the bones. And even if I somehow managed to run the street-gang gauntlet I would probably only stumble straight into the path of one of the city's mentally ill taxi drivers. In Naples the cars literally drive *at* you, giving way to no man, woman or back-packing brontosaurus, and in the city's labyrinthine, cobbled streets there aren't even any pavements on which to take refuge. It is like the Pamplona Bull Run with Fiats.

It seemed the city had given up on any hope of progress around about 1972. I lost track of the number of museums, churches and other sights that were 'closed indefinitely for repair' (come to think of it, I believe we have our alternative tourist board slogan for Naples right there). The buildings are crumbling, the streets are piled high with rubbish, the transport infrastructure is antique and the fashions are ten years out of date. None of the public clocks work. In fact, you can't help wondering if the people in charge of capital investment in these parts know something about the future activities of Vesuvius that the rest of the world doesn't . . .

When Andersen first visited Naples in early 1834 Vesuvius was aflame. It was just one example of the timeliness that typified his arrivals in foreign places. He had arrived in Rome on that same trip just in time to see the exhumation and reburial of Raphael (recording how, when the pall bearers tipped the coffin to ease it into to tomb, he heard all the bones slide to one end); later in his *Poet's Bazaar* journey in 1841 he sees Venus in a unique position in the skies above Malta – it was just the kind of thing that led one exasperated friend, on hearing Andersen's latest travel story, to exclaim: 'It's a lie, a downright bloody lie! That kind of thing never happens to any of us!'

Vesuvius was a 'river of fire flowing downward . . . the crater was burning like a bonfire . . .' Andersen wrote. 'It was the world's great pulse I heard.' Mustering all his courage, he and some friends set out to get as close as they could to 'the black cauldron' (as the Snow Queen calls it), taking donkeys most of the way, but then wading onward, knee deep in ash: 'It burned the soles of our shoes. If the crust had broken we would have fallen into a sea of fire. Then we saw the monstrous stream of fire pouring slowly, thick and red like porridge, down the mountain.'

Vesuvius plays a potent role in *The Improvisatore*, the novel he was working on at the time. His virginal hero, Antonio, also visits Naples during an eruption, and an older woman attempts to seduce him: 'She drew me towards her: her lips were like fire, that flowed into my very soul! Eternal mother of God! Thy holy image, at that moment, fell down from the wall . . .' Antonio, taking this as a sign of divine intervention, runs from the room.

'Everything was aflame, just as it was within me! The current of the air wafted forward the heat. Vesuvius stood in glowing fire – eruptions in rapid succession lit up everything around.'

It's clear Naples aroused Andersen like no other city. He seems to have been on heat during virtually his entire first visit there in 1834, yet he claims to have remained pure. 'I can feel the climate affects my blood,' he wrote one night. 'I felt a raging passion, but resisted.' After one particularly heated evening walk in which he came close to buckling when tempted by a virginal thirteen-year-old prostitute, he wrote: '. . . Went home and had a good supper with a glass of Malaga. Thought about Louise [Collin – his most recent unrequited love] and the others at home. If they had seen me this evening they would certainly be worried about me. Naples is more perilous than Paris, because you freeze there, but here your blood boils. God lead me to what is best and most sensible.'

Back then Andersen had been spurred on to leave Rome – to stay one step ahead of his sorrows, as ever – by the news of the disastrous response to 'Agnete and the Merman' and the death of his mother. This time round, in 1841, he was fleeing the scene of illness, loneliness, awful weather and, of course, his latest theatrical disaster, *The Moorish Girl*. He travelled with Holst and Rothe, and they arrived to find Vesuvius dormant and sealed with snow.

In the mid nineteenth century most of the Grand Tourists who visited Naples gravitated towards the Chiaia (beach) district, on the western curve of the bay. Goethe loved it here, as did the Shelleys. Admiral Nelson stayed here when he arrived in the city in 1793 to seek reinforcements for the defence of Toulon, promptly getting off with the ambassador's saucy young wife, Emma Hamilton, at her home on vico Santa Maria. Andersen would not have been especially pleased to hear this as, like all Danes, he detested Nelson on account of his bombardment of Copenhagen in 1801, but he and his chums stayed near by in a place owned by a Signor Ferrari, on 'piaza dei fiori in Locanda dei fiori'.

According to a nice man I spoke to in the city archive, this is most likely Fiorentina a Chiaia, a narrow alley, perhaps no more than a car's width, leading inland from the Riviera di Chiaia. The church Andersen describes here is gone, levelled by a bomb in 1943; as are the sixteen shoemakers and the fruit shop that also stood in his time, but the street/square is still paved with the 'broad lava stones' that Andersen notices caused the local horses such distress: 'The poor horses cannot keep their footing, and are therefore beaten amidst screams and shouts.' Actually, I have to be honest with you, the broad lava stones are hardly admissible evidence as virtually the whole of Naples is paved this way. (Buggy-bound Neapolitan toddlers must see life as a complete blur for the first few years of their lives.)

Andersen continues: 'In all the houses, the ground floors are without windows, but with broad, open shop doors', commenting also on the profusion of washing that hangs – undies and all – from every balcony and window. In fact, Neapolitans still live like this. Often, while walking around the back alleys of the city, what I initially assumed to be dark, poorly stocked shops would turn out to be someone's living room, some of them virtual museum pieces with bakelite phones, fuzzy TVs and the obligatory pictures of the Pope and Maradona on the wall.

Holst and Andersen are still bickering like a married couple as they arrive in Naples; Andersen records several 'scenes' between them in his diary. It is hard to figure out the cause of these tiffs. Initially, I imagined Andersen was probably tense as he waited to hear whether he would receive the royal travel grant that would allow him to continue to the Orient, but the disputes actually continued long after 1 March, when he hears the joyous news that Christian VIII has decided to give him 700 *rigsdaler* (*c.* £7,000).

He is ecstatic, and immediately sits down to write a letter of thanks to Jonas Collin before going out to the theatre to celebrate, afterwards inviting Rothe and Holst to drink a toast to the king with white wine from Capri.

But again on the fifth there comes another falling out: 'A scene with Holst! He said that I had got a bitterness, a rudeness that he had never known.' And on the eighteenth Andersen notes in his diary: 'Holst was grumpy and answered me hard and angrily several times as I knew I had answered him on other occasions.' Whether this was down to Andersen's lingering envy of Holst's success or some other reason, it is impossible to fathom, but they usually seemed to make up and spent every day sightseeing together.

Having dropped my rucksack off at the hotel and at least now with a sporting chance of fending off the pickpocket piranhas (who, in fairness, never actually materialised), I walked down to the shore for my first view of the bay.

I sat on an abandoned Lambretta – which, minus its ancillaries, looked remarkably similar to a toilet bowl – staring across the water to Vesuvius, a glowering presence despite being topped with snow, as it had been in 1841. The mountain has been significantly remodelled since Andersen last saw it, of course. Dickens witnessed a minor rumble in 1845, and the most recent disturbance was a massive, so-called 'Plinian' eruption (after the Roman historian, Pliny the Elder, who witnessed the AD79 eruption) that happened just after the Americans landed in 1944.

My only other company on this blustery day were an elderly gentleman stroller, some pigeons and a young couple, down on the rocks below me who were, I swear, beneath their puffa jackets, having it off.

I admired their fortitude, it was freezing. The weather had been similar in March 1841, but five years later in 1846 Andersen elected to travel to Naples in the midst of summer for a change. He had found the heat almost unbearable but the intense sunlight did inspire him to write one of his most psychologically menacing tales, 'The Shadow', Andersen's take on the already popular doppelgänger theme.

This was a pivotal story for Andersen, marking his coming of age as an author of serious short stories for adults. A.S. Byatt, in her introduction to the most recent edition of *The Annotated Brothers Grimm*, talks of how Andersen's tales have the power to 'twist your spirit with sick terror', describing the author as a 'psychological terrorist'. Nowhere is he more so than in 'The Shadow', and anybody who still believes he belongs in the nursery would do well to read this macabre, haunting tale to their kids and watch their reaction.

The story is about 'a learned man from the cold countries' who loses his shadow in the glaring sun of 'the hot countries' when he instructs it to peep on a beautiful woman in a neigh-bouring apartment. He returns home having grown another shadow and thinks nothing more of the loss until, some years later, his original shadow turns up, a rather nouveau riche, worldly figure, now a fully formed man. The beautiful woman, it turns out, was Poetry and from her the shadow has learned as much, he says, 'as if I had lived three thousand years and read every-thing that was ever composed or written . . . I've seen every-thing and I know everything!' He has used his newfound freedom to spy on people around the world and then to terrorise and blackmail them. 'I look where no one else can look . . . and saw what no one ought to see. What an ignoble world it really is!'

Understandably, this unsettles the man who becomes ill and loses weight – '"You look a shadow of yourself," people told him' – and so his former shadow, 'who was now the real master', invites him to recuperate at a health spa where the shadow is hoping to grow a beard (like Andersen, he has trouble in this department). There the shadow woos a princess and, indeed, is about to marry her when the learned man finally has enough, and attempts to expose the shadow as a fake. The shadow, in his new position as royal fiancé, is able to use his influence to have the man impris-oned, claiming that the man is *his* shadow. The story ends with the marriage of the shadow to the princess: 'The learned man heard none of it, because by then they had taken his life.'

The modern satire and fantastical allegory of 'The Shadow' has warranted comparisons with Saki and Kafka, and it is unquestion-ably one of his finest pieces of work. An Andersen fan can while away countless lonely hours deconstructing his presence in both of the two protagonists and trying to fathom the workings of its author's mind as he wrote it. Is it, for example, an allegory of his suppressed sexuality? Or is Andersen attacking his critics, who persecuted the 'real' artist and championed mere shadows? Jackie Wullschlager points out that at the same time as he was writing it, Andersen was also writing what she calls the 'fraudulent' *Fairy Tale of My Life* – his whitewash of an autobiography. 'As Andersen was posturing, shadowless, to the world in his autobiography, the terrors he was suppressing came back in spades in "The Shadow",' she writes.

(I might add that it can surely be no coincidence that Roger Moore, a man who knows a good script when he sees one, cites as his greatest performance the lead role in a film loosely based on 'The Shadow', called *The Man Who Haunted Himself* – an early seventies B-movie, about a man who momentarily dies on an operating table and releases his doppelgänger into the world. His 'shadow' assumes the man's identity and pushes him to insanity.)

Andersen often ends his diary entries *Bridget Jones*-style, with mention of what he has had to drink that day, and in Naples that was often the local tipple, Lacryma Christi. Employing this as the kind of feeble excuse characteristic of a deviant lush such as myself, that night I bought myself a bottle of this blood-red wine, whose grapes are grown on the lava fields of Vesuvius, and took it back to my hotel room.

No wonder he had all those rough mornings! It made my mouth feel as if I had eaten ten cream crackers. As I made my way to the bottom of the bottle, just to make sure that it didn't just need a little time to breathe (nope, it really was undrinkable; at least metaphorically so), I watched a Napoli game on TV. Unable to afford the rights to screen the match itself, the local TV station instead simply filmed the crowd and the reactions of its team of commentators. (A novel solution, but I felt that it wouldn't work with all sports. Fat ladies knitting and boys gobbling packets of Quavers at a snooker match would hardly be the same.)

What with the Lacryma Christi and the nightclub next door booming out the current hit by Caparezza (Italy's answer to Eminem, only without the tunes), sleep was an elusive mistress that night. At one point I did ring down to reception, hoping to be told, perhaps, that Sharon Stone was doing a photo shoot in the next room.

'Nothing we can do,' said the receptionist.

'Well, you could call the police,' I suggested.

She let out a derisive snort and hung up. Complaining about the noise in Naples is, it would seem, as futile as complaining about the cold in Copenhagen.

I must have fallen asleep at some point, though, as I do remember dreaming that I was due to play tennis with Madonna. This seemed to be a regular arrangement, but as I arrived at the courts it became apparent that I had made an embarrassing double booking. Janet Jackson was waiting for me on court number one with all her entourage. Madonna was on court two, alone, and there ensued an awkward scene as I tried to explain to Janet that she would have to wait until I had played Madonna. This culminated in Janet exposing both of her breasts at me. And when I finally arrived on court two, all Madge could talk about was her concern over her daughter's facial hair.

Perhaps I, too, was beginning to be affected by the Neapolitan sensuality that had sent Andersen into such a tailspin. The more I walked around the city, the more I realised that, in a slightly twisted, Readers' Wives kind of a way, Naples is a remarkably sexy city. The fact that the locals all look like a young Gina Lollobrigida or Al Pacino helps, of course, as does the relative absence of tourists – rucksacks and guidebooks are such a passion killer, don't you find? This, though, only goes some of the way to explaining the unbridled, inherent *horniness* of Naples.

More pertinent, I think, is the fact that, unlike Verona, which is essentially a living museum, Naples is a real, living city. But unlike, say, Huddersfield, which *is* a real, living city (yet about as sexy as haemorrhoids), the Neapolitans live under the permanent threat of sudden annihilation. This, I think, is the key to the city's erotic charge. Any second now, Vesuvius could explode and bury them all in a duvet of white-hot cinders, and if not that, then God, who really seems to have it in for the place, is just as likely to dispatch floods or earthquakes, both of which have struck Naples in the last twenty-five years. Neapolitans thus live every day as if it could be their last. Ask yourself this: what would you do with one day to live? Clean the streets? Direct the traffic? I don't think so.

In 1841 both the mountain and Andersen's libido had calmed down somewhat. It was being monitored by the newly inaugurated Osservatorio Vesuviano (the mountain that is, not his libido), but a not insignificant reminder of its destructive might (still, Vesuvius) was close to hand. On 18 March Andersen accompanied Rothe and Holst on a day trip to Pompeii, riding on Italy's first railway around the Bay of Naples. The excavations of the AD 79 eruption – which had smothered the town with a 400-degree vapour cloud – started in the mid eighteenth century, albeit in an ad hoc fashion. More methodical work took place later in the eighteenth century and new discoveries were being made virtually every month. Andersen comments in his diary that the prison is newly unearthed, but on leaving he begins to feel a bit of a sore throat – the first signs of the illness that he described in *A Poet's Bazaar*: 'Fever raged in my blood. I was, perhaps, near death. I believe the grim tyrant looked through the door at me, but it was not yet time; he went away, and the goddess of health stood where he had stood.'

So just how sick was he? I sent a copy of his diary entries detailing this illness to a Danish doctor friend of mine. His diagnosis? Tonsillitis.

Nevertheless, Andersen allowed himself to be persuaded by his landlord, Ferrari, that he be bled immediately, and Holst and Rothe hurried off to find a barber – it seems in those days it was normal for hairdressers to undertake simple surgical procedures. ('Hello, love. A bleeding? Of course. Do your roots while I'm at it? Been anywhere nice on your holidays?')

'Ferrari held me in his arms, one vein was opened on my hand, which was held in warm water,' Andersen writes in his diary. 'I was close to passing out; after the dressing I felt the feverishness gone; I had vomited a couple of times; weak I fell back and slept moderately well in the night.'

Two days later he is up and fit again. The 'grim tyrant' didn't linger that long, then.

I had dreamed of seeing Pompeii since I was first traumatised by hearing about it in primary school (my parents had to take me up to the South Downs to convince me they weren't volcanic), and so the next day I took myself along to the Stazione Circumvesuviana.

Shortly after the tannoy had announced that 'the train to Sorrento is now departing', the train to Sorrento (and Pompeii) arrived. We trundled through sinister container yards, an unregulated mess of cheap housing, and great shimmering glasshouses filled with orchids and tomatoes, gently serenaded as we went by some buskers banging out Led Zeppelin numbers on accordions and tambourines.

At the entrance to the ruined city I bought an audio guide. Initially I couldn't get the thing to work properly and spent the first hour peering through railings trying to reconcile what the guide was telling me with what I was seeing. 'And this is the twenty-thousand-seat Anfiteatro,' the guide would say, as I peered into what looked like a sewer. Once I realised I had been reading the wrong number on the plaques, I spent a fascinating and informative day trying to find the dead people.

Andersen calls Pompeii 'the city of the dead' and I had expected to find it strewn with petrified corpses contorted into paroxysms of burning agony, but this is not the case. I did eventually find a few stiffs hidden behind some railings and rubble at the back of a kind of Roman railway arch. They were clearly not intended for public display, and were apparently just being stored there, but I could just about make out the ghoulish silhouettes of straining limbs laid out on a trestle table. Most surreal.

A group of teenage American girls had been following a few paces behind. Earlier, one had asked me: 'Which one is Vesuvius?' and I had pointed out the vast, looming mountain with its rivulets of snow above us, 'Oh, right, thanks.'

Now, as they caught up once more, I nodded in the direction of the cadavers. 'Look!' I said. 'Bodies!'

They stood next to me, peering into the darkness trying to make out what on earth I was going on about and then recoiled, squealing, in girly horror. They hurried on ahead, occasionally looking back at me warily as if I had something to do with it.

When Goethe had visited a few years before Andersen, he had described the Pompeians' living quarters as 'doll's houses', and it is true, they are remarkably small. But with their narrow streets, cramped dwellings and all-consuming obsession with sports, the people of ancient Pompeii seemed surprisingly similar to modern Neapolitans – except that Pompeii is in slightly better repair.

Fascinatingly, as well as being told that the ancient Romans ironed their clothes (something I had never really considered before), the audio guide also told me that urine was highly prized in Roman times. The ammonia was used for washing, and was collected daily from public toilets. Presumably this means there was someone whose full-time job it was to collect other people's wee. Well, I suppose that moves us journalists off the bottom rung.

Rather understatedly, the guide also told me that 'cremation was the customary funerary method' for ancient Pompeians. No kidding.

Finally the guide led me to the fresco depicting the god Priapus weighing his ginormous sex vegetables which decorates the wall of one of the villas. It was an impressive sight, but merely the entrée for the barrage of filth and degradation I was to find at the Cabinet of Obscene Objects the next day.

But first, a night at the opera (no skipping).

Andersen was a keen opera-goer and gave his verdict on several performances he saw during his journey to and from the Orient in 1840. On his first visit to Naples six years earlier he had been enthralled by the performances of the legendary contralto, Maria Felicita Malibran Garcia, whom he had seen at the grand San Carlo opera house. But she had died in 1836.

In *A Poet's Bazaar* Andersen uses her absence this time round, and the temporary closure of San Carlo, as a metaphor for the gloominess that casts a pall over his second Italian trip: 'It was at the same season of the year as now that I heard Malibran in Naples. Everything had then the fragrance of newness; a southern warmth and radiance lay over the whole – and now, how changed! . . . Now, on the contrary, many of these pictures are dashed with strong shadows . . . the odour of freshness and newness was gone.'

Luckily San Carlo was open when I was there and I bagged myself a ticket to *La Traviata*. Although Italy's second most important opera house – after Rome's La Scala – is faded, with flaky stucco, crumbling masonry and blackened marble, it remains ineffably grand. On a glitzy Friday night it rapidly became all too apparent that my baggy cords and anorak were entirely inappropriate dress. As I ascended the stairs to the sixth tier, where I could almost touch the magnificently frescoed ceiling, the other opera-goers, in their furs, stilettos, suits, ties and shiny leather shoes, looked at me as if I were a bag lady on a spree.

In my experience, opera is not one of those art forms that leaves you wanting more, no matter how professionally executed. This production was, to my untrained eyes, magnificent, but after a while my private amusement at the girth of the performers soon began to overshadow the action. From what I could make out, this was your classic love triangle, played out by the local Weight Watchers club dressed with costumes from *Flash Gordon*. I enjoyed it, but I soon found myself yearning for a blast of Caparezza.

The next morning I climbed Vesuvius. I say 'climbed', I took a bus to a large car park near the summit and then walked the remaining half mile or so along a well-maintained pathway. As I walked I had to dodge golfball-sized lava boulders, which rolled past me as they were released by the thawing snow. In the silence they made an ominous clacking noise, like the stones in the *Blair Witch Project*. I had read on the train that we are currently in the midst of Vesuvius' longest period of quiescence ever and, for all I knew, these sinister snowballs could have signalled the start of the Big One that will hit sometime soon, though no one quite knows when.

I soon forgot all this, along with my name and any doubts about the existence of God, when I arrived at the crater rim, 1,281 metres up. So awesome is the view here, and so infinitesimally small and feeble does it make one feel, that this moment should by rights be accompanied by the crescendo of timpani from 'Also Spoke Zarathustra' (better known as the *2001: A Space Odyssey* music), played at a bowel-loosening decibel level through hidden speakers. Looking down into the crater is like looking into the very pit of mortality; one is reminded of the frailty of existence, the futility of all human endeavour and the fact that one hasn't had an ice cream all morning (something to do with the conical shape, and the snow, I think).

The inner walls of the crater were gently steaming but there was only the faintest trace of a sulphur smell. Behind me, way below through the haze, I could make out the suburbs of Naples and, across the Sorrentine Peninsula, a patchwork of *pomodorini* greenhouses glinting in the sunlight like giant solar panels: Ischia was a shimmering illusion. As I walked around the crater rim the railings eventually disappeared, as did the steps, until I was climbing onward in an almost manful fashion – although the intrepid tone was undermined by the gift shop at the end of the path.

Back in the city later that afternoon, I set out on another Andersen art hunt, first at the Capodimonte, a massive, moth-eaten palace overlooking the city (home to all those kitschy, collectible figurines: grandmothers' Pokemon), before walking back down into the city to the fabulous Museo Archeologico Nazionale, my last stop in Naples before catching the ferry to Malta that evening.

This is one of the great European collections, founded in the early eighteenth century by Charles II of Bourbon. From the list of artworks Andersen had written of in his diary, I found here the epic Farnese *Hercules*, a proto-body builder 'muscular and living', notes a wide-eyed Andersen – though, yet again, with the privates of a chipmunk – as well as *The Bull*, a mountain of marble depicting the myth of *Dirce*.

With marble sculptures this size it is always interesting to figure out how the sculptor has managed to support the tremendous weight of the figures. Look closely and there are invariably tree trunks growing out of unlikely parts of their anatomy, as is the case with Dirce's bull friend, who has a tree coming out of his stomach. He fairs slightly better than the male figure holding his horns though; he has a tree growing out of his backside.

But the rooms everyone wants to see in the archaeological museum (at least, those of a mucky-minded disposition like myself) are those containing the fabled Cabinet of Obscene Objects, a collection of art so sexually explicit and perverse that it remained hidden for centuries, the source of lurid gossip and wild speculation throughout the salons of Europe.

The Cabinet of Obscene Objects – today called the Secret Room – very much lives up to its billing. These are the pictures, frescoes, statues and reliefs (if you'll excuse the pun) enjoyed by the ancient Pompeians and Herculaneans. So blue are these one hundred and two pieces that, apart from a brief airing when Garibaldi let Italy's hair down for a while, for more than a century anyone wanting to view them was required to obtain a special visitor permit from the Ministry of the Interior. The collection only went on public display in 2000, following a great deal of soul searching in the Italian media.

For a man of the world, such as I, who has plumbed the depths of Hamburg, it was all very mundane of course. It takes much more than some low-cut togas and a thong to get me goi . . . wait a minute, good grief! Would you look at *that*! Not a stitch on! And what's that he's holding? A club of some kind? Is that actually possible with chickens! And what's that sticking out of her . . . ? Good Lord! Nurse?

Men, donkeys, lions, gladiators, birds, satyrs, nymphs, hermaphrodites – in the ancient world no gender, species or mytholog-
ical beast was, it seems, excluded from the carnal carousel. One
statue found in Herculaneum, for example, depicts a gladiator
fighting his own, oversized penis; others found in Pompeii show
Pan pleasuring a goat (to the goat's apparent pleasure); given this
evidence, it is hardly a surprise that ancient Pompeii had something of a reputation as a Roman Sodom. They certainly liked
it up 'em, and no mistake.

As I took notes, sketches and photographs (for research, you
understand), I noticed a heavy-breathing middle-aged bearded
man with a video camera diligently filming every single exhibit.
Well, you've got to have a hobby, I suppose. We can only be
thankful, I thought to myself, that Andersen never got to see
this. It would have sent him into a fit of the vapours from which
he might well have never recovered.

How wrong I was. When I returned home and did a little
more reading, I found in the most recent Danish biography of
Andersen (by Jens Andersen) that, incredibly, he *did* gain access
to the collection on his visit to Naples in February 1834. He
borrowed the key to what he called the 'Camera Obscena' and
its 'drawings of the Greeks' debauchery' – then hidden in a room
in the basement – from the museum director. What's more, much
to his credit, he didn't seem scandalised by it at all, using words
like 'movingly drawn' and 'lovely' to describe this pagan porn in
his diary. This was quite a contrast to the occasion, six years
earlier, when he had been shown around the *Cabinet Mysterieux*
in Paris – by a *woman*, he notes with particular horror in his
diary. 'It was dreadful! All the sexual parts depicted with the most
terrible diseases, cold sweat sprang from my fingertips.' By his
second visit to the collection in 1846, he has even picked out a
favourite: 'Saw the secret cabinet, satyr and goat in coitus [still a
highlight, I have to say] is in terms of expression masterly . . .'[+]

I shouldn't have been so surprised. As Jens Andersen
comments, the collection was merely a literal manifestation of

the way in which Italy had become one giant, erotic diorama for Hans Christian Andersen.

This set me thinking, yet again, about his perplexing proclivities. Forget the latent bisexuality; could it be that the voyeurism he exhibited here and during his brothel visits is, in fact, the simplest explanation for Andersen's odd behaviour? Maybe Andersen just liked to look. Maybe the penis–biting incident, the unfortunate encounters with women in his childhood and his insecurity regarding his looks determined that, throughout his life, all Andersen really wanted to do was enjoy the visuals. Perhaps he was just not the interactive type.

By the time Andersen reached Naples at the end of his first European tour in 1834 his money had run out. He was forced to return, with a heavy heart, via Munich and Vienna, to Copenhagen. This time though, he would stay one step ahead of his sorrows for a few months more as he set sail instead for Malta; the mysteries of the Orient his goal.

Holst – who clearly by this stage had had enough of Andersen – was not impressed: 'Heaven only knows what he will do in Greece and Constantinople for he spends his time in the most ridiculous way. He sees nothing, he enjoys nothing, he delights in nothing – he does nothing but write. When I see him in museums, his pencil going all the time to write down the keeper's information about statues and paintings rather than looking at them and enjoying their beauty, he reminds me of the executor of a will going through the property of the deceased and itemising every one with meticulous care, constantly afraid he may have forgotten something.'

But the voracious traveller of March 1841 was moving onwards, further into the unknown than he had ever dreamed he would venture, to lands full of fantasy and danger that would transform him for ever.

Pencil poised.

Chapter Six

MALTA

'Constantly in motion, always striving to employ every moment and to see everything.' This is how Andersen once described himself as a traveller, and the single day he spent in Malta on his way to Athens exemplifies this whirlwind spirit better than anything. In the ten or so hours that he was on land, he managed to see enough to fill the itinerary of a normal sightseer for a week – he saw pretty much all the island had to offer in fact – and, as this was an unplanned stop, he did it all without the guidebooks he normally used.

This single day in Malta was a pivotal point in his journey to the Orient, as is the chapter that describes it in *A Poet's Bazaar*. The book seems to shift up a gear as its writer becomes re-energised by the novelty and exoticism of this fantastical island. Up until this point, he has seen it all before. In terms of Germany and Italy, he had been there, done that and got the I ♥ Dürer T-shirt. But from Malta onward Andersen's senses would be assaulted by improbable sights, alien races and unfamiliar customs, virtually all the way to Vienna. What's more, from Naples he travelled alone, free to go as he pleased and not be dragged around all the familiar sights as he had been with Holst in Naples and Rome.

I was buoyed by the prospect of leaving Italy myself, and there is nothing like a sea crossing to make one feel one is properly travelling. As I was keen to reach Athens in time for the Independence Day celebrations I, too, would only have one day in Malta. Thus, Andersen and I would go head to head in a titanic day-tripper challenge.

It was a mismatch from the start.

In fact, Malta had given me problems before I had even arrived. Andersen took the French steamship, *Leonidas*, directly from Naples to Valletta, but that route no longer exists. So I had departed aboard the Tirrenia Line's *Rafaele Rabattina* – a chintzy, nine-storey luxury liner, crewed by elaborated brocaded young men and women – from Naples' seedy Stazione Marittima, to Palermo, Sicily. From there I would have to cross the island by bus and take another ferry to Malta. I left Naples on the first leg of this trip on Sunday night, and was due to arrive in Palermo at 5 a.m. on Monday morning.

As we sailed out of the harbour I went up on deck for one last look at the Bay of Naples. Unfortunately it was shrouded in mist, as if someone had finally brought down the fire curtain on Vesuvius, albeit 2,000 years too late.

Andersen was impressed by his boat, describing it in great detail over four pages of *A Poet's Bazaar* – from the 'pretty house for the captain' to its 'handsome mirrors', 'polished marble columns', 'wine cellar' and even a theatre in which the male crew members played the female roles. 'It was not only comfortable, but elegant,' he comments approvingly. In his later autobiography he recalled his joy of being at sea in 1841: 'We frolicked, sang, danced, played at cards, and chatted together – Americans, Italians and Asiatics; bishops and monks, officers and travellers . . . A few days of living together on the sea makes close fellowship.'

The exclamation count is high as he bids farewell to: 'Naples, thou white, sunlit city!' telling us that, like Vesuvius, 'fire burns . . . in my heart; everything is a volcano!' He sails past Capri and Stromboli, glowing diabolically at night. Approaching Sicily – 'thou mighty tripod in the deep, clear, air-covered sea, we greet thee!' – he is on the look-out for Scylla, the six-headed monster, and the whirlpool Charybdis – according to *The Odyssey* they guard either side of the Straits of Messina – 'but there was no particular motion of the waves to be seen'.

The exclamation marks disappear and his mood darkens once again as, from the coast of Syracuse, he hears a bell chime. It seems to reawaken the sadness that has accompanied him during the journey so far: 'Its clang was so melancholy, it was like the last tones of a dying swan as it bends its head, and descends on its large, extended wings, from the air into the calm, the deep blue sea.'

Having disembarked at five in the morning, I wandered around Palermo for a couple of hours, waiting for things to open and looking, as all visitors probably do, for signs of Mafia activity. Realising that it would be at least twenty hours before I saw a bed again, I sat down in the main square to conserve energy and watched some boys playing an impromptu, pre-school game of football. Italian males grow up with a football at their feet so it must be a nightmare to have no footballing skills, doomed, like I was, to being picked last for matches, along with the fat asthmatic Belgian exchange student. Even supporting a football team is anathema to me. I could never really figure out who or what it was you should be supporting. Is it the players? But they change clubs with a frequency directly proportionate to their agents' cocaine habits; the managers likewise. It is also not unknown for entire teams to move grounds, so you aren't necessarily demonstrating a geographical loyalty either. Team strips are redesigned every season so the supporters have to cough up fifty quid for a new jersey, which means that, as a comedian I once heard discussing this pointed out, they travel the length of the country every second weekend, pour small fortunes into satellite subscriptions and season tickets, and stake their mental health and happiness on a set of contrasting colours.

As I ruminated on this, a football hit me on the side of the head and I realised I was being used as one of the goal posts. It was time to go.

The high-speed catamaran wasn't due to leave for Malta until late that night from the harbour at Pozzallo on the other side of the island but, just to be on the safe side, I set off early on a bus from Palermo station. At least I would be travelling along the coast that Andersen had observed from the *Leonidas*.

Needless to say, the steely resolve of the Sicilian planning authority has not quite been enough to prevent the wholesale rape of its coastline by warehouse developers, breeze-block housing, gaudy villas and high-rise apartment blocks. So catastrophically hideous is it that one almost feels embarrassed for the Italians that they could be so short-sighted as to destroy what must once have been one of the most captivating coastlines in Europe.

Lemon trees so laden that their fruit outnumbered the leaves, massive cacti and pink blossoming almond groves alleviated some of the wilful squalor, but nothing could draw my eye from the massive electricity generating plant we passed, which looked like it was built from all the backs of all the fridges ever made. And I didn't once see Mount Etna, which Andersen calls 'an amphitheatre for the high gods themselves'. (But then I wouldn't rule out the possibility that they've levelled it to make way for a ceramics factory.)

I arrived in Pozzallo just in time, with only four and a half hours to spare. The small harbour town had a sleepy, Wild West feel to it. Its main feature was a profusion of traffic wardens in pseudo military uniforms, which was odd because there was virtually no traffic. I assumed it was siesta time, but it soon became apparent that siesta was Pozzallo's permanent state.

Walking down the high street I heard an extraordinary commotion just ahead. As I approached, this grew to a deafening white noise, like a million silver spoons being shaken in a giant metal bucket. It was a large flock of finches, presumably returning from a winter sojourn in Africa. It was the first birdsong I could recall having heard in Italy – a testimony to the Italian male's pathological need to blast anything with wings out of the sky. I would be surprised if they made it to the mainland.

For Andersen, leaving mainland Europe was like beginning his journey over again. 'It was now as if a new life had arisen for me,' he wrote years later in his autobiography. 'As I saw my European home lie far behind me, it seemed to me as if a stream of forgetfulness flowed of all bitter and rankling remembrances: I felt health in my blood, health in my thoughts, and freshly and courageously I again raised my head.' Indeed, the moment when the *Leonidas* docks in Valletta harbour at 3 a.m. and he comes up on deck for his first view of Malta has an epiphanic ring: 'Such a radiant firmament I had never seen before – neither under the clear sky of Italy, nor even in our northern winter nights. Venus seemed to be a sun, immensely distant, so that it could only show itself as a point – but it was a sun's point . . . My hands were clasped involuntarily, my thoughts were with God in contemplation of his magnificence.' He is, again, worshipping in his preferred manner, in the open air.

As he also notes in *A Poet's Bazaar*, the island, which was once the impregnable bastion of the Knights Templars, was by that time the Mediterranean base for the English navy – having been placed under its protection following the Treaty of Paris of 1814. Following the advent of steamships, Malta was flourishing as a stopover for the more adventurous Grand Tourists, en route to north Africa and the Levant.

The prospect of the mighty baroque fortress of Valletta, cross-pollinated over the centuries by a melange of tribes and races, must have thrilled a man like Andersen who so often sought to supplant the troubling reality of his life with the distractions of travel or fantastical fiction. The Grand Harbour of Valletta offered both, thronging, he says, with 'Turks, Bedouins, monks, and Maltese', and, once again, the *Arabian Nights* are invoked by way of comparison.

As the sun rises over the battlements of Valletta, Andersen is eager to go ashore and does so in the company of a young Russian officer, called Christoforoff (probably chosen in preference to the other nationalities on board because he would have spoken German). Together they hire a Moorish guide.

'This, then, was the island which Homer has sung of, and of which the Phoenicians had possessed themselves,' he writes. 'Calypso's Isle, where Ulysses passed years of his life [not strictly true, but we'll let that pass]; the Greeks' and the Carthaginians' *Melita*. The island has seen Vandals, Goths and Arabians as conquerors.'

It was as if he had stepped into one of his own fairy stories. Which brings us – with a neatness that almost suggests I planned it this way – to the one part of Andersen's life leading up to his 1840 journey that I have yet to tell you about.

Back in 1834, returning to Copenhagen from his first trip to Italy to face the music about his dire epic poem 'Agnete and the Merman', Andersen had miraculously pulled his career out of an apparently terminal nosedive with *The Improvisatore*. That success was nothing, though, compared with the fame, glory, wealth and adulation that his follow-up work, in a very different genre, would eventually bring. While *The Improvisatore* was still at the printers, Andersen had commenced his next project. 'Now I am beginning to write some Fairy Tales for Children,' he wrote to a friend, adding with semi-accurate prescience, 'People will say this is my immortal work! But that is something I shall not experience in this world.' These tales would indeed bring him the immortality he always craved, but he would reap the fame and success while he lived.

Just a few months after *The Improvisatore* was published, his first volume of short stories, *Eventyr, Fortalte for Børn, Første Hefte* (*Fairy Tales told for Children – First Instalment*), came out, almost as an afterthought. The pamphlet contained four stories: 'The Tinder Box', 'Little Claus and Big Claus', 'The Princess on the Pea' and 'Little Ida's Flowers'.

'The Tinder Box' is a splendidly amoral tale about a soldier who fetches riches for a witch from within a magic tree, avoiding three guard dogs, each of which has larger eyes than the last. The witch asks only for the tinder box that he has also retrieved, but he decides he wants that too. When she complains he chops her head off. Soon the soldier has spent his ill-gotten gains. He strikes the tinder box to re-light a candle stub and discovers he can summon the dogs from the tree to grant him wishes. He has become fixated on a princess, and he orders one of the dogs to bring her to him. The king and queen find out, imprison the soldier and order him to be hung. On the gallows he strikes the tinder box once more: 'And the dogs flew right at the judge and the whole court, took one by the leg and one by the nose, and tossed them many miles up in the air so they fell down and broke into pieces.'

The same fate befalls the king and queen, and the terrified populace makes the soldier king in their stead. And so it ends. The princess is happy because she is queen and the soldier is happy with his endless wealth and the hand of the princess – never mind that he is guilty of grand larceny, homicide, regicide and treason, not to mention appalling ingratitude to the witch and highly questionable financial mismanagement.

'Big Claus and Little Claus' is, if anything, even more morally dubious. At one point Little Claus puts the corpse of his grand-mother in his bed to see if the warmth will bring her to life; later Big Claus wallops her on the head with his axe, believing her to be Little Claus; and she then suffers the indignity of being dressed up in her Sunday best and taken out for a ride in a wagon, where an innkeeper throws a cup of mead in her face to try to wake her up. '"GOOD LORD!" shouted Little Claus, running out of the door and grabbing the innkeeper by the collar. "You've killed my grandmother! Just look, there's a big hole in her forehead!"' Little Claus accepts a bushel of money as a bribe from the innkeeper. And so the story continues on the wonderfully anarcho-grotesque course that so many of Andersen's tales would follow.

Typically, Andersen complains in his autobiography that the critics knifed him for the stories – 'I reaped a harvest of blame,' he moaned. It is true that the Danish critics, perhaps in a state of shocked confusion (if we are being kind), didn't know how to handle these remarkable stories and attacked their light tone and often ambiguous morals as being unsuitable for children. One Danish critic wrote that 'The Princess on the Pea' was 'not only indelicate but quite unpardonable, in so far that a child may acquire the false impression that so august a lady may always be terribly sensitive.' Another chided: 'It is no empty convention that one must not put one's words together in the same disorderly fashion as one may do perfectly acceptably in oral speech.' Even Andersen's friend, B.S. Ingemann, reckoned the stories were 'a waste of time'.

But both H.C. Ørsted and Heiberg (who at that time was still on Andersen's side) both agreed that the stories would make Andersen's name and, of course, the children of Denmark reacted with an unprecedented fervour. 'Wherever I go and there are children,' he wrote to Henriette Wulff, 'they have read my fairy tales, and bring me the loveliest roses and give me a kiss, but the girls are very small, and I have asked some of them if I cannot be allowed to draw the capital with interest in about six or seven years' time.'

From the start, though, he was keen to make it clear that these tales were not just for children, as he wrote in the preface to the first collection: 'They were told for children but their elders should also enjoy listening to them.'

With the next volume, published seven months later (featuring three stories: 'Thumbelina', 'The Naughty Boy' and 'The Travelling Companion'), he began to grow in confidence and to develop the genre further, and by the time the third volume came out, in 1837, he could already boast two more master-pieces: 'The Little Mermaid' and 'The Emperor's New Clothes'. From then on he published a new volume every Christmas. In 1838 came 'The Galoshes of Fortune', 'The Steadfast Tin Soldier', 'The Daisy' and 'The Wild Swans', followed a year later by 'The Garden of Paradise', 'The Flying Trunk' and 'The Storks'.

This was not the plan, of course. Andersen's dream had always been to write for the stage but of the thirty or so plays that he wrote, only a third achieved any success. He tried his hand at novel writing (if you count his first, bizarre attempt – *Christian IV's Dwarf* – he wrote seven in all), but the scope, discipline and demands of forming plausible, complex characters and sustained plots were, in truth, beyond him. With the fairy story, however, he had found a literary form that perfectly suited his talents and personality. In his hands it took a quantum leap forward. By writing displaced allegories, stories set in far-away kingdoms with a cast of talking toys and tin soldiers, Andersen found he could write about politics and royalty and society and sex and hypocrisy, without any of his politician or monarchical friends being able to point the finger. As Elias Bredsdorff wrote: 'In some of Andersen's tales the satire is so general in its purpose that it hurts no one in particular.' This, of course, means that his stories are open to endless interpretation, which is one reason why they have remained so universal for so long.

Also, by creating fantasy worlds and fantasy characters Andersen was able to manage and manipulate his own experiences. 'The Top and the Ball', for example, was his way of coming to terms with his rejection by Riborg Voigt. He often created worlds in which he would either triumph – as in 'The Ugly Duckling' – or at least bow out with a tragic dignity like the Tin Soldier. They reflected his life as if in a fairground mirror so that he was able to wrestle his demons at a safe remove.

There is only one mention of Malta in his stories: a reference to the fortifications in his Greek story, 'The Pact of Friendship' (which was included in *A Poet's Bazaar*), but he must surely have had this astonishing island, and particularly its capital, in mind when creating many of the palaces, castles and fortresses that appear in his fiction. Valletta is built on Mount Sciberras, a small hill-peninsula, jutting out between Marsamxett Harbour (where the *Leonidas* docked) and the Grand Harbour. Virtually every building in the town is constructed from the same warm, yellow local stone, even new apartment blocks. Imagine Royal

Tunbridge Wells crossed with Marrakesh and you will have a (very poor) idea of the place.

Like many former British colonies, Malta slumbers like a pleasant theme park version of provincial 1970s Britain. It still has traditional red postboxes, Perkins buses, Hillman Hunters and manners. At one point I sat down on a bench next to an old man who, simply by greeting me with a 'good morning', almost reduced me to tears; it was the first unprovoked friendliness from a stranger since Munich. The old part of Valletta is mostly traffic free. What cars there are do their best to avoid scything you down. After my fraught weeks in Italy it was like sliding gently into a nice warm bath.

Andersen, his Russian companion and their Moorish guide arrived in Valletta through the city gates and made first for the Hotel de Mediterannea. The building, which was just a few steps from Siege Square in the centre of the old town, was levelled by the bombing of the Second World War and is now the site of the Embassy cinema and bingo house (leading one local historian, writing about Andersen's visit, to comment: 'Little would he have imagined that . . . a "film" in which a Mr Danny Kaye impersonated him would be shown there. But that actually came to pass!')

At the hotel a fracas ensues when Christoforoff pays the Moor half the agreed fee. The Moor throws the money on the floor in disgust, Andersen reports, 'and with a look which, on the stage, would have had its effect, expressed his pride and anger. I would have given the man more money, but the Russian placed himself between us, gave the servants a wink, and they turned the dissatisfied man out of doors.' Andersen follows him outside, and tries to give him three times the amount the Russian had offered but, 'he would not accept anything; shook his clenched fist toward the house, and went away proud as a mortified noble. This first scene in Malta put me out of humour.'

My humour was rather put out too when, walking towards the Grand Master's Palace – now the parliament building – I almost found myself mounting the bonnet, *Starsky and Hutch*-style, of a large BMW.

I had stumbled, literally, into one of the most important events in the recent history of the island – the resignation of its seventy-year-old Prime Minister, Dr Eddie Fenech Adami – who had chosen that very day to quit after leading the country for nineteen years. The car that had nearly embedded me in the walls of the palace belonged to the President, arriving ahead of the PM to receive his resignation.

All this I learned from some excited locals who had gathered behind hastily erected barriers on the other side of the street. I stood with them for an hour or so waiting for the Prime Minister to arrive. This was, of course, precious time lost in my race to retrace Andersen's Malta itinerary, but I justified it to myself because, a) this was history being made (albeit the history of a people I knew little about, by a politician I had never heard of), and, b) Andersen travelled at a time when there seemed to be an awful lot more history happening, and this was my chance for a piece of the action.

As the incoming PM arrived – an identikit European politician, tall, smooth, blank, with his dutiful wife in tow – I asked a man in a grey suit standing in front of me how Adami was thought of. 'We love him,' he said. 'He fought hard for us to join the European Union. He is a very great man.'

'They say he might run for President, that's why he is retiring,' added a middle-aged woman with unfeasibly large, gold glasses standing next to me. (Why is it that as they approach middle-age some women begin to buy larger and larger glasses until, around about the age of fifty-six, they reach dinner-plate proportions and obscure most of the upper part of their faces; and then, just as suddenly, they begin to shrink until no more than Miss Marple-style wire rims at about seventy-eight? Surely there has to be a doctoral thesis in this?) There were keen nods from all assembled.

Finally a black Mercedes pulled up and out clambered a short, round, elderly man. The crowd rushed to embrace him; the TV news men sprang to life; and I am proud to say that I even got to shake his hand. I realise that this was hardly in the 'Where were you when JFK was shot?' league, or even, 'Where were you when you heard Richard and Judy had switched to Channel Four?' come to that, but it was obviously a moment of great importance to the Maltesers.

It was only after he had disappeared into the Grand Master's Palace and the TV crews had begun to pack up, that I remembered why I had been heading there myself. While I felt privileged to have witnessed this important moment in the history of the island, I was also mightily pissed off that the resignation meant that this was the only day in living memory that the palace museum would be closed. 'If you can get into the State Rooms today you will be doing better than Rambo!' the guard told me as I tried to sneak through the turnstile while he wasn't looking.

Andersen enjoyed a lengthy tour of the palace; he even got to go up onto the roof, from where he claims to have been able to see Etna 'like a pyramid of Carrera marble'. He turns to face Africa: 'Malta now became like another north to me,' he writes. 'I felt a desire like the bird of passage in harvest. My thoughts flew to the land of the lions; they followed the caravan over the sandy deserts; they flew to the woods of the blacks, they rested on the gold-producing streams, and dreamt with Egypt's kings in the cloud-wreathed pyramids. Shall I ever go there?'

Amazing! Even when he is in the midst of the most exciting, intrepid and exotic journey of his life, standing in the centre of an island that is the living embodiment of his beloved *Arabian Nights* and, according to him, the 'most densely populated on the whole earth', Andersen is *still* yearning to travel somewhere yet more outlandish. As it turned out, he did reach Africa – on a day trip to Tangier from Spain in 1862 – but more interestingly for me, this spoke volumes about Andersen's insatiable wanderlust; as much as all of his travel memoirs combined. He was the eponymous Fir Tree, 'forever wanting to push on' and dreaming of the excitement of city life as it sits in the forest: 'There must be something greater, even grander! But what? I'm yearning! I'm pining!'; and he was the clerk in 'The Galoshes of Fortune': 'Oh, to travel, to travel! Surely it is the most delightful thing in the world. It is the great desire of my heart! If I could travel, this restlessness which comes over me would be quieted. But it must be far away!'

Anyone who loves to travel, who relishes even simply the atmosphere of airports and gets so excited by seeing names like 'Hyderabad' and 'Rostov' on the departure board that he will drone on and on about it until his wife eventually gives in and says 'Oh just get a ticket, will you?' will empathise with Andersen in this. But what planted the travel seed? Was it one of his earliest memories when, in 1808, a platoon of Spanish soldiers allied with Napoleon stopped in Odense for a few days on their way to attack Sweden? Though Andersen was only three at the time, he claims to remember 'the brown foreign men who made a disturbance in the streets'. One of them took the toddler up in his arms and pressed a silver religious icon, which hung around his neck, to Andersen's lips – much to the annoyance of his mother who resented such papist superstition.

Then there was his short but torrid time in Helsingør where, to escape the psychosexual taunts of his headmaster, he would wander the harbour to see the foreign ships docking and hear the babble of foreign languages from the sailors, intoxicated by the exoticism of it all.

Many of Andersen's literary heroes, like Heine and Goethe, had written about their travels and they, too, were undoubtedly an influence on his desire to travel. But there is something missing from these explanations of Andersen's incessant need to leave Denmark.

We have already seen how his libido was liberated by foreign travel. He wasn't the first sex tourist, and he certainly wasn't the last. (I hate to suggest this, and I can hear the sharp intake of breath from Danish readers as I write, but I suspect, had the jet engine and cheap package tours been available, Andersen might have been a familiar sight on the less salubrious beaches of Thailand.)

He also had an insatiable need to experience the new, the now, the next. Travel was an educational experience for Andersen. He was an observant anthropologist, fascinated by the human condition and the differences of peoples – the more exotic, the better. One of the most memorable encounters in *A Poet's Bazaar* is his meeting and burgeoning friendship with the Persian – replete with sabre and silver earrings – whom he meets on board the *Leonidas*. Though they barely exchange a word, the Persian's alien charm bewitches the Dane.

Andersen was remarkably open to new people and a keen observer of their peculiarities; it thrilled him to be sharing a boat with this man, along with Bedouins, Spanish monks, Americans, Russians and Englishmen. He was fascinated not just by their differences, but their similarities. Later on, as his boat stops in Belgrade, he is tickled to observe the same kind of social pretensions he had seen at home: 'Toward evening the chief persons of the good city of Semlin came on board; they greeted each other, as we could see, according to rank; some got a whole bushel of compliments, they were the very tip-top inhabitants; others got gracious compliments by the dram; it was quite ridiculous to see. I thought I was at home! How mankind resemble each other everywhere.'

As my Italian Andersen friend, Bruno Berni, pointed out, *A Poet's Bazaar* is, essentially, its writer's prolonged shopping trip in search of such characters, rituals and places. Andersen craved new experiences and his curiosity needed feeding at least once every year or so.

Copenhagen was (is) a small, inward-looking city and it had been relegated to the cultural and political minor leagues by events of the late eighteenth and early nineteenth century. At the time of Andersen's birth, Denmark had been ruined by a succession of ambitious yet dim-witted kings (always a lethal combination, that), and humiliated in various conflicts at the hands of the Swedes (something the Danes are still smarting over). As a consequence it had lost Norway, Iceland and its territories in southern Sweden, all of which it had ruled for centuries. Further indignity awaited when Nelson bombarded Copenhagen (again, I can tell you from personal experience that the Danes are still sore about that). Denmark was finally declared bankrupt in 1813, and forced to sell its meagre colonies in India and Africa. From this most wretched period in the country's history there ensued a prolonged period of introspective wound-licking, from which some might say Denmark has never really emerged.

Andersen soon outgrew Denmark and its introspective cliques, just as he had outgrown Odense and its small-town mentality. As he once wrote to Henriette Hanck: 'I do not belong here in the Northern countries and regard it as one of my earthly accidents that I was born and brought up on the corner of Greenland and Novaja Sembla.' Later in life, when he had been beaten into submission by the Danish critics, he found much of the adoration he sought abroad – another reason to travel.

A fairly typical rant on this subject came in a letter he wrote in 1843 to his good friend, Henriette Wulff, from Paris (where he had been lauded by the grand literary lions of the day):

I wish my eyes may never again see the home which can only see my shortcomings but fails to realise what great gifts God has given me! I hate those who hate me, I curse those who curse me! Always from Denmark there comes the cold air to petrify me abroad! They spit on me, they trample me into the mud, and yet I am a *Digter* [from the German, meaning a particularly high-flown poet] of a kind God did not give them many of – and in my dying hours I shall ask God never to give any such to that nation again. Oh, what poison has come into my blood at these hours! ...The Danes can be evil, cold, satanic! A people well suited for those damp, mouldy-green islands from which Tycho Brahe was sent into exile . . . I wish I had never seen that place, I wish the eternal God will never again let anybody with a nature like mine be born there; I hate the home, just as it hates and spits on me. Please pray to God for me that I may find a speedy death, that I may never see the place where I'm made to suffer, where I'm a stranger, a stranger like nowhere abroad . . . I do not believe in love in the Northern Countries, only in evil and falsehood – I myself feel it in my blood, and only thus can I feel where I belong.

He wrote to Edvard in a similar vein from England some years later:

At this moment I am at the pinnacle of my success . . . it is a fact; I am a famous man. The aristocracy here, so discouraging to their own poets, have welcomed me as one of their circle. Today and during the next fourteen days I have been invited out every day . . . I am being inundated with requests for my autograph . . . but to Denmark, to Copenhagen, I am nothing, there is not one jot of interest or sympathy . . . At home they have spat on me, while Europe has honoured me.

One has to sympathise: shortly after returning from London, Andersen recorded an incident in which two men had looked up at him as he stood at his living-room window: 'They saw me, stopped, laughed, and one of them pointed up to me and said in such a loud voice that I could hear every word: "Look! There's our orang-utan so famous abroad!"'

The poor man found himself an outsider at every turn. His traumatic youth dislocated him irrevocably from his surroundings. After he became the 'Fyn Nightingale', singing for his supper in the grand houses of Odense, he never really fitted in anywhere. For all his efforts, the Copenhagen bourgeoisie never really accepted him. He was always the upstart from the provinces, with a patchy education, odd manners and a vulgar ambition.

'He simply had no idea how to act in the homes of upper-middle-class sophisticates,' writes Wullschlager. 'He had no role models, no friends of his own age, no proper schooling . . . All his social intercourse, therefore, turned on the desire to impress a class above his own, for his very survival in the city depended on [them]. This left a terrible legacy . . . So much of his energy was pouring into self-education and theatrical training, as well as into sheer physical survival that none was left for emotional or social maturing.'

Meanwhile, on his return visits to Odense he was, again, the famous orang-utan. One of the most poignant moments in his autobiography comes when he describes his first return visit to the city after he had started school. While sailing on the river in Odense with some local notable or other, he looks to the banks and sees his mother, crying with pride for her fledgling. Already he had left what remained of his family behind him; his roots had been severed, and he would spend the rest of his life trying to lay new ones.

Denmark is not the easiest place to gain acceptance, even today. The children of immigrants are, for example, routinely described as 'second-generation Danes'. This is not necessarily a term of racial abuse, but simply how they are ordinarily referred to by the media, politicians and otherwise well-educated, liberal Danes. So while it would be preposterous to call someone a 'second-generation American' or even a 'second-generation Briton', in Denmark they use this as a handy catch-all for anyone who isn't, well, you know, 'one of us'. But in the nineteenth century the Danes found their outsiders from within – the newly mobile lower classes – and Andersen was one of the unfortunate pioneers: a first-generation middle-class *arriviste*.

Even though it is mostly free of the class baggage that can make Britain so insufferable, Denmark still has its myriad unwritten social conventions that can take a lifetime to learn. As an outsider in Denmark myself, I can empathise, to a degree at least, with Andersen's sense of social displacement (I learned the hard way, for instance, that a dinner invitation for seven means just that; if you are ten minutes late they will have begun eating and it all gets terribly embarrassing).

This permanent outsider status made foreign travel both more appealing and, in a way, less of a shock for Andersen. If you are an outsider at home, you aren't so likely to find it that uncomfortable being an outsider away from home. It breeds a peculiar, blithe confidence – a self-reliance – that Andersen, for all his anxieties and frailties, had in abundance. In other words, if others travel in hope, Andersen travelled to cope; he lived his life with his bags half packed, and the car waiting outside with the engine running.

In his memoir of his Spanish trip of 1862 he wrote something that I think is quite revealing about his travel impetus: 'In a foreign country where no one knows you or indeed wants to know you, you can, without reservation, be yourself; you are not preoccupied, consciously or subconsciously, with untold doubts – you need not fear that your opinion will be trumpeted forth like the cracking of a whip in the Alps causing an avalanche of mortification to roll over you.'

Of course, all of us, in some shape or form, attempt to retreat from the world from time to time. Some drink, others support a football team, or, like my friend Alan, build a model of Gatwick airport out of lolly sticks. To his credit, Andersen's escape from his world was to get out and interact with it. Though travel was more stressful for him than for most, the worries about passports and catching something nasty from a loo seat were infinitely preferable to dark nights spent nurturing a colossal persecution complex, convincing himself that his career was on the skids and that, one day, he might be exposed as a homosexual and drummed out of Denmark.

And it is no coincidence that Andersen toyed with the idea of suicide virtually his entire life. After all, what is death, but the most exciting journey into the unknown? In his first travel book

– about the Harz Mountains in Germany – Andersen directly connected his restlessness with this curiosity about death: 'To be in a strange haste with everything is, in reality, my chief characteristic . . . even in my travels it is not that which is present that pleases me; I hasten after something new, in order to come to something else. Every night when I lie down to rest, I hanker after the next day, wish that it was here, and, when it comes, it is still a distant future that occupies me. Death itself has in it something interesting for me – something glorious, because a new world will then be opened to me. What can it in reality be that my uneasy self hastens after?'

Was this an intimation of some kind of death wish? Was that why he took so many risks on his travels? I am not sure. What is certain, though, is that the adolescent, alienated and malformed by a unique set of circumstances, grew into a desperately unhappy, restless man doomed, like Karen Marie in 'The Red Shoes', to an eternal dance across Europe and beyond in a desperate search for love and acclaim.

Away from the tourist attractions of its high street, *Triq ir Repubblika* (in 1840, called *Strada Reale*), Valletta is evocatively dilapidated; at times it resembles a disused film set for an *Indiana Jones* sequel. Even before the locals began their exodus to the suburbs, Evelyn Waugh called the area 'the most concentrated and intense slum in the world' and today there are countless boarded-up palazzos. Placed anywhere else in Europe, they would be worth millions but here they remain neglected, with weeds slowly prising apart the stonework, and streaked with pigeon poo.

In Valletta's side streets you still find tiny, hole-in-the-wall workshops making coffins and suits, as well as some wonderfully eclectic little shops. In one window I noted a motley collection of Franklin Mint-style *Star Trek* figures; an inflatable policeman; some scissors; an artificial limb; toothbrushes; a guide to Hickman Field air base in Hawaii; and a signed photo of Charles Hawtrey – the flotsam of a retail twilight zone.

Mdina and the neighbouring town of Rabat, where Andersen heads next, are the centre for the island's mini-St Paul industry, with a cathedral, grotto and catacombs named after him. It is said that the apostle lived in the grotto for three months after being shipwrecked off the coast of the island in AD 60, spending his time baptising the locals. This empty underground cave, which Andersen also visited, was made by the Romans in 100 BC and used as a prison (you can still see the hook where, the museum guide told me with ghoulish relish, they used to suspend torture victims).

On their way back to Valletta the daytrippers pass the house of Prince Emir Bechir, who had fled to Malta from Lebanon with a hundred staff and a family of fifteen. In *A Poet's Bazaar* Andersen notes that: 'Numerous black slaves sauntered about in the yard, and a fine giraffe stood by the wall and ate the green leaves', but he makes no mention of the giraffe in the diary entry he made that night, back aboard the *Leonidas*. In fact, this giraffe has exercised Andersen scholars for some years. In an essay that accompanied a one hundred and fiftieth anniversary exhibition about Andersen's day in Malta, a local historian dismissed the sighting and suggested he might have seen a camel instead, but I am not so sure. The house and San Anton Garden are today the official residence of the Maltese president, but the walls, which appear to be the originals, are too tall for a camel to have been visible. Maybe he saw a camel standing on a box.

Andersen returned to the *Leonidas* at five in the afternoon, but notes in his diary that the Russian goes back into Valletta that evening, returning with some souvenirs: 'The Russian showed me on his arms traces of bites, which a woman last night had given him, in sexual excitement; he had visited her together with one of our officers.' It doesn't seem to occur to him that his Russian friend might have been some kind of sex criminal, but it is perhaps the memory of this that he refers to in his story 'The Collar' (1848), when the sex-mad hero (a detachable shirt collar – not the first item of clothing that might spring to mind for this role, but still) recounts his conquests: 'Then there was that prima ballerina, she gave me the scar that I still carry. She was so wild!' Later in the trip, he does, however, confess in his diary to an unease about the man: 'polished, and yet has Russian blood. He showed us his copper engravings; some were missing. They've been stolen, he said, by the officers on the other ship. I said it was possible that he had forgotten them, like today when he'd supposedly thrown away *Correspondance et Mémoires d'un voyageur en Orient* [by Eugène Boré], which I had lent him; it was found in his bed.'

By the end of my day on Malta I felt I had put up a good fight in the whistle-stop Malta tour stakes. Admittedly, I had the advantage over Andersen of having the internal combustion engine and proper roads at my disposal – he travelled to Mdina in a two-wheeled carriage – but I had also been delayed by the Prime Ministerial musical chairs.

There was, though, one non-Andersen question that chased around in my thoughts like the last pea on the plate as I took a taxi to the airport the next morning: why are chocolate Maltesers so called? I vowed that when I got home I would investigate but having trawled through a good many of the 18,400 references to Maltesers on the Internet and got nowhere, I rang Nestlé Mars, the company that makes them. Eventually I was put through to External Affairs and a nice woman called Barbara, who admitted she was flummoxed. She promised that someone would ring back and a couple of days later, remarkably, they did. They told me that the name has nothing to do with the people of Malta, but is, of course, a reference to malt, a prime ingredient of said spherical chocolate treat. They are, you see, 'malty teasers'! So now you know.

So anyway, I arrived in Athens the next morning and . . . okay, okay, I'm not going to get away with this, am I? There are no longer any boats from Malta to Athens, and I am deeply ashamed to admit that I flew. Trying to distract you with the Malteser thing was a cheap trick, but worth a try.

About the only way I could possibly have sailed to Athens would have been to wait until late spring and hope that I could stow away on a passing cruise ship. The odds of that were slim, and my money would have run out while I waited. I would have been forced to fend for myself on the streets of Valletta, grubbing for charity, living off rotting vegetables and cigarette butts. Had I been Michael Palin, my team of dedicated researchers would doubtless have smoothed things for me before I arrived, and arranged passage with a tame merchant navy crew. Paul Theroux would have simply unfolded his pocket kayak and rowed across the Med. But me? I brought dishonour upon my family by giving in and flying. Before setting out on this trip I had pledged to travel in Andersen's footsteps as authentically as possible, but, short of wading out into the harbour and swimming to Piraeus, there was no alternative.

The description of Andersen's departure from Malta is as romantic a piece of travel writing as you might ever wish to read. 'The cannon sounded, the flags waved, and we glided out of Malta's road at a rapid rate, into the open Mediterranean, which lay as blue and still as a velvet carpet spread over the earth; and the sea was like bluish ether – a fixed starless sky beneath us; it extended in the transparent air, further than I have ever seen it; neither dark nor light stripe bounded the horizon; there was a clearness, an infinity which cannot be painted, nor described, except in the eternal depth of thought.'

I flew to Athens via Rome – the last place I wanted to see by this stage – at exorbitant cost, and my rucksack got lost and didn't arrive for two days.

Chapter Seven

ATHENS

As he steams across the Mediterranean towards Athens aboard the *Leonidas*, Andersen is consumed by the ecstacy of escape. 'The time went on delightfully,' he writes in *A Poet's Bazaar*, 'joy and mirth reigned at the dinner-table. The sunsets were extremely beautiful. The stars streamed forth so clear and bright! . . . My northern home has granted me but a few minutes in my life so delightful as I enjoyed here for whole hours.'

The crossing is calm, dolphins frolic in their wake and the company on board is everything a travel writer could wish for: there is a papal envoy en route to the Lebanon; the Spanish monks and the Persian, of course; and the brooding Bedouin, sitting on the coal sacks – 'silent as a ghost, the eyes sparkled in that brown face, under the white burnoose, and his naked, dark-brown legs stuck out.' The bird-like, black-clad Andersen must have seemed equally exotic, although his fellow passengers seem unclear as to his origins: '"From Denmark!" repeated our Roman ecclesiastic, who was going to Jerusalem. "Denmark! You are then an American?"'

Andersen and the Persian witness a small bird land on the boat, exhausted from its migration. A crowd of other passengers gathers too; it appears this is the most exciting thing that has happened for some time. True to form, the Roman priest immediately suggests that they kill and eat it. Andersen is aghast: '"Our little winged pilgrim shall not be eaten!" said I', so one of the crew takes it and looks after it, releasing it the next day. 'It was a great event for us all.'

That night the Persian and he cement their friendship with an exchange of fruit. Andersen points towards the night sky using the universal gesture: 'Cuh! Would you look at that?' The Persian touches his turban in a less universal, but still effective response. The dialogue floundering, Andersen dredges up the only Hebrew he remembers from school, '*Bereschit Barah elohim Et Haschamaim Veet Haaretz!*' ('In the beginning God created the Heaven and the Earth' – the first line from Genesis). 'And he smiled, nodded, and in return gave me all he knew of a language that he thought was mine: "Yes, sir! Verily! Verily!" This was the whole of our conversation. Neither of us knew more; but we were good friends.'

It is here, in the middle of the Mediterranean, that the most remarkable example of Andersen's Clark Kent eyesight occurs. So far on the journey he has claimed to be able to see a) both the Adriatic and the Mediterranean from a hilltop south of Lojano in northern Italy; b) the Mediterranean from the Palatine Hill in Rome, and c) Mount Etna from the roof of the Presidential Palace in Malta. This time his Superman vision picks out snow-capped Etna and the coast of Greece simultaneously from the deck of the ship. The captain pooh-poohs the idea, and none of the other passengers can see Greece, but Andersen is adamant.

After dinner, a few hours later, he looks to the horizon again, and sees both land masses still. 'The captain took his best telescope and cried, "Land!" It was the coast of Greece! It was a mountain top near Navarino [now Pylos, in the Peloponnese], covered with snow, and it shone in the clear air. I had discovered Greece the first of them all.' The captain is astounded: '"I have never before heard," said the captain, "that any one could see both Etna and the coast of Greece at the same time, with the naked eye! It is remarkable!"'

This was quite an important trust litmus, as far as Andersen's fantasy-prone journalism was concerned. So I decided to check it out. Etna is 3,350 metres high and the highest mountain in the Peloponnese is Taigetos at 2,520 metres, so these are fairly large targets, but the *Leonidas* would have been at least 200 miles away from each at the time. If you factor in the curvature of the earth – at eight inches per mile – throw in a little Pythagoras theory, and then get your friend Jacob whose brain is so big he works with computers to do the maths, you will discover that to see them both is, sadly, impossible. Even presupposing superhuman eyesight and perfect conditions, Etna would disappear after about 120 miles, Taigetos just after the 100-mile mark.

The prospect of Greece excites Andersen immensely. At school, under Meisling, he was force fed the classics, and, more recently, as with the rest of Europe, he has been gripped by the country's fight for independence after almost 400 years of Turkish rule. 'Greece! I saw then before me this great father-land of spirits! Under yonder mountains lay the beautiful Arcadian vales! A thousand thoughts, one different from the other, flew towards that shining mountain, like a flock of migratory birds!' he writes, exultant.

His excitement at landing on the island of Syra (or, Syros) – where he must wait for a few hours before boarding another French steamer, the *Lycurgus*, bound for Piraeus – is tempered only by the sadness of parting from the friends he has made aboard the *Leonidas*. As he steps on to the quayside he describes what is, for him, a recurring conflict between the desire to keep moving and the attachment he so readily forms with strangers: 'Gratitude toward God, joy at being here, and yet a certain feeling of desolation.'

On Syra he has just enough time for a shave and to experience yet another case of mistaken nationality: 'The barber asked me if I was an Englishman; and when I said I was Danish, he pressed me to his heart and shouted: "*Bravi Americani!*" I assured him that I was not an American, but a Dane; he nodded quite pleased, laid his hand on his heart, and said, as far as I could make out, how dear the Americans were to all Greeks, from the time of their struggle for liberty, when the American ships brought them provisions.'

Outside the local hotel, he meets a Russian who has been

robbed on the way from Constantinople – a reminder of the
dangers that lie ahead. The Russian curses both the Greeks and
all travel writers, whom he blames for luring him from home:
'"They are all scoundrels," said he; "as well as those writers and
Lamartines [a reference to Alphonse de Lamartine, the author of
Souvenirs d'un Voyage en Orient] who describe these countries so
that one feels a desire to visit them. I wish I had one of the
fellows here; I would break his bones!"'

Many of Andersen's Danish friends would have heartily agreed
with the Russian. Their 'Danish self-sufficiency and provincial
glorification', as Elias Bredsdorff called it, was a great irritation
to Andersen and he often parodied the insularity of these 'Danish
super-patriots' (and, boy, have I met a few of those) in his stories.
In 'The Beetle', for instance, one frog says to another: 'I should
very much like to know whether the swallow [a common
Andersen cipher] – that gadabout creature – on its many journeys abroad has ever found a better climate than ours, with all
its drizzle and damp. It's like lying in a soaking-wet ditch. If you
don't revel in that, you can't really love your native land.'

When Andersen arrived back in Hamburg at the end of this
journey he met an elderly Danish lady who had asked him: 'Tell
me, Mr Andersen, have you ever, on all your many and long
journeys abroad, seen anything as beautiful as our little
Denmark?' 'I certainly have', he replied, 'I have seen many things
more beautiful.' 'Shame on you!' she said. 'You are not a patriot!'
In 'Olé Luköié' (sometimes known as 'The Sandman' or 'Willie
Winkie'), the old woman becomes a hen who berates a swallow
– again – for its constant travelling, saying: 'We get warm weather
too, sometimes. Don't you remember, only four years ago, we
had a summer that lasted five weeks! . . . And then we don't
get all those poisonous creatures they have abroad . . . anyone
who doesn't think our country is the best of all is a scoundrel;
he doesn't really deserve to live here.'

The Collin family took a similarly dim view of Andersen's
travels, particularly the eldest daughter, Ingeborg. 'Heaven knows

why you do not stay at home to see the many lovely things we have here!' she wrote to him in response to a complaining letter he'd sent from Rome a few weeks before. 'What is the pleasure of being cold in Rome? You may as well be cold in Copenhagen.' It was probably Ingeborg Andersen had in mind when he was writing the frog's speech in 'The Beetle'.

You can understand why so many Danes thought like this at that time. The world had been fairly beastly to them in the preceding years and, in fact, they remain an insular tribe to this day. A remarkable number of Danes still prefer to spend their July fortnight sitting with gritted teeth, all three bars blazing on the heater, in their summer houses – many, essentially, glorified garden sheds – staring out at the rain and playing endless games of Cluedo, than leave their beloved homeland for Spain or France. They are not quite the adventurers their Viking forefathers were, that's for sure.

In 1841 Greece was still coming to terms with its newfound freedom from the Turks. Independence had been ratified by the Treaty of Adrianople in 1830 and would ultimately signal the beginning of the end for the Ottoman Empire as subsequent revolts in the Balkans sent its Danubian territories tumbling like flaming dominoes over the next few decades. Rather improbably, following the assassination of their first President, Joannis Capodistrias in 1831, the Great Powers of Europe had imposed a seventeen-year-old Bavarian prince – the son of Ludwig I – on the Greeks, crowning him King Otto I, King of the Hellenes.

On his arrival, Otto had made Athens the capital (up until then it had been Nafplion – but Otto was not the brightest light on the tree and perhaps had pronunciation issues with that), and commenced a massive neo-classical building programme. He was determined to create a fitting capital for a nation that wished to reclaim its position at the heart of western civilisation, and throwing up grand public buildings was very much the Bavarian way of going about it.

Andersen describes the state of chaos that ensued in a letter to his friend Carsten Hauch: 'Athens grows by the hour; houses and streets shoot up from the gravel.' He likens the city in size to Helsingør – a comparison that seems ludicrous today as Helsingør has about 60,000 residents, and Athens four million. But in 1840 it looked, he said, like 'a town that had been built up in the greatest haste for a market', and there were less than 10,000 inhabitants.

So Andersen arrived in Athens at a pivotal moment in the country's history. As, in a way, did I.

The Greeks were flustered, having just dumped their government in the build-up to the Olympics. The Athenians were running around like panicking dinner-party hostesses with their make-up half done, the table not laid and a collapsed soufflé in the oven. If the international news coverage was to be believed, none of the preparations for the games had been finished – not the surface of the marathon route, not the roofs of the main stadium or the swimming pool, not even the basic transport infrastructure. CNN had just rendered the Greeks incandescent by reporting all this: 'It's true there are some things not finished,' one indignant local told me on the bus from the airport to the underground station. 'But there are lots of things we *have* finished and they didn't talk about any of them!' It seemed impolite to mention that the very fact that we had to take a bus for that part of the journey was because the Greeks had abandoned the original plans for the new metro to go all the way to the airport.

From the air Athens had looked like a massive, dirty snowdrift. If ever any city warranted the cliché sprawling, it is the Greek capital, but in Andersen's day it could barely muster a cluster. The majority of Otto's ambitious buildings and palaces had yet to be completed. In 1841 even the king was living in a makeshift palace, which Andersen described, rather condescendingly, as 'an extremely modest building . . . it would in any other country in Europe, be taken for a private gentleman's summer villa.'

At the exit of the new Acropolis metro station I paused by a large reproduction of a watercolour of the city painted in 1836. In the foreground was the Military Hospital, one of the first neo-classical buildings constructed by Otto. Behind it is the Acropolis, crowned by the Parthenon. But other than that the picture shows nothing on the south side of the city bar a few palm trees, the odd camel and scrubby desert. And guess what? As I exited the station on the edge of the Plaka district, there was Otto's hospital, newly restored (although work had not *quite* finished), standing proudly among rubble and makeshift fencing in the shadow of the Acropolis, high rises all round.

Andersen knew Plaka well – there wasn't much else to Athens then, after all. And, despite large sections having being spruced up for the tourists and entire streets selling nothing but plastic Parthenons, calendars of ancient Greek porn and Athens Olympics merchandise (most perplexing slogan: 'Athens 2004 – Overcome Yourself'), away from the main tourist drag, there are still numerous decaying nineteenth-century houses, in a state of picturesque Miss Haversham-style dereliction, just like those Andersen drew.

Deciding that I would rather gouge my own eyes out with a rusty nail than dine in the restaurant opposite the station with a sign in the window saying: 'As recommended by *Lonely Planet!*' – 'Come! Dine with sanctimonious, unwashed, bleating hippies!' – I strolled into Plaka and found a lovely old 1970s corner taverna, with heavily varnished wooden panelling, ceiling fans and tartan tablecloths. Here I dined on 'octopus on vinegar', followed by a satisfyingly rich veal stew, laced with lumps of salty feta.

I opened my by now rapidly disintegrating copy of *A Poet's Bazaar* on the table in front of me. As the journey had progressed I had begun to employ various combinations of sticky tape and glue to hold its brittle, tea-stained pages together – the spine having exploded over lunch in Verona. The book was now beginning to resemble some kind of holy relic and drew curious looks

from the waiters in the restaurant. As I toyed with my compli-
mentary dessert, which they had insisted I try despite my extravagant 'full-tummy' mime, I turned to the chapter entitled 'Arrival
in Athens'.

After three days of quarantine in Piraeus harbour, during which
time several Danes resident in the city had taken the trouble to
row out to meet him, Andersen and his fellow passengers were
released: '. . . Above a dozen Greek boats [lay] about our vessel.
I sprang into the first at hand, and we rowed briskly toward land,'
he writes. 'We rolled rejoicing out of Piraeus. Sailors, in their
glazed hats, sat outside coffee houses . . . [and] gave us a "hurra"
emptying their wine glasses.'

Even the dirt and the beggars were now cause for celebration: 'We went at a gallop; there was a terrible dust, but then it
was classic dust . . . Whilst our horses baited, there came beggars
with large pewter cups; we gave something to all, for they were
Greeks . . . Before us lay the Acropolis, which I had so often
seen in pictures; but now it was before me in reality! . . . I could
not rightly bring myself to think that I was in Greece, and that
I was entering Minerva's city.' Years later, writing in his autobiography, he likens these first moments on Greek soil to 'standing
on the great battlefield of the world, where nation had striven
with nation . . . How little appear the inequalities of daily life
in such a place!'

Andersen was welcomed into Danish–German circles like a
visiting dignitary and invited to dine at the city's highest tables.
Though in his autobiography he complains about Danes sticking
together in foreign lands – 'It is a weakness of my country-people
. . . they must dine together, meet at the theatre, and see all the
lions of the place in company' – he was as guilty of this as the
rest of them. When he visited Paris he was a regular in the Café
de Danemark, for instance; in Rome he seemed to have virtually nothing to do with the locals; and upon arrival in Athens he
wastes no time in calling on every Dane and German in the city
– the architects Christian Hansen and his brother Theopolis (both

of whom had been in the city for some years, Christian as royal architect to Otto); the archaeologist Professor Ludwig Ross; a Dr Ulrich; the Danish Consul Travers, who promises to introduce him to the King; as well as the queen's chaplain, Reverend Lüth and his wife Christiane.

'I walk up to the Acropolis every day,' he wrote to Hauch. 'The view is marvellous and the place itself a ruined fairy world; wild cucumbers grow over the steps of the Parthenon; scattered around are unburied skulls of Turks and Greeks; here and there are whole bombs from the time of the Venetians.' (This is a reference to the bombing of the Parthenon by the Venetians, which took place in 1687 when it was being used as a munitions store; the Venetians must have done one of the greatest double takes in military history that day.)

I didn't spot any cucumbers or skulls, but rosemary, olives and tortoises still flourish on the slopes of the Western World's foremost ancient site – 'the world's most perfect poem in stone', according to Lamartine. The ruins (which Andersen describes as looking as if an earthquake had just struck), their setting and the view are so overwhelming that, as you stand there, you feel nothing can ever quite whelm you the same way again. It is the landfill of the gods, with sliced Ionic columns, naked stylobates, and Pentelic marble spheres lying hugger-mugger on the pink-veined limestone bedrock, gay poppies and dusty cedars sprouting from the wreckage. The columns of the Erechtheum Temple look like well-sucked sticks of rock; so fragile you feel a strong gust could reduce them to rubble. Some were held together with Sellotape (honestly – I took a picture to prove it). And, of course, though a twelve-year restoration programme began in 1983, the Parthenon repairs are still not completed, which, I couldn't help thinking at the time, did not augur well for the Olympic projects. In fact, in all my time in Athens I never once saw anyone working on the Parthenon. They are, apparently, so resigned to it never being finished that they have now colour-coded the cranes and scaffolding to blend in better with the masonry.

'It is 11.12 now, I said we had until 11.35, so you have twenty-three minutes!' barked an American tour guide to her herd of elderly cattle as I passed them by the entrance to the Acropolis museum. I hoped she was referring to the time they had on the Acropolis, but it could just as easily been their allotted time for Athens as a whole.

They reminded me of Andersen's future fantasy, 'Thousands of Years From Now', in which Americans 'do' Europe in a week: 'Onward they speed under the Channel Tunnel to France . . . The airship flies on, over the land where Columbus sailed forth, where Cortez was born . . . Through the air and over the sea to Italy, where ancient eternal Rome once lay; it has been wiped out, the Campagna is a wilderness. Of St Peter's Church, only the remains of a solitary wall are shown, but its authenticity is doubted. To Greece, in order to sleep for one night at the luxurious hotel high on the top of Mount Olympus . . . "There's a lot to see in Europe", said the young American. "And we saw it in a week!"' (The story predates Jules Verne by several decades, by the way.)

Inside the Acropolis museum the curators had let no opportunity pass to carp about the rape of their monuments by the British and, clearly, they have a case as it was the Turks who gave permission for much of it to be removed in the first place. Here, along with a ravishing array of statues and friezes – all somehow rendered with a more delicate lightness of touch than their Roman counterparts – I learned that the Athena Nike Temple frieze was 'removed by Elgin, cut down to a thickness of 0.12m and sold to the British Museum' (Elgin got £35,000 for them). We should give it all back, of course but, then again, where would the repatriation of colonial booty end? The Queen's da Vinci sketches to Italy? (Would she even notice?) Gibraltar to the Spanish? (Would they even want it?) But *Kylie back to the Australians*? See the danger?

Actually, Andersen himself witnessed this plunder. On 27 March he drew a Greek vase that caught his eye in a display on the Acropolis. It is just the kind of *objet* you would expect to attract his attention: fantastical, pretty and begging for a story to be written about it. This, it turns out, is the Aigina griffon jug, made in 675 BC, and also swiped by the British Museum, where it remains to this day.

Outside the Acropolis museum, a group of American teenage boys, with giant-tongued sneakers and trousers at half mast, were discussing the view:

Dude #1: 'Seriously.'
Dude #2 'Du-ude, seriously.'
Dude #1: Like, dude, seeeriously dude.'
Dude #3: 'Seeeriously, dude, seeeriously.'

And to think, the haze and smog meant that their view was *seeeriously* limited compared to Andersen's, who with his amazing eyesight had claimed to see Accro Corinth, sixty miles away (theoretically possible, according to Jacob, but not with twenty-first-century smog).

Descending the Acropolis, I came to the foot of some stairs cut into a large, red boulder. Two thousand years ago this served as the pulpit from which St Paul delivered his missives to the Athenians. Plato spoke from here too. Today the hill is covered in cigarette butts and populated by clusters of pretty, giggling teenagers. On the far side a group of Greek men had launched into a spot of traditional dancing – chillingly similar to Morris dancing, right down to the hanky waving.

In *A Poet's Bazaar* Andersen mentions the hill and that he visited Socrates' prison near by, plucking a red flower from the entrance to the cave to send to his friend, the poet Adam Oehlenschläger. The truth is that this shallow cave is closer to the Athenians' answer to Juliet's house in Verona (it was probably just a troglodyte's dwelling), but it still looks exactly like Andersen's drawing. The cave, where the philosopher is said to have been incarcerated for his dubious relations with young, male

Athenians (including Plato), is carved into the side of Filopappou Hill. This preposterously idyllic mound adjacent to the Acropolis thronged with poets in ancient times, and is now home to birds, bees and blossoming bushes – Louis Armstrong singing 'What a Wonderful World' should be piped here round the clock.

From there I walked up into Anafiotika, a rambling, ramshackle village, which grew up around the base of the Acropolis in the nineteenth century as a home to the builders who had come to work on Otto's new projects. It is essentially a two-hundred-year-old fishing village plonked right in the centre of a brutal concrete city; a dislocated Cycladis oasis with tiny whitewashed cottages with blue shutters and doors, strung together by mazy alleys so slender I could barely squeeze my rucksack through, taking care to avoid the plates of congealed spaghetti left out for local strays as I went.

I felt a sudden chill of excitement while wandering around Anafiotika as it dawned on me that Andersen would almost certainly have walked here, and that it hadn't changed a bit. It was precisely the kind of evocative, time-warp place I had hoped to find when I left Copenhagen.

The main retail artery of central Athens is Ermou. It is another Andersen haunt, but somewhat altered over the last century and a half. I know you are waiting in a high pitch of nervous antic-ipation for the latest gripping instalment of my Andersen Hotel Hunt, so, from the clues given in *A Poet's Bazaar*, the eastern end of Ermou is my best guess for the location of the Hotel de Munich, where Andersen stayed throughout his time in Athens.

Ermou is another of those lively avenues, like Toledo in Naples and Il Corso in Rome, that Andersen loved. Always on his travels he was drawn to the places in a city where people gathered to socialise and where he could observe their peculiarities. Still today, whatever time of night and day I visited it, Ermou seemed as if in the throws of a carnival, with a cast of characters including a living statue of *Sesame Street*'s Big Bird (well, it's a living); a clown brandishing a snake (quite possibly one of the most disturbing sights

I have ever seen), and numerous Africans selling counterfeit sunglasses and those hideous posters of kittens and Lamborghinis (now kittens *driving* Lamborghinis really would be something). That said, is it not time that there was an amnesty for killers of Peruvian pan pipe players? It would surely be a vote winner, probably even in Peru.

In *A Poet's Bazaar* Andersen tells us that his new best friend in Athens fought to preserve a palm tree that was growing slap bang in the centre of Ermou. 'Professor Ross begged that it might be spared; and it was permitted to stand,' he writes. 'I therefore christen it "Ross's palm" – and from this time all travellers and writers of travels will be pleased to call it by its proper name!' I suspect the axes came out the moment Ross was looking the other way; the palm tree is certainly not there now, although the little, biscuit-coloured Kapnikarea church, which Andersen drew, still stands, dwarfed among the high-rises.

Nearby is a café, which, given its location and period high ceilings, old carved wooden bar and furniture, I felt sure Andersen would have frequented. Perhaps it was the one that he said made Rome's Caffé Greco look like 'a sand-hole under the stairs', and was packed with Greek dandies in national dress so tightly laced 'that they must have been blue and green about the ribs, with eye-glass, and glacé gloves, smoking their cigars, and playing billiards'. I sat and had an orange juice. Greek waiters have a nice habit of bringing you a glass of water while you decide what to order (Italian waiters reading this might care to note that it is free), and I asked how long the café had been there. 'Fifteen years,' he said.

I borrowed their phone to call Myrto Georgiou Nielsen, a Greek psychologist and scholar who had written two books on Andersen – the first a psychological study, the second about his time in Athens. She was friendly and welcoming; she sounded lovely actually, but she couldn't meet me that day. 'Oh no, it's Independence Day today. None of the locals stay in Athens on Independence Day – that's just for out-of-towners!' she said.

Instead, she invited me to her apartment in Kolonaki the next day.

As an out-of-towner myself I had deliberately timed my arrival in Athens to coincide with the parade, which Andersen had seen and written about, reserving special praise for the ranks of 'pretty Greek boys' whom he ogled as they marched past. 'The handsome men and boys were pleasing to look upon. Of the women there were not many, and those we saw were ugly,' he writes, rather ungallantly.

I walked up to the parliament building – designed by Christian Hansen as Otto's new palace – an hour before the parade was due to begin. The crowd was already five or six deep when I took my place in front of his brother Theophilos' Hotel Grande Bretagne and, over the next hour, we became so tightly compressed that fossilisation seemed inevitable. I couldn't bend to scratch my knee, or place my empty Coke can on the ground. I was close enough to the man in front of me that I could tell what kind of shampoo he used (and that, judging by his dandruff, he ought to change brands), but still, I was excited to see what kind of spectacle would materialise. Would it be big, fun floats and bikini'd dancing girls? Or majorettes and waving celebrities? Surely all these people wouldn't endure all this for one of those slow trundle-bys of military hardware . . .

First came three Jeeps, and then nothing for another twenty-six minutes. As a warm-up act this had little to recommend it and, furthermore, suggests that, if you ever find yourself in the Greek army and there is a war, on no account let them make you ride in the Jeeps. I had not endured two hours standing with my face in someone's armpit, while a toddler on the shoulders of the man next to me tried to blind me with a plastic Picachu, to applaud camouflaged sports utility vehicles. That said, the marching nuns, who came next, were a highlight (as a crack troop, I can hardly imagine anything more terrifying than a gang of tooled-up, highly trained Sisters), but by then my enthusiasm was waning. As the jets flew over, I pictured a few more crumbs of the Parthenon tumbling to earth and it crossed my mind that this would be the perfect moment for Turkey to invade.

I had by now been standing in one position for so long I was considering calling Sky to offer myself as the new David Blaine, so I crow-barred my way through the crowd, finally bursting free of the throng like a champagne cork from its bottle.

The carnival atmosphere continued into the evening with Plaka's tavernas heaving with Athenians sipping frappés and eyeing up each other's labels. It was in front of these carousing crowds that I fell victim to the hilarious antics of a street comedian who, in the absence of an actual routine or anything, got cheap laughs by imitating passers-by behind their back. At the time I, of course, laughed along with everyone, slapped him heartily on the back ('Aha, yes, you got me there, you, *you* . . .'), and congratulated him on his wit. But, later, I followed him home, knifed his guts open, and stamped on his entrails.

I had, it seemed, finally become an orang-utan myself.

I ate outside in the balmy early-spring air, beneath the Lysicrates Monument (which Byron had once used as a study). I had been braced for the worst as far as Greek food was concerned, my single previous experience of it being as a spectator to my dad's almost instantaneous regurgitation of an attempted moussaka, made by my mother during one of her pioneering food experiments in the late '70s. But actually, I had the best food of my entire trip in Athens: twitchingly fresh cod, battered and deep fried so briefly that it remained sushi-ish in the middle, and then served with a sauce that resembled wall-paper paste but was deliciously garlicky (if you can imagine such a thing); rich, meaty stews; refreshing tzatziki; and simply gallons of ouzo.

Sitting outside that night I also first became aware of the Athens Noise. Most cities have a defining sonic characteristic. In Copenhagen it is the whirr of dynamos on bicycle wheels; in Rome it is the peel of church bells; in London it is the nasal whine of Ken Livingstone, and in Istanbul, as I was to discover, it is the cracking of pistachio shells.

Athens' distinctive sound came from the rosaries that were habitually rattled by the men as they walked. All men will fiddle idly with something noisy given the chance. Most of us make do with loose change in our pockets or car keys, although the sound can often be drowned by the tutting of nearby women. But Athenian men have cunningly disguised their fiddling as some kind of religious observance and so contrive to appear simultaneously sanctimonious. Sometimes they even swing them as they walk, like Dixon of Dock Green with his whistle.

The next day, on my way across town to my meeting with Myrto, I popped by the Danish Institute (glad to hear the Danish government is spending its 60 per cent income tax revenue wisely), located in the heart of Plaka. I wanted to hear what, if any, preparations were being made in Greece to celebrate Andersen's two hundredth anniversary and hoped for help locating a few of the things he mentions in his chapters on Greece in *A Poet's Bazaar*.

I was met by Panagiota, who is charged with promoting Danish cultural events in the city. Panagiota told me that the main programme of events was to take place at Athens' Children's Museum where there would be puppet shows, theatre and dance. She also helped me track down one or two things Andersen had mentioned in *A Poet's Bazaar*. There was one thing, though, that she could not help with. Something he sees and refers to in an almost throwaway comment at the end of a description of a visit to the theatre. 'The people say that it is the pillar to which Christ was bound when his executioner scourged him,' he writes, 'and they believe that the Turks have thrown it into the sea, but that it returns here every night. The white pillar stood in the solitude, and pointed in the starlight night toward heaven.'

It is a fairly confusing description of a hardly credible legend, but I still thought it unlikely that he made it up entirely. And, surely, a legend as powerful as this would still be known about, even after 163 years. Columns to which Christ was tied do not just disappear, do they? We went off on a hunt through the Institute's many rooms and asked several archaeologists, but none knew.

Maybe Myrto could tell me more.

Myrto was a jovial, welcoming woman in her early sixties, with platinum hair and a beaming, warm smile. She exuded the curiosity and appetite for life of someone decades younger. Her eyes were set on permanent twinkle. I think I was in love.

As she made me welcome in her tastefully furnished living room, we bonded over our common grievances about Denmark. Myrto's late husband was Danish and they had brought up their children in Copenhagen. She had taught psychology at Copenhagen University and during that time had developed a fascination with Hans Christian Andersen. I was keen to hear her diagnosis.

'He was a special man, and he is particularly fascinating for a psychologist,' she began. 'His neuroses are so clear and, though he is not a sympathetic character, there is a pathology in him which is fascinating. If you think back to his childhood, I think his ugliness played a great part in the man he became – that and the fact that as a seventeen-year-old he was forced to go to school with eleven-year-olds must have left terrible scars.

'As a child he had nothing he could be proud of but when he became famous and found himself the centre of attention at all those manor houses and palaces around Europe, that became a substitute. He found his need for love in fame, although, of course, I still think he suffered.'

What did she make of his sexuality? 'Well, he was not gay,' she said confidently. 'No, I think it was more that he was very, very scared of sexuality. Sex is physically and emotionally explosive and that frightened him, so he turned inwards. His sexuality remained at a very childish level – no, I should say he was not childish or childlike, he was *infantile*. I don't think he had the guts to have sex.'

But what about the visits to prostitutes? 'Maybe he kept going back thinking, Now, *this* time I am going to do it . . . I think if he had had intercourse it would have been like a "Gloria" moment for him, but there are no signs of this. Instead he made his stories his erotic world. He used them to avoid reality, to make a world he was safe in and could control.'

This sounds like a scared, cowed man, frightened of life, I said. So how, then, did he have the courage to travel around Europe in a time of great upheavals and danger? 'Maybe he was not aware of the danger,' replied Myrto. 'In his head he knew what could happen, but I don't think he was courageous. He had no sense of reality.'

The phone rang and Myrto answered it, switching seamlessly into fluent French. When she returned I asked whether, after all her research into his personality and writing, she actually liked him as a person?

'Yes, I like him because he was special, I am attracted to people who are different,' she said. 'He was something, he was a character and he was so transparent.' But didn't she find his incessant complaining and self-pity grating? 'Of course, but you must never forget that he was very, very unhappy throughout his life, and though he became very famous, rich and successful, it was never a real cure for loneliness. He was alone almost all of his life.'

In his diaries and letters Andersen always seemed to be surrounded by friends, dining every night at a different house in town or out at the theatre, so one might not automatically think of him as lonely. But Myrto was right, it is one of his defining characteristics. Like Gerda in 'The Snow Queen', Andersen 'understood the word "alone" and knew how much there was in it'. From the moment he left Odense for Copenhagen he was alone in the world.

That self-reliance is, I think, part of what made him such a determined and successful traveller. He was accustomed to loneliness and though he often travelled with a friend, his two most rewarding trips – the trips where he seems to have best left

behind the petty anxieties of his day-to-day life – were this one
and his trip to Portugal, where he also travelled alone. Without
a companion to whinge at and bore with his various ailments
and fears, he seems to have just got on with things and coped
so much better; by looking outward at the world, he found a
brief inner peace.

Myrto generously offered me the use of her driver the next
day to see a couple of Andersen-related things outside the city
– one of which was the monastery at Dafne (which, I discovered, now sits beside a six-lane highway with a BP petrol station
as a neighbour, and was closed for repairs, just as it was when
Andersen was there), the other, a statue of a stone lion.

'It was strangely impressive to find [it] here, in this desert,'
Andersen writes of this enigmatic statue in *A Poet's Bazaar*. 'With
the exception of the feet, the lion is whole; the expression of
the eyes intimates that a cunning hand has wielded the chisel.
The mane is only partly executed. Strong creeping plants wound
up around its sides, as if they would bind it to the grave it
adorned.'

'No one knows about this statue,' Myrto told me. 'It is in
Kanza near Peania and I only know about it because I used to
take my children up there to play when there was nothing else
there. The poor lion has a cage around him now, but he used to
just stand there out in the open. I remember when I first saw
the cage I couldn't help but cry a little. He looks so sad now.'

The lion did indeed look rather glum when I saw him the
next day, propped up on his crude concrete replacement 'legs',
his nose hacked off. Andersen was right though, his eyes do have
a certain charisma.

As he stands admiring the lion Andersen hears a local herdsman
singing a melancholy song from within a nearby house. Inside
he meets the man and his wife; their small son plays in the
doorway. The boy's name is Demetrius, and Andersen gives him
a coin, reflecting afterwards: 'That dark cabin was his paradise;
the marble lion his riding-horse: his mother had often placed

him on its back, whilst she gathered heath-berries by the walls of the ruined church.'

Beside the lion I was pleased to see that both the tiny chapel (dedicated to St Nicolai, and now rebuilt) and the large olive tree he also mentions are still there. As for Demetrius' house, I assume this is the ruin – little more than some stone foundations – that stands near by.

Kanza is a fair drive out of Athens, and Andersen had reached it on horseback. 'I have a great talent to be an excellent rider,' he wrote to a friend, 'but I have no wish for you and your sister to see me on a horse with tall Greek hat and billowing silk tassel. Yesterday I rode for five hours in a row, but I can also feel it now.'

Having once tried to ride myself, I can attest that it is one of the most terrifying mistakes one can make. Nothing would ever induce me to mount so much as a Shetland pony ever again, not even with a St John's ambulance on standby, but here was Andersen romping off across the rugged Greek countryside with no decent medical facilities this side of Vienna. Very impressive.

He had taken lessons from Prokesch von Osten, the Austrian ambassador to Greece. Prokesch was a figure of great gravitas who had written two books about Napoleon. So smitten was Andersen by this mighty statesman that he dedicated an entire chapter of A Poet's Bazaar to lavishing praise upon him – listing everything from his schoolboy talents as a swimmer and skater, to his military record, even at one point describing his taste in home furnishings. He then quotes Prokesch's poetry at length, writing of this 'handsome, powerful man, with dark expressive eyes'. Reading on, you soon discover one possible explanation for this hagiography: Prokesch is an Andersen fan. '. . . He was requested by the company, after dinner, to read one of his poems. He promised to comply; but first he took a volume of Chamisso's poems, and read those of mine which Chamisso has translated; he read them with such effect that they sounded like music . . . He and his lady seemed to be fond of my "Eventyr" in particular, and begged me to write more soon.' A sure way to Andersen's heart.

That same day Andersen and his party met a cavalcade from the royal court which included a striking young woman, with jet-black hair and a 'daring carriage'. Andersen gushes that, 'She darted like a beautiful vision through the wood – like the Queen of Grecian elves! She was the daughter of the hero Marco Bozzaris, the most beautiful woman in Athens, and one of the ladies of honour to the Queen of Greece.' This is a notable celebrity sighting. Her father was a legendary rebel leader who died during a battle in northern Greece in which 1,200 of his men defeated 12,000 sleeping Turkish soldiers. The date, 20 August 1823, had gone down in the annals of Greek history and the name of Bozzaris carried as far as America – which, as with Europe, was in a state of 'Greece fever'.

Andersen encounters his daughter twice more and I do believe he starts to develop one of his periodic heterosexual crushes on her: '. . . She follows her young queen like the beautiful genius of Greece; her long, dark eyelashes are set like silken fringes over her fiery eyes. She is beautiful as she rides on her noble horse, and she is beautiful when she tarries so that we can fully see her face . . . Among the many different pictures that my memory has brought from Greece, Marco Bozzaris' daughter is the beauteous ideal of the daughters of that land.'

As I had been leaving Myrto's I asked if she knew anything about the column he refers to in *A Poet's Bazaar*. She shook her head and chuckled, 'You know Andersen; who knows if the story was true or even if there ever was such a column.'

I hoped to find a clue at the Museum of the City of Athens on Klathmonos Square. In a former life this was the humble 'private gentleman's summer villa' that Otto and Amalia lived in when they first arrived in the city as they waited for their new palace to be built. This is where Andersen was introduced to the young royal couple, after much lobbying and several, clearly very annoying, last-minute cancellations (Diary, 7 April: 'Waited the entire evening to be called to the king. It didn't happen. Desire to leave tomorrow for Constantinople. – Sensual wild disposition').

King Otto finally received Andersen with gratifying warmth, as he records with satisfaction in *A Poet's Bazaar*. 'The King and Queen showed me a kindness and favour which, in connection with the inward prepossession I had felt for the royal pair in that new, flourishing Greece, made the impression of both indelible in my heart.' The Queen, he notes, is 'young and hand-some; she has an aspect of mildness and wisdom'; the king, meanwhile, 'appears very young, but somewhat pale and suffering; he has lively eyes, and there is a very mild and amiable expression in his features.' Having waited all this time you would think Andersen would have prepared some scintillating conver-sational gambits, but he records that they talked about the rela-tive beauty of the Greek and Italian mountains, and how many ships he had seen in Syra. He also has to shout as the king is, apparently, stone deaf.

He sympathises greatly with this young couple, exiled from the heart of European cultural life to this desolate backwater: 'It is no happiness to reign in Greece. How much they have given up by living here! How many troubles must inevitably touch the King's heart for this people, and this land's sake! He who reigns alone in a devastated classic land, rich in noble monuments; alone with a people – well – I know them too little to pronounce upon them – but I love not this race. The Turks pleased me far better; they were honourable and good-natured.' He notes that when Amalia and Otto first arrived in Athens, the Queen was given a bouquet of potato flowers by the people – potatoes had only just arrived in Greece and were deemed the most exotic blooms available. All in all it must have been quite a comedown from the idle luxury of Bavaria.

As an inveterate snob and royalist, Andersen went to great lengths to wangle introductions to monarchs and aristocrats on his journeys. In the back of his 1845 almanac, for example, is a list of all the kings of all the kingdoms – plus the princes and the principalities – of the countries he hoped to visit during the year, as well as the names of their wives and their birthdays. He planned his regal stalking with military precision.

His strident, unquestioning royalism can probably be traced to his childhood in Odense, which was also home to Crown Prince Christian. Andersen's mother often worked at the palace and he himself played with the young Prince Fritz (later Frederik VII) as a child. He had further contact with the Danish royal family as he grew up, being presented to Fritz's father – later King Christian VIII – at the time when he was doing his turns at the homes of the well-heeled to raise money for his Copenhagen adventure.

And then there are the persistent rumours that he was actually the *son* of King Christian VIII and a noblewoman, Elise Ahlefeldt-Laurvig – rumours that have fuelled several treatise over the years. The most notable was Jens Jørgensen's *H.C. Andersen: A True Myth*, published in 1980. Jørgensen claims that Andersen was born to Elise in Broholm Castle after an assignation with Christian, then crown prince.

How else do you explain Andersen's extraordinary high self-esteem? Jørgensen asks. Why does he write in his autobiography, 'there *lay* here on April 2nd 1805 a living weeping child' instead of saying he was 'born'? Why was his mother so protective of him to the extent that she forbade teachers from hitting him, and excused him from work when he came home crying – an extraordinary indulgence for a woman of her class? Then there was the 'unusual' interest shown in him from such a young age by the royal family and the fact that the anecdote about him playing with Fritz as a child only appeared in Andersen's first autobiography, which wasn't intended for publication. It was omitted from all the other editions. Why on earth should successive kings have given money – to fund his education and early foreign trips – to this mouthy urchin from Odense, the conspiracy theorists ask, unless he was one of the family? Also, it is well known that Christian VIII fathered illegitimate children, including a girl who was given away to a servant a year earlier. Then there was the large cache of coins, hoarded by Andersen's grandparents, but rendered obsolete after the collapse of the Danish economy in 1813. Where else might they have come from, if not as a gift from the king to finance his illegitimate son's upbringing? Plus we know that Anne Marie fostered children; might Andersen not just have been a rather special foster child?

A more recent biographer, Alison Prince, revisited Jørgensen's theories, placing great emphasis on the fact that in 1842 the king gave Andersen a ruby ring with thirty diamonds. 'It seems odd,' writes Prince, 'that such a notable gift should have been bestowed for no particular reason. No birthday was being celebrated, no rite of passage marked – or was it?'

The ring, so the theory goes, was a bribe, or a 'welcome to the family' gift. It was at this stage that Andersen was told the truth about his parents. By way of evidence, Prince states that Andersen's recent stories, notably 'The Emperor's New Clothes' and 'The Princess and the Swineherd', 'had started to express a satirical disrespect for the court . . . Andersen was a loose cannon which urgently needed to be chained down.' The story he was working on at the time, 'The Ugly Duckling', can be read as a codified declaration of his secret identity, particularly the famous line: 'It doesn't matter if you are born in the henyard so long as you have lain in a swan's egg.'

Opponents of the theory point out that all of this is circumstantial. What's more, if Andersen and his dipsomaniac mother had the slightest inkling that he was to the palace born they would never have been able to keep it to themselves. She would have blurted it out and it was his greatest dream to be of noble birth – as a child he had fantasies along just these lines. In his autobiography, *The Fairy Tale of My Life*, Andersen writes that: 'I continually heard from my mother that I was brought up like a nobleman's child.' He would hardly have written that if he had been sworn to secrecy by the royal family, but nowhere does he raise any such suspicions (nor, while we're at it, does he give any evidence to support the *other* rumour – that his father was Nicolas Gomard, his French godfather who, by all accounts, sewed his oats like Odense's answer to Mick Jagger).

This would be enough to dismiss the theory entirely, but for one thing. Andersen was, actually, extremely good at keeping secrets. His bisexuality was one rather notable example of this (although you could argue that he was in such complete denial of it that it doesn't count as a secret), but there is another instance that I know of where he held his tongue, despite severe temptation to do otherwise.

The incident took place in 1845, at a time when Andersen's plays had virtually been hounded off the Danish stage by the villainous Ludvig Heiberg. He hatched a cunning plan to circumvent the Heiberg mafia, submitting a play to the theatre under a pseudonym. The play, a comedy, was accepted by Heiberg, Johanne took the leading role, and it ran for sixty-one performances, during which time Andersen only told his close friend, H.C. Ørsted, and the Collin family that he was the author. This must have been a sweet satisfaction to Andersen, but he never went public with the truth. When the rumour spread that it was he who had written the play, people dismissed the idea for the very reason that they believed he could never keep such a secret.

Not bad, eh? I grant you that knowing that you are the son of the king is of an entirely different magnitude, but it is fairly good evidence of Andersen's inscrutability. Indeed, I might even begin to convince myself were it not for the fact that, as recent research has confirmed, Christian VIII wasn't even in Denmark at the time Hans Christian was conceived, while Lady Elise was performing on stage in a concert in Odense on the day he was born.

Oh well, nice try. I am sure Andersen would have relished the intrigue.

★   ★   ★

The building that houses the museum of Athens is, as Andersen says, an unremarkable early-eighteenth-century, two-storey house. One ground-floor room houses a scale model of Athens in 1842, built in the late 1970s. From this I learned, among other things, the location of Dr Ulrich's and Prokesch von Osten's houses (both long gone but they once stood close to the new university buildings on modern-day Panipistimiou); and the former location of the Boukourus Theatre, a little out of town to the west. But of the pillar there was no sign.

While I was inspecting the model I got talking to another visitor, a large, bear-like man called Demetrious – an academic who was working on a history of Athenian place names over the last 2,500 years (which put my unstructured meanderings into perspective). Demetrious, like virtually all the Greeks I met, was friendly and eager to help. When I told him about the column he offered to have a look in his various books on the city when he got back to work. I rang him the next day and could hear the disappointment in his voice when he was forced to admit he could find no reference to it. 'Bye bye, friend', he said sadly. 'Anything at all you need, you give me a call.'

Upstairs, much of the mansion is given over to the living quarters of Otto – a little piece of eighteenth-century northern Europe in which Andersen would have felt immediately at home. The walls are hung with various portraits of the dim-looking royal stooge whose reign was already causing dissent in 1841. 'Certain it is, that the Greeks do not favour these strangers; but during my stay I never observed any visible signs of dislike,' Andersen writes. Had he hung around a little longer the signs would have been all too visible. A peaceable insurrection in 1843 forced Otto to abandon his Bavarian cronies and create a new constitution but, by 1862, his time was up and he was left with no choice but to abdicate and return to Munich. Ironically, the British replaced him with George I, the son of the then Danish king, and, therefore, according to the conspiracy theorists, an indirect relative of Andersen.

Alongside the picture of Otto looking every inch the Bavarian in-bred, is the requisite portrait of Byron – the spit of Rupert Everett – there in recognition of his sterling PR work for the cause of Greek independence. Byron's death in 1824 at Mesolongi pretty much determined the blueprint for the Romantic hero and, as with all young men of a sensitive, arty disposition, Andersen had been a great fan. In 1825 he had, rather improbably, likened himself to the club-footed, sexual adventurer. 'Read Byron's biography,' he wrote in his diary. 'Oh! He was just like me, right down to his love of gossip, my soul is ambitious like his, contented only when admired by everybody, even the most insignificant person who will not do so will make me miserable.' He was delighted when, in 1838, Byron's widow wrote to him after she read about his childhood.

That night I was determined to escape my hotel room and sample some of the city's nightlife. Though Andersen was still in his mid-thirties when he came to Athens, he was not what you would call a raver. 'At home by 5.30 every evening,' he had written a couple of months earlier in Rome. 'I am tired of reading and constantly glancing at the clock to see if it isn't past nine yet so that I can go to bed and sleep my way to another day!' Aside from the odd evening with Prokesch von Osten or Ross, things were much the same in Athens.

In this way Andersen conforms perfectly to my Pigeon People theory. Pigeons develop to maturity far quicker than other birds as a survival mechanism, which is why you never see any baby pigeons, but the point is that some people do likewise. That is why it is virtually impossible, for example, to imagine the likes of Margaret Thatcher, Alfred Hitchcock, Albert Einstein, Yasser Arafat, Humphrey Bogart or Barbara Bush – my quintessential Pigeon People – as teenagers. They were born middle-aged.

I *have* seen pictures of Andersen as a relatively young man, of course – looking callow, lanky, fragile and foppish – but, as with many Victorians, he seems to have slipped directly from his early

twenties into his early fifties. Though he remained child-like in so
many ways, he never had the luxury of an experimental teen period
(unless you count writing poems about dying babies); he was too
consumed with survival and climbing the class ladder. He never
seemed to let his hair down and when he found himself among
groups of men of a similar age, as in Rome in 1833, he appears
to have been the butt of their jokes.

Being a bit of a Billy No Mates myself in Athens, I was not
even in the happy position of having friends to be ridiculed by
but, steeling myself for the inevitable stares, I put on my best
shirt – the 'Scacchi shirt' as I had come to think of it – and hit
the glamorous streets of Kolonaki.

About four hours too early.

It soon became apparent that in Athens only the younger
Saturday-night crowd venture out much before midnight. I felt
very, very old and very, very lonely. So this is why Andersen
never bothered with nightlife, I thought to myself as I trudged
back across town, my lonely walk interrupted only by an alarming
ambush by three goose-stepping soldiers with pom-poms on
their clogs, and yet another sleazy old man.

This was the third time that a dishevelled, middle-aged man
had approached me while walking on the streets of Athens.
Before, I had reacted by suddenly finding something completely
fascinating to look at on the other side of the street, but this
time I decided to get to the bottom of it all. Were these men
selling something? If so, what? Drugs? Women? Pom-pom clogs?
The approach was always the same: 'Excuse me, sir, do you know
the time?'

This time I answered, and lingered in what I thought was a
significant manner. The conversation went like this:

Him: 'Where you from?'
Me: 'England.'
Him: 'London.'
Me: 'Kind of, yes.'

Him: 'I've been in Manchester.'

Me (unsure of the appropriate response to this bombshell; was it a drug reference?): 'Oh.'

Him: 'Very rainy.'

Me: 'Yes, not like here. Ha ha!'

Him: 'Chmmerummerghunnger.'

Me: 'Pardon?'

Him: 'Chummerungnergummer.'

Me (puzzled look): . . . ?

Him: 'Chemical engineer.'

Me: 'Oh, erm, journalist.'

Him (already making to leave): 'You not speak Greek?'

Me: 'No, but, hey, wait, where are you going? What do you want?'

If he was gay, was he put off by my wedding ring? Or, worse, did he just not fancy me quite so much close up? Was it the fact that I said I was a journalist that put him off? In the end, I preferred to conclude that he was sizing me up for a mugging but thought twice when he got a closer look (unlikely in largely crime-free Athens, but still).

Back in my hotel room I caught the last part of a made-for-TV version of the story of Odysseus with an all-star Hollywood cast that included Isabella Rossellini as Athena, Armand Assante as Odysseus and – well, I'll be! – my close personal friend Greta Scacchi as Penelope. It was rather good actually, and the perfect preparation for my impending journey across the Aegean.

During my days in Athens I had encountered significant frustrations while trying to arrange my onward journey. Andersen had sailed back to Syros – where he was briefly held on suspicion of being a German spy, until he brandished his letter of introduction from Prokesch von Osten – and from there to Smyrna (now Izmir) in Turkey, but this route no longer operated.

Clearly, after my Malta debacle, flying was not an option, but

at that time of year many of the ferry routes were not yet up
and running, at least not regularly, and I risked being stranded
for up to a week if I chose the wrong one. The official Greek
ferries website claimed there was a fast boat to the island of
Chios that took a couple of hours, and from there I could take
another hour-long boat ride to Turkey. However, when I asked
about this in the high-street booking office, the girl behind the
desk seemed able only to repeat the phrase: 'This is not in my
computer.' Instead the journey would take a dozen hours and I
would have to stay two nights on Chios before making a connection to Turkey.

What's more, there was no ferry service from Izmir, north,
along the Turkish coast and through the Dardanelles to Istanbul.
I was determined to arrive in Istanbul by boat, however, and to
do this I would have to catch a bus across the western part of
Turkey to Bandirma, and take a high-speed catamaran from there
to Istanbul. It was as close as I could get to Andersen's route
using public transport. All I would be missing would be the
journey by boat along the coast of Turkey, and Andersen had
done that by night anyway so I was able to convince myself that
was no great loss.

I consoled myself further with a visit to Athens' market (there
is nothing like a good market to raise the spirits, I find), full of
salted cod, severed cows' heads and great curtains of some uniden-
tifiable animal's intestines – not the place to come with an ouzo
hangover. Big, hairy men in bloodstained aprons shouted at each
other, hurled octopi like mop heads and brandished strangely
rude pigs' trotters. In my daze I nearly tripped over some escapees
from a bucket of snails. I looked down to see a writhing
gastropodous mass, several of which were making their way diligently up the side of the bucket to the rim, their bid for freedom
signalled by a *schluup* as they lost suction, followed by the
inevitable crack as they hit terra firma.

The market was a detour from my final attempt to solve, once
and for all, the Christ's column mystery. A guidebook reference to

a church called St John of the Column sounded promising. The map had the church opposite the market, but the small chapel there didn't have a column protruding from its roof.

From here I wandered among some of Athens' less picturesque back streets, home to Indian mini-marts, shops selling Taiwanese alarm clock and cafés with outdoor tables populated entirely by pot-bellied old men wearing proper jackets and hats and playing backgammon. I had been heading towards the National Theatre, in the vain hope that it was the same theatre that Andersen had visited, but it was clearly built more recently.

Eventually I found a street called Theatrou, dominated by a monolithic twentieth-century office block. If there had been an ancient column here, in what is now the home of the city's Indian, Pakistani and Arabic communities, it would surely not have survived the architectural brutalism of the 1970s. And anyway, I had by now wandered far too far from where the map in my guidebook said the Church of the Pillar was. Something wasn't quite right.

As it transpired, I had walked past the church several times in the last few days without realising it. My guidebook had the wrong address for St John's. I found the right one in a phone book and hurried there straight away. Sure enough, there, opposite a Chinese laundry, was a small chapel, locally known as Agios Ioannis Kolonastis: not much more than a breeze-block hut, with a weathered Corinthian column – believed to be part of a temple to Apollo – protruding from its roof like an improbably grand chimney. This, surely, was the pillar Andersen had seen. In his day it would have stood alone and been visible from the steps of the theatre. The gates were locked, but by a freak coincidence, just as I was reeling off a roll of film that I was sure would prove of earth-shattering importance to Andersen scholars, a group of Danish tourists filed past, lugging their suitcases behind them.

I grabbed the last straggler, and pointed towards the column: 'Look!' I said in Danish, with what must have been a disconcerting, wild-eyed intensity. 'That's Hans Christian Andersen's column!'

'Oh, aha, good,' said the poor girl, casting a desperate eye towards her friends who were rapidly disappearing around the corner.

'He wrote about it in 1841. It was the column Christ was tied to when he was whipped!'

'But wasn't that in Palestine?' she asked, dubiously.

'Well, yes, but it was washed up every night, you see and . . . and . . .' But she had already hurried off, smiling politely, clearly in fear of her life.

This monumental discovery (as yet, I still await the various honours due me from the Danish and Greek governments) seemed a fitting way to end my stay in Athens. Later that afternoon I boarded a rattling local train, which took me out through the city's dust-covered suburbs to the harbour at Piraeus where I would board my slow boat to Chios.

On the train I re-read the final part of Andersen's Greek chapter in *A Poet's Bazaar*. This takes the form of another short story – 'The Pact of Friendship' (sometimes called 'Friendship's Covenant'), which I referred to earlier – a romantic tale about a Greek boy, his adopted sister and another boy who at one point saves the girl from drowning – set against the backdrop of Turkish occupation. The story is unremarkable but for one incident, in which the two boys pledge eternal friendship before the eyes of God in church. It seemed to me, for all the world, like the first gay wedding in literary history. See what you think (the brother narrates the story):

I had my best clothes on; the white fostanelles [pleated skirt] folded richly down over the hips; the red jacket sat tight and narrow; there was silver in the tassel on my fez, and in my belt were knife and pistols. Aphtanides [the other boy] had on his blue dress, such as the Greek sailors wear. A silver plate with an image of the Virgin hung on his breast, and his sash was as valuable as those which only the rich nobles wear. Everyone saw that we two were

about to celebrate a festival . . . We knelt on the steps of
the altar, and Anastasia [the adopted girl] placed herself
before us.

We all three said our prayers in silence, and she asked
us: 'Will you be friends in life and death?'

We answered: 'Yes.'

I do realise this *isn't* a gay wedding. In fact, what Andersen is
describing here is the wish fulfilment of the kind of sibling love
triangles he had sought to create with Riborg and Christian
Voigt, and Louise and Edvard Collin. Most peculiar.

Andersen counted 100 houses in Piraeus but, after the Corinth
Canal was finally finished in 1893 (having been started in AD 62
– quite a delay even for Greek builders), it would become one
of the world's busiest ports. Today it remains the main hub for
ferries to the Greek islands. I lugged my rucksack around the
perimeter of the harbour, past massive, shiny new catamarans and
luxury liners until, finally, I found my ferry, a rusting hulk, sagging
in the middle like a Thelwell pony.

I had paid for a cabin all to myself, so thought it odd that
there was a 'Bed Number' on my ticket. If there were two or
more beds in the cabin, what did it matter whether I slept in
one or the other? Perhaps it was meant for crew use only, I
thought to myself. It was only when I came to collect the key
from the purser that the full enormity of my predicament became
apparent: I had been assigned a bed number because I was to
share the cabin WITH A COMPLETE STRANGER.

Andersen shared rooms, and even beds, with strangers all the
time during his travels – remember the awful Englishman? – but
how anyone could think that a grown adult male would wish
to disrobe, close his eyes and go to sleep in a room no bigger
than a walk-in larder with a strange man doing the same in a
bed just an accidentally outstretched arm's length away from their
groin is beyond me. My mind whirred into a fevered overdrive,

calculating the various scenarios that might ensue, none of them very appetising.

I went to the cabin, but it was empty. I lay on the bed, my restlessness hardly soothed by the fact that the boat was full of fifteen-year-olds who, bless their little hearts, found endless amusement in knocking on my door and running away again. Every five minutes or so an announcement in Greek would come over the tannoy to set my mind buzzing further still – what if these were important safety messages? Ding, dong! 'On no account must passengers flush the toilets twice within the same minute, as the ship will sink.'

With the boat having now left Piraeus and just as I was beginning to think that I had been lucky and I would have the cabin to myself after all, there was a rattle at the door. This time, instead of some stifled giggling followed by the patter of Nikes, it heralded the arrival of my partner for the night, a walking B.O. bomb no more than five feet four inches high, by the name of Carlos.

Despite the Spanish name, Carlos was Greek. Through the magic of mime, for he spoke no English and my Greek was a little rusty, I deduced he was a lorry driver (either that or a fairly inept nightclub dancer), and that he was taking some fridges to Chios. My Marcel Marceau moves proved limited when it came to my turn to explain how I came to be sharing his cabin, so I offered him some mineral water as a distraction and we sat drinking and staring at our shoes.

I don't know what was going through Carlos' mind ('Good grief, this guy has B.O.!'), but I was delaying the awful, inevitable moment when I would have to prepare for bed. We wouldn't arrive in Chios until 3.30 that morning and I was exhausted – what with the excitement of the column hunt and everything. Eventually, I yawned ostentatiously and got up to go to the bathroom. Suddenly Carlos sprang up too.

Here we go, I thought.

Though he was short, Carlos was powerfully built and I didn't fancy my chances should he decide to attempt a deflowering. Visions of Hamburg shop windows flashed across my mind, and I braced myself for a struggle. Maybe I could fell him with my washbag, or gouge his eyes with my biro – enough to allow me a precious second to scramble for the door, for, surely with the noise of the engines, no one would hear me scream.

Carlos wanted to offer me his toothpaste.

At 3.30 a.m. the harbour at Chios was thronging with people, perhaps as many as a hundred, there to meet loved ones and friends. I made my way, blearily, to my hotel on the seafront and slept the sleep of a man who didn't have to listen to Carlos' snoring.

The next day, with nothing of an Andersen nature to occupy me (he never set foot on Chios – the island was at that time still reeling from a notorious massacre of 27,000 locals by the Turks), I hired a car and went for a drive. As it turned out, this gave me as authentic an impression of nineteenth-century Mediterranean life as anything I would experience on my entire journey. There was little traffic, other than the odd walnut-faced man on a donkey; the countryside was largely undeveloped; and the island was garlanded by pink blossoming almond trees, ancient olives and a spectacular hilly coast. And, in terms of perform-ance and comfort, a knackered Daewoo Matiz was as close as I would probably ever get to mid-nineteenth-century horse-drawn transport too.

The following morning the weather had taken a turn for the worse and the sea was on spin drive. Even for a footstepper as obsessive as myself, the fact that Andersen had also experienced a rough crossing on this leg of the journey was little consola-tion. 'The women shrieked, the ship creaked and I thought about my Danish friends, those I expected never to see again,' he writes. 'Greek women clung to each other and howled. On the deck children lay as if half dead, and the sea smashed over the ship so that everyone was soaked.'

As I read this over breakfast I looked out at the yacht masts, ticking like metronomes in Chios harbour. Beyond them was the rusty biscuit tin on which I would sail to the Turkish town of Cesme; it appeared to be undergoing *USS Enterprise*-type last-minute emergency repairs.

As I made my way around the harbour to face my watery doom, the dead-man-walking scenario was completed by a doleful stray dog that followed me all the way. The church bell tolled. It didn't ring, it tolled. I chewed my potent anti-seasickness gum until my entire mouth was anaesthetised. At least I wouldn't taste the vomit, I thought.

I did though. No amount of gritting my teeth with my eyes fixed on the horizon could quell the inevitable chunderous spew as we rocked and roiled across the sea towards Turkey. The final straw came when a man with dirty fingernails, eating a souvlaki that appeared to be filled with pus, came out of the toilet next to me, carrying the full force of his effluvial odour in his slipstream. I caught the toilet door just as it was closing, but failed to make it to the robustly patinated lavatory bowl in time, delivering last night's kebab into various pockets of my corduroy trousers.

Chapter Eight

CONSTANTINOPLE

If the resonances of classical Greece had appealed to Andersen's intellect, Asia stirred his fantasies. 'I saw a part of the world of which Egypt's Moses was also vouchsafed a sight – that part of the world where Christ was born, taught, and suffered,' he writes in *A Poet's Bazaar*. 'I saw the coasts from whence Homer's songs were sent forth over the world. The East, the home of adventure, was here before me; and I was now about to set my foot upon its soil.'

Disembarking at Smyrna (modern-day Izmir), his senses are assaulted by this alien continent. He sees minarets for the first time in his life; there are women dressed 'in Muslim veils, so that only the tip of the nose and the dark eyes were to be seen . . . I met a half-naked black boy driving two ostriches before him with a stick. Each of them looked like a worn-out trunk on stilts, to which was fastened a dirty swan's neck. They were two ugly creatures, but they produced an effect in the picture. A scent of musk and myrrh streamed out of several of the shops; others were filled with fruit . . . Clothes from three parts of the world made the most varied show here. All tongues jangle amongst each other – Arabian, Turkish, Greek, Italian.'

Though there is a risk of plague, he can't resist diving headlong into this extraordinary city, the birthplace of his beloved Homer. He plucks a rose from the poet's grave and presses it in his copy of *The Iliad*. While out walking he meets the Danish consul, Herr Jongh: 'I presented myself to him as a Dane, and we were soon walking arm in arm through the long street.' Jongh is on his way to Constantinople ahead of Andersen and promises to smooth the social path for his arrival.

I also wanted to see something of Izmir; it was not a city I had ever imagined visiting, but I have a perverse attraction to big, ugly cities that no one ever goes to unless they have to (hence the visits to Jakarta, Ulan Bator and Sheffield I mentioned earlier). I had arranged to meet someone from the tourist office for a brisk whisk through the city's sights before catching my connecting bus to the harbour at Bandirma, from where I would take the high-speed catamaran to Istanbul.

My guide, Mustafa, led me, first of all, to the three-thousand-year-old fort overlooking the city. 'Built by Alexander,' he told me. He then pointed to a small cluster of red roofs below us, which stuck out amid the otherwise relentless concrete clamour of modern-day Izmir. 'Roman Agora.'

He wasn't what you would call a talker, Mustafa.

Though it grieves me to say this of what was the only city on my entire journey to offer me a guided tour for free (and lord knows I tried with the rest), Izmir is phenomenally unprepossessing. Most of it was destroyed by the Greeks on their way – or so they thought – to reclaiming Constantinople decades after Andersen's visit. It boasts a Rio de Janeiro-esque location beside a magnificent crescent-shaped bay, but apart from the taxis nothing seems to be much older than thirty years.

Even Mustafa seemed bored and drew my attention instead to a nearby tree. From it he plucked a small green nut, which he invited me to taste. I guess it was a betel nut, but it didn't seem to be ripe. I munched on it for a while, but in the end had to spit it out when he wasn't looking. Except he was looking. Very embarrassing.

As for the location of Homer's grave, nothing is known of it today. In fact, the only sign that one of the greatest story tellers of antiquity was born in Izmir is a monument on a roundabout, somewhere. Mustafa was unable to find it. Then again, this shouldn't surprise me. There is no mention of a visit to Homer's grave in Andersen's diaries until much later in Vienna, when he notes: 'Homer is buried near Smyrna and had lived on Chios.' He made the whole thing up.

Izmir's charms, such as they are, lie mostly in the hairbrained methods employed by its citizens to make a buck. Down on the harbour front there was a man with a set of bathroom scales, offering to weigh passers-by for a small fee (presumably they kept their clothes on). Another enterprising young man had somehow managed to tether five balloons a few metres out in the water and was inviting people to shoot them with an air rifle. A shoeshine man almost lured me into what would certainly have been an unhappy transaction for both parties with an elaborate preamble, in English, in which he asked about my home, my family and my favourite football team before finally addressing the subject of my shambolic footwear. 'Very dirty,' he said.

I did, however, have a pleasant surprise when I proffered a bunch of notes to a taxi driver, only for him to return half of them, saying, 'Too much.' From a similar experience with a water taxi in Constantinople Andersen concluded that 'the Turks are the most good natured and fair dealing people I have ever encountered'.

Of course it may have been because he simply couldn't be bothered to carry all that paper around. Turkish notes are not worth a great deal. Even paying to take potshots at water-borne balloons requires the exchange of a quantity of currency ordinarily reserved for a house purchase. One million Turkish lira bought me a manky doughnut from a street vendor, for instance, and I couldn't help wondering how this affects a society as a whole. The Turkish version of *Who Wants to be a Millionaire?* was unlikely to be quite as suspenseful, for instance, and I seriously doubt whether the lower denomination coins are worth more than the metal they are made of. It was like a scene from *Brewster's Millions* when I tried to offload my remaining lira leaving the country a week later.

From Smyrna Andersen sailed aboard the French steamer *Rhamses* up the Aegean and into the Straits of Marmara, together with yet another exotic cast of passengers. As they come aboard, everyone is first required to discharge their firearms and then place their weapons in a pile in the middle of the deck. Andersen – who obviously had no weapons himself – positions himself by the gunwale to best observe the passing scenery, admitting it also affords him the best view of the veiled Turkish women who so fascinate him: 'They were eating, and had therefore taken the veil from their mouths. They also regarded me. The youngest and prettiest seemed to be a merry soul: she certainly made remarks about me . . .' A young Turkish man jokingly admonishes Andersen for gazing upon the women without their veils, and indicates that the husband of the women is beginning to take umbrage. Andersen resolves to charm the man via his young daughters, something I would be inclined to think might actually make matters worse, but, he writes, 'If a man would be on good terms with parents, he must make friends with the children.'

He targets the man's youngest daughter and coaxes her with some fruit, but the eldest girl turns out to be the 'more tame' of the bunch and they soon become 'the best of friends'. 'I placed her on my lap,' he writes, 'and she took hold of my cheeks with her small hands, and looked up into my eyes so affectionately and confidentially, that I was obliged to speak to her. I spoke Danish, and she laughed so that her little heart hopped within her.' Andersen's technique works; the father orders the girl to bring them some coffee, which they sip together on his rug as they sail past a 'dark and ruinous' Gallipoli on the coast of Greece.

The girl has a clay jug in the shape of a horse with a bird behind its ear. 'Had I been able to speak Turkish with her, I should at once have made a story about it for her,' Andersen writes. This ability to conjure a meaningful and amusing narrative from inanimate objects was one of Andersen's greates talents, of course. 'It often seems to me as if every hoarding, every little flower is saying to me, "Look at me, just for a moment, and then my story will go right into you," and then, if I feel like it, I have the story,' he once wrote. After his death an acquaintance recalled going for a walk with him: 'For the first quarter of an hour he would not talk much, but shamble along, poking his stick into every hole and corner, or touching with it every odd thing that lay in his path. Then something would attract his attention – a bit of old glass, a faded flower, or a half-eaten insect – no matter what it was, he would stop, and pick it up, touch it tenderly, and bend over it caressingly, and then, in a kind of low, half regretful tone, he would begin and tell the story of its life, its joys, its sorrows, and the sad destiny which brought it to the spot where he had found it.'

Indeed, a few paragraphs on in *A Poet's Bazaar*, he actually does concoct a story from the girl's clay jug, imagining that the horse has grown large enough to bear the two of them and take flight: 'and when we touched the earth there amongst myrtles, she had become a full grown girl, charming as she was in child-hood, and glowing as the sun that had poured his beams into her dark eyes . . .' Had her father known this was what the odd-looking foreigner was thinking, I suspect he might not have been quite so generous with his coffee.

Their boat arrived in Constantinople on 25 April at five o'clock in the morning. Andersen is transfixed by the city's spectacular setting on the Bosphorus Strait and Golden Horn, and its fairy-tale skyline of minarets, palaces and towers. 'Constantinople was poorly lit,' he wrote in his diary, 'but extremely large and fantas-tical. It was a Paris, combined with Venice and the phantasy.'

Then as now, Constantinople – renamed Istanbul by Atatürk in 1935 – was the only city in the world to straddle two conti-nents. A new liberality – the so-called *tanzimat* or 'reform' era – had allowed freedom of religious worship, making it perhaps the first truly secular, multicultural city in the world. The then Sultan, Abdül Mecit, welcomed foreign visitors, and Andersen was among the first wave of modern tourists to arrive.

Looking a bit lost at Bandirma harbour while waiting for the boat that would take me to Istanbul, I had been adopted by a group of very charming, female architecture students, all of whom spoke English. They joined me on the catamaran to Istanbul, where they were attending a weekend of seminars on steel construction techniques. And so it was that I found myself bonding over the unlikely topic of the glory of Camden Sainsbury's, as we sped through the darkness towards one of the most exotic cities in the world.

My hotel, the Pera Palace, is legendary in these parts, boasting Hemingway, Agatha Christie (who wrote *Murder on the Orient Express* in the room next to the one I was given), Garbo and the spy Mata Hari as former guests (although, you have to wonder, if everyone knew Mata Hari was a spy, how did she actually get to do any spying?). It was built by the Orient Express company for their passengers but these days it is the very definition of faded grandeur. The bar in particular is awash with period atmosphere. It is the kind of place where arms dealers rub shoulders with impecunious eastern European royals seeking funding for a revolution; where caviar smugglers do deals with Russian Mafiosi in exchange for pink diamonds and Volga virgins; and where dishevelled backpackers live out absurd Graham Greene fantasies.

Having checked in at around eleven at night, I hit the streets, desperate to find somewhere to eat. So desperate was I that all my usual restaurant criteria were rashly cast aside. I headed up a steep side street opposite the hotel and into the first restaurant I could find: a hideous one-room joint, with bizarre Portacabin-style plastic cladding on the walls. *Who Wants to be a Millionaire?* was playing on a fuzzy, wall-mounted TV screen in one corner, and around it were gathered most of the staff. Another waiter arrived shortly after me, carrying food for them all, which he had bought from a nearby takeaway. Not the most encouraging sign.

There was no menu, and my Turkish being rather rusty, it seemed that I would have to be satisfied with getting what I was given. This turned out to be a bowl of deep-fried breaded fish – more like bait actually. These were not quite small enough for me to comfortably crunch whole, yet neither were they large enough for de-boning to be a practicable option. I asked for bread; the owner laughed.

If the restaurant had been full I would have paid and left at that point, but I was the only diner, sitting in full view of the staff and owner, all of whom were watching me intently.

Millionaire built to its climax and to enliven the atmosphere I started shouting out random answers. By coincidence, I got the first four questions right, despite not having a clue what they were about and the staff began to regard me with a mistrustful awe. Following a quick calculation, I reckoned I could have walked away with the tidy sum of no less than two pounds eighty.

I gave up on the fish about a quarter of the way through – if I wanted to eat skinny pin cushions I would . . . actually I don't know what I would do if this were the case, but the whole scenario is pretty unlikely, so let's just say I had little confidence that any of the waiters could administer the Heimlich manoeuvre, and leave it at that. I asked for a receipt; the owner laughed. It had been one of the worst restaurant experiences of my life (and that includes the time vomit came out of my nose after a rogue knickerbocker glory in the Haywards Heath Wimpey *c.* 1977).

After the modern concrete wasteland of Izmir, it was satisfying to be back in a city so evidently layered with history as Istanbul. Wandering around the steep side streets of Pera and Galata (modern-day Beyoglu) the next day, the nineteenth-century Constantinople Andersen described was still much in evidence. Here were the traditional Turkish gravestones that he drew, as well as the ancient churches and Italianate balconies – many of them clinging on by their fingertips – he described.

Pera and Galata used to be the Italian and Jewish quarters of the city. Foreign visitors have traditionally stayed here since the early nineteenth century, and many European embassies and consulates remain as a reminder of that time. The area's main landmark is still the Galata Tower, a fat, round fourteenth-century lookout tower, a bit like the cardboard core of a toilet roll, with a conical roof. These days there is a lift that takes you to the top floor – now a nightclub, which, though empty when I visited, was instantly recognisable as the type of place where middle-aged men with gold jewellery and double-breasted suits dance awkwardly with women old enough to be their first wives.

As I lolloped further down the steep Galata hill towards the Atatürk Bridge, I passed a man pushing a trolley laden with elaborate, cream-filled desserts for sale, and another carrying trays suspended by chains and loaded with tumblers of Turkish tea. Just before the bridge were stalls piled with bananas, rubber bands, TV remote controls and mountains of pistachios (the entire city is carpeted with their shells). I bought a pastry from one of the glass-sided carts that you see throughout the city. It seemed to have been made, not from a mixture of flour, eggs and water, but an inedible by-product of the construction industry. I placed a sample in an envelope and posted it to NASA for possible use in the space programme.

The incessant hawking of goods continued on the bridge itself, where fishermen traditionally drape their curtain of lines into the Golden Horn – the modern equivalent of the iron chain that once stretched across the Bosphorus to keep out enemy fleets. Surely no fish can pass beneath this bridge alive.

The fishermen were vying for pavement space with men selling cigarettes, mobile phone cases and pirate copies of Office 2000. One enterprising soul was pushing a photocopier on a hostess trolley, powered by a generator on the lower shelf. Kebab grills, roasting chestnuts and candy-floss machines provided the olfactory backdrop – along, of course, with the choking fug of diesel fumes.

Down by the harbour-side small boats contravened every fire safety rule imaginable with skillets of frying fish balanced precariously over open fires as they rocked in the wake of the elderly passenger ferries that ply non-stop from Europe to Asia. Watching this I was accosted by the rapacious postcard sellers who cling

like limpet mines to tourists as they wait for the ferries. Some
people simply will not take a 'Look, please, I do not want to
buy any postcards, I have already bought loads of postcards, now
will you please leave me alone before I kill you NOW!' for an
answer.

Walking on I passed a man tending to a large white rabbit on
a small folding table. Beside the rabbit was a tombola. What in
God's name was this all about? I stood and watched for a while.
He was raffling the rabbit! I bought a ticket, but the rabbit and
I were not to be. A short while later a man walked past dressed
in a comedy convict's costume, replete with black-and-white
stripes and a ball chained to his leg. Not one passer-by batted an
eye. Then, a street-cleaning machine drove past. Nothing unusual
in this, except that it was driven by a woman in her early twenties in full make-up and dressed in platform heels, a long fur coat
and sunglasses. It was as if she had been en route to a party, but
had decided to tidy the place up a bit on her way.

You come to believe anything is possible in Istanbul. It is a city
of relentless surprises, most of them amusing, some surreal, a few
alarming. Andersen felt the same way: 'Every street is a masquerade
ball, so different from anything other European cities can boast.' It
is, in other words, the ultimate poet's bazaar – a place to go shopping for extraordinary sights and experiences.

'What a swarm of beings!' he continues. 'In the midst of the
crowd there was a Bulgarian peasant dancing, with a calot on
his head, miserable sandals on his feet, and a long sheepskin jacket
on his back. He dances like a bear springing up on its hind legs.
Another Bulgarian played the bagpipes for him. Six or eight
brown, muscular fellows were dragging along large blocks of
marble, which were placed on round pieces of timber. They
continually cried out their "Make way!" We met Armenian priests
with crape fluttering from their hats. Now sounded a mumbling
song; a young Greek girl was borne along to be buried; she lay
in her customary clothes, and with her face uncovered in the
open coffin, which was ornamented with flowers. Three Greek

priests and two little boys with lighted candles walked before. What a crowd! What tumult!'

Later, he sees children playing with a dead, skinless horse: 'Five or six little Turkish boys, almost naked — one, at least, has only a turban on — skip about, with a wild howl, around a dead horse, which, as the hide is flayed off, lies there in a corner, reeking, and stretching its four legs in the air. A naked brat gets up to ride on the raw animal, and then jumps about: it is an original sight!'

As with Naples, the sultry heat and exuberance of the locals also set Andersen's sensual antenna twitching. 'An Asiatic sensuality is torturing me here. Oh, how I'm burning with longing! . . . The rowers had powerful, naked arms sticking out of their wide, gauze-like sleeves,' he wrote in his diary. 'No one rows more beautifully than the Turks . . . Feeling sensual.'

And just when you think Istanbul can't get any more intense, you come to the Grand Bazaar — Andersen's 'city of bees, where every bee is an Egyptian, an Armenian, a Turk, a Jew'.

The Grand Bazaar's 5,480 retailers put any modern shopping mall to shame. If you have a pressing need for painted ostrich egg lamps, Iranian caviar, Viagra, clockwork dervishes, fabulous carpets, gold, counterfeit Louis Vuitton, mother-of-pearl chess sets, jewelled daggers, clothing with tempting labels such as 'Fashion', 'Design' and 'Trend' and pointy-toed slippers, this is your one-stop shop. There is no Swarovski, no Benetton, and no monster dildos; it is, however, the only place in the world where you can still buy those patchwork leather pouffe covers that your hippie aunt had in the 1970s.

The Bazaar remains one of the world's great crossroads. I sat for while in a corner café, watching faces from virtually every ethnic background pass by — from Georgian to Somali to Californian. And if you close your eyes it really does sound like a beehive, with the buzz of a hundred deals being done; the air being sucked through a hundred teeth.

Andersen bought a fez, and so did I.

In the Bazaar, he who hesitates is fleeced. You soon learn not to make eye contact with any of the traders; their powers of persuasion are relentless, they will leave no ploy unturned in order to get your attention, hold it and then sell you something against your will. One man selling Turkish Delight and candy noticed that I was writing something down, and cornered me: 'Hey! You write my name? My name Eddie Murphy! You see my face? Ha, ha!' I looked at him. The resemblance was uncanny. I don't know who his resemblance was uncanny to, but with six billion to choose from I am sure there must be someone – although it wasn't Eddie Murphy.

Stallholders kept approaching me in French for some reason, and I began to sympathise with Andersen's frustration at being constantly mistaken for an American. That said Americans can actually be useful in the Bazaar. I soon learned that if you can get in the slipstream of a group of them, their outgoing, guiless-ness acts as a kind of minesweeper through crowds of touts. By such means I was eventually able to find my way out of the labyrinth, although the American family I had attached myself to began to cotton on towards the end – I think they thought I was stalking their daughter. Leaving the frenzied commotion of the Bazaar, with its cacophony of 'Yes, my friend, you say hello? You buy? You buy carpet? Why not?' I felt like a pearl diver surfacing for air.

I spent the rest of the day touristing round the sights of Sultanahmet beneath a watery spring sun. I visited the Topkapi Palace, the museums and the Hippodrome, with its ragbag collec-tion of ancient obelisks, pyramids and columns. The female slave market that Andersen described with hushed horror – 'A young mother gives the breast to her child, and they will separate these two' – is no longer there (I mean the building that housed it, obviously I was hardly expecting to find women on sale), but the palace, the Blue Mosque and the Haghia Sophia remain the city's great tourist attractions. Outside the latter, much to my delight, I came across a man selling tickets to see the whirling dervishes.

Chapter IX, 'The Dervishes' Dance', is the great setpiece of *A Poet's Bazaar*. Witnessing this arcane religious ritual was one of the most memorable experiences of Andersen's life and he referred to it for years afterwards.

The chapter begins: 'It is well known that the Turks, speaking generally, regard all imbecile persons as inspired by a divine spirit. Therefore the insane have places in the mosques. The terrible Isani are objects of respect and awe; the Dervishes are included in this category by reason of their dance, which is a positive self-torture. They chew a sort of intoxicating root, which increases their delirium.'

Ever since his childhood visits to Odense's lunatic asylum with his grandmother, madness had held a morbid fascination for Andersen. A visit to a dervish cloister was irresistible and, in fact, he saw the dervishes dance twice in Istanbul. On the first occasion he travelled with an old dervish hand who had seen them dance in Tripoli. On the journey across the Bosphorus he tells Andersen about the experience: 'In order to see the wildness of the Isanis, we ordered a Moorish slave to bind a living goat outside the house where we stood. As the crowd came on, the Moor was directed to kill the animal: he stuck his dagger into its neck, and then sprang in behind the door. The goat sprawled in its blood, and at the same time, the howling Isanis pressed forward. One of them thrust his hand into the bleeding wound, lifted the goat up with a howl, tore it in pieces, and flung the bleeding entrails up against the walls of the house. The whole crowd fell upon the animal, and literally ate the flesh, hide and hair!'

They travel to the Ruhani cloister in Scutari (modern-day Üsküdar). On entering, Andersen hastily cuts the straps that hold his boots to his trouser bottoms, while his companion merely pulls a pair of slippers over his boots. '"This is a good person!" said the Turk to my servant,' he notes proudly. Though there is no live goat action, what they see is shockingly visceral nonetheless: '. . . there came a man whose appearance was calculated to excite the greatest horror I have ever as yet seen any human being capable of producing . . . I have never seen a man in whom insanity was so clearly visible in the eyes as this . . . One of his hands was withered, probably his own doing; his mouth was one bleeding wound; both his lips had lately been cut off, so that the white teeth grinned; it was horrible to look at! His mouth began to bleed, his eyes rolled, and the veins in his forehead swelled. The dance became more and more violent, and yet not one moved an inch from his place. They seemed not to be men, but machines . . . My companion whispered to me: "For heaven's sake do not laugh, or we are undone! They will murder us!"

"'Laugh!' I replied: "I am ready to weep! It is afflicting – it is shocking! I cannot bear it any longer!'"

He flees for the door, professing to loathe this kind of brutal, grisly violence, which is odd, because his stories are full of this kind of thing. Andersen specialised in the arbitrary, no-consequence violence kids love but that parental watchdog groups routinely condemn in everything from Roald Dahl (who, interestingly, had Scandinavian parents) to *The Simpsons* (whose creator, Matt Groening's, surname, now I think of it, sounds suspiciously Nordic to me). You find it in 'The Wild Swans' where we meet 'a group of hideous ghouls who took off their tattered garments . . . and then dug down into the freshly made graves with their skinny fingers, and tore the flesh from the bodies and devoured it'; and in the soldier chopping off the witch's head in 'The Tinder Box'; and in the gothic horror of 'The Marsh King's Daughter', in which we learn that the eponymous Helga's 'greatest pleasure was to dabble her white hands in the blood of horses slaughtered for sacrifice; in her wild freaks she would bite the heads of the black cocks which the priest was about to slay.' Her saviour, a Christian priest, meets his end when a robber 'swung his iron club with such force at his head that the blood and the brains were scattered about'. All rather Ozzy Osbourne, isn't it?

Andersen's second visit to a dervish cloister comes the next day with the Mewlewis dervishes in Pera. This is a rather better class of whirler: 'Everything was clean and handsome: the view through the open windows to Scutari and the distant Asiatic mountains certainly contributed much to the embellishment,' he writes. 'It might almost be called graceful . . . The dance, in unison with the low sameness of the music, gave the whole the character of silent insanity, which affected more than disturbed the spirits. The whole performance could scarcely be called edifying: it appeared to me like a sort of ballet, whereas the dance of the dervises in Scutari remained in my memory like a scene in a mad-house.'

I knew that it was still possible to see dervishes in shows laid on for tourists, but the whirling dervish timetable is about as reliable as that of the Greek ferries. Before arriving in Istanbul I had been told that they only whirled from June to September, and so had given up hope. That tickets were on sale, then, was very welcome news, even more so when I realised that this particular 'whirl' would take place in the very same dervish cloister in Galata that Andersen had visited.

So overcome is he with the whole dervish experience that Andersen doesn't seem interested in finding out why they dance or the background to their beliefs, but I thought I would at least try and learn more. Browsing the Internet in a back-street café, I found a site dedicated to dervish culture and their Sufi religion. It was based close to the Blue Mosque, in a third-floor office above a restaurant and, though I turned up unannounced, I was warmly welcomed by Mehmet, who seemed to be in charge.

We sat down by a window overlooking the minarets and I asked how the dervishes were thought of in Istanbul today. This prompted a monologue on the Sufi faith of such length and intensity that it suggested he had been waiting all his life to be asked this very question. 'Atatürk closed us down but in the 1950s we re-opened. Today it is not a problem. Last five years, not a problem. After 9/11 we have had more and more interest. Terrorist groups, fundamentalists don't like us because Sufism uses music, we dance, we are very sociable, for them this is not

the Saudi Arabian way. We are not Arabs, we came from Asia.'
That was the gist.

The whirling, Mehmet explained, is a ritual of the Sufi religion, which in turn is a spin-off – if you can excuse the double-
pun – of Islam. It was founded by the son of Mevlana Muhammed
Celaluddin-i Rumi, a Persian poet, born in what is now
Afghanistan. He fled the Mongol horde in 1219 for the Anatolian
city of Konya (still a dervish hotspot), where he wrote the
Mathnavi, often called 'the Persian Koran', and gathered various
disciples. He renamed himself Mevlani (Our Leader), and founded
what remains a refreshingly tolerant branch of Islam.

I asked if Mehmet was a dervish. He laughed. 'Me? No, I
could never be a dervish, it takes time and patience, real Sufis
study very hard. It is not just about learning the dance.' He then
lowered his voice, leaning forward conspiratorially. 'You know,
you are very, very lucky today because just over there is the first
female dervish to dance together with the men. She is French.
She has had problems with the newspapers in France and does
not want to be in the newspapers, she is not for tourists, but I
can go and ask her if she will talk to you. If she says yes, it is a
big chance for you.'

It seemed ungrateful to refuse this scoop and so, a few moments
later, a slim, middle-aged French woman with her brown hair tied
back into a ponytail came and sat beside me. She was wearing
jeans, a black leather jacket, a souvenir sweatshirt from Jerusalem,
and a serene smile. Around her neck was a gold pendant in the
shape of a whirling dervish. Her name was Lily, she was a painter
from Lyon, and from the awed expressions on the faces of the
people who had gathered around us, it was clear that I was in the
presence of someone special. I was wholly unprepared to conduct
the interview that everyone now seemed to be expecting. So, to
give myself a moment to think, I asked Lily how she came to be
a dervish.

She commenced her elliptical explanation in a dreamy voice:
'My thoughts, my beliefs put me far away from Christian roles.

I was feeling more wild, like a bird in Islam. Islam is the most free religion that I know. There is no hierarchy, like in Christianity. I became a Muslim in 1988. Ah, it was a beautiful time in Üsküdar, winter time, but sunny like summer. After three years of Mevlevi living, my thoughts and my behaviour put me little by little away from that to Sufism.'

Judging by the look of horror that passed across her face, my follow-up question instantly betrayed my ignorance: 'How did it feel to be the first female dervish?'

'Oh no!' cried Lily. 'It has always had women dervishes, but they have practised separately. Now I dance with men, but I am not proud of it, oh no, because it has been naturally. It is stupid to be proud. Stupid! How can you be proud? Istanbul is Istanbul, you break the rules. And anyway, when I dance with the men I cannot reach communion. When women dance with men it is more folkloric like in Galata. I hate to go to Galata, because it is a show, you see.'

Folkloric, it turned out, was just about the worst insult that could be hurled at a dervish dancer, implying a kind of dervish-lite show put on for tourists. Lily, quite clearly, was the real deal, committed to the whirl with all her heart.

I asked about the dancing and its meaning. Was it a kind of trance? Or were they, as Andersen believed, mad? 'Trance is very wrong, yes, no. Dancing is the Mevlani prayer, a meditation. He discovered that everything must turn, the flowers, the atom, everything has cycles for living. I don't like the word trance, because that means you have lost consciousness, but my religion does not accept losing consciousness. We cannot drink alcohol. It is a frenzy of love, it is joy, not ecstasy – no, you must be careful of this word. God brings us to this frenzy, it is a happiness that explodes outside of your body.'

From then on virtually everything Lily said served only to compound my bafflement. Each answer raised more questions, but before I had a chance to clarify one point, she had leaped to another. My eyes were beginning to glaze over.

Have you ever woken from a daydream and found yourself a spectator on your own life? It happened to me now as Lily was suddenly struck by an idea. She was on her way to see her Sufi guru, Feyzullah, for the first time in three years (she was visiting Istanbul for one day, she lives elsewhere). I had inadvertently convinced her that I was deeply interested in Sufism and she decided there and then that she would take me along to meet him so that I could learn more. 'He is the chief of Semazan, he symbolises the moon in the dervish ceremony, he is the teacher, the under chief. He is so wonderful. It is Mevlani who has brought you and me together today, Michael, I can feel it. He means it to happen.'

Before I had the chance to think up a plausible excuse, Lily and I were walking arm in arm at high speed down past the high walls of the Topkapi Palace to catch a ferry to Üsküdar, on the Asian coast of Istanbul.

On the ferry Lily began to fill in a few biographical gaps. She told me that her husband had died twenty-one years before, and that they had no children. She had worked as an archaeologist and, latterly, a painter. As the boat chugged past the University of Istanbul where she had studied for two years, she became emotional and blew kisses to it. She frowned when I told her that I had doubts about the existence of God. 'But God created everything, God is love, he decides everything. He has decided that we should meet today!'

We drove in a taxi for about half an hour alongside the Bosphorus, passing frilly, faded Ottoman mansions and peaceful waterside villages, and beneath massive suspension bridges. Soon I was being ushered into the front room of a dervish moon master – who lived in an apartment above a laundrette – and finding myself on the receiving end of yet another enigmatic, rambling monologue.

Lily had fallen into Feyzullah's arms like a long-lost sister, playfully patting his bulging tummy, before introducing me as her 'friend'. We sat in a room furnished with the kind of sofas and chairs you find abandoned in lay-bys, with a view of the Bosphorus.

Feyzullah was a rotund man in his mid-forties, with matted grey hair and stubble, wearing an old red check shirt and jeans. Not your typical spiritual leader then; more like a Turkish Alexei Sayle. I asked how important it was that Lily was the first female dervish to dance with men. Wrong question.

Lily flashed warning eyes at me. Feyzullah launched into his sermon: 'There is no difference between men and women in Islam spiritually. Mevlani in his works says openly that woman is the creator on a mystic logic basis, but after the prophet Islam they create the separation. In reality there is no order but Koran.'

Ah, I see, that's clear then. So what is the difference between Islam and Sufism?

'The duty of a Sufi is to enlighten people. The real Islam is to work for the knowledge twenty-four hours, for the happiness of others. This is the aim of the Sufi. He must work with his ego, control his desire and be very modest. If he does not have this in his character he is not Sufi. All the prophets are the brothers descended from God, God is one. Since then there has been an almost political development, with all religions, but in Sufism the concept is the reality of the prophet. Mevlani was a mystical successor, not a prophet. He said that you must forget everything around you and liberate yourself from your ego and your possessions. He says that reality will not appear before the church bells stop and the minarets come down. You must forget what has come after in the name of Islam and read the Koran. Drink from the source, not from the sea.'

'Wow,' I said, 'that sounds pretty revolutiona—'

'Whirling is an expression of love,' Feyzullah continued unabated, 'a kind of prayer. People think that the whirling brings the person to a divine ecstasy – this is wrong. The whirling is a real concept. If there is no action inside it is only physical. This is just automatic whirling, for tourists.'

'Oh, what, you mean like the folkloric dervishes in Galat—'

'The first to give real rights to women was Mohammed, but those who came after him in the name of Islam, they did not follow Mohammed's teachings. Women can whirl, and they can whirl with their brothers, just not in front of the public.'

'Ah, *oui, absolument.*' Lily nodded vigorously.

'Why is that?' I asked.

'Well, what does Mevlani say?' asked Feyzullah; he wasn't expecting an answer. 'In his book he said if anybody put his treasures in front of a thief he will lose them.'

Onward he ploughed for about an hour, my questions sliding off him as if he were coated with Teflon. Each time I looked up from my notebook to ask a question, he took it as a sign that I had finished copying down his last speech and commenced another. He was a conversational glacier; I, a minor topographical feature to be flattened.

He embarked on a long fable about how Sufis got their name. The word Suf means wool in Arabic, and if you add an 'i' it means 'to be like it'. 'Take a piece of wool and throw it up in the air,' he said, 'and it comes down slowly because it is not heavy. Gravity can not touch it. This is the start of Sufi logic. A person must not be in the gravity of earthly desire, he must not be pulled down by ego and possessions.'

Feyzullah was beginning actually to make some sense and, in fact, I suspect Sufism has an awful lot going for it in terms of its tolerance, compassion, emphasis on education and anti-materialism. But I was not in the market for a new faith, or any faith come to that. It would also appear – and I can only hold my hands up to this – that when it comes to issues of spirituality and mystical depths, I have the attention span of a hyperactive goldfish. But how to extricate myself from this tricky situation? How does one cut and run on a guru without hurting his feelings?

I eased my right hand into one of my trousers pockets and, silently, began to press keys.

My phone rang!

'Sorry, I'd better just answer that,' I said. Feyzullah stopped speaking, and eyed my phone with distaste. 'Hello. Yes. Oh. Oh *no*!' I said, pulling a face. 'Yes, yes, I'll come at once. Bye.'

I stood up. 'I'm awfully sorry but I really have to go. My hotel is on fire.' It seemed to work. A taxi was called and I made my escape.

The next day I went along to the Galata dervish cloister – renamed after Atatürk's Sufi ban, the Divan Edibiyati Müzesi museum – to see for myself the dance of the dervishes. Feyzullah and Lily had led me to expect a kind of Disney tourist show. I was in for a surprise.

I arrived early and entered the cloister through a low, unmarked stone archway that led into an open, paved courtyard in front of a two-storey, wooden clapboard lodge. To the left was a mausoleum of Sufi sheikhs containing six enormous sarcophagi, each covered in felt, trimmed with silver brocade and sporting the traditional dervish headgear – a kind of felt turban that looks like those cartoon cranial bumps Tom and Jerry sometimes inflict on each other. Next to this was a small, ancient Sufi cemetery, with its slender gravestones topped with stone turbans, lying amid the undergrowth, beneath dusty cypress trees. Blossoming rose bushes and lounging cats were scattered about.

Other than the strays, the courtyard was empty. This timeless, spiritual oasis in the middle of Istanbul was perhaps as close as I could ever hope to come if I were to summon the spirit of this great traveller, Hans Christian Andersen.

I sat, on a bench in a corner of the very courtyard that he had described in A Poet's Bazaar. Looking around at the wooden cloister, the flowering roses and the timeworn tombs, there was little to indicate that a century and a half had passed and, for the first time, I rather wished it hadn't. What would it have been like to meet this lonely nomad? Could we have understood each other?

I looked up from my shoelaces to see a tall, thin man, dressed in a black frockcoat, black trousers, bulbous boots and a top hat standing on the other side of the courtyard. He had entered through the stone archway on my left as I had sat staring at the ground with my face in my hands, and made his way in hesitant strides across the cobbles, pausing here and there to bend forward and inspect the roses, read a headstone and take some notes. He looked like a great, flightless bird, comical yet melancholy, self-conscious and dignified.

We were alone for a moment, this improbable phantom and I. He glanced over in my direction, but didn't seem to see me. And then he was gone.

There was so much I wanted to ask him; so much I wanted to share with him. Most of all I wanted to put my arms around him, give him a big hug and tell him everything was going to be all right; to stop fretting so much. Time would win his battles for him. Immortality was assured. I could spend a lifetime speculating on his impulses and fears, and never come closer than I was right now, sitting among the tombstones he had drawn, but even had I met him I doubt I could have reached beyond that haunted façade.

A few people began making their way inside the temple and I followed them into a graceful octagonal room with a large, galleried 'dance' floor in the centre, open right up to the ceiling. This was the first dervish temple, or *Derga*, built in Istanbul on the orders of Iskender Pasha, the governor general and imperial guard chief of Sultan Beyazit II, in 1491. The current building was restored in 1972, but it still oozed history and mystery.

Judging from the way they greeted each other, many of the hundred and fifty or so people gathered to watch the ceremony were clearly regulars. This was the first sign that, despite being a ticketed event, which, by definition, ought to imply it was bogus (you don't pay to watch Mass in a Catholic church, after all), this wasn't entirely the tourist show I had been expecting.

The congregation ranged from men in suits to old ladies in headscarves, young children, plus a smattering of people who were obviously tourists. I took my place in the front row behind an ornate, knee-high balustrade next to a woman in her early

thirties. As we waited – for about half an hour – for the ceremony to begin, I tried to make conspiratorial 'Cuh, they're a bit
late, aren't they?' kind of faces, but she didn't respond. Eventually
five wooden chairs were placed on one side of the arena. A jolly,
old sailor lookalike in a green, sleeveless cotton smock and green
trousers entered and made a speech in Turkish. When he had
finished, six musicians – two recorders, one large drum, twin
bongos, a mandolin and a kind of lap-based mandolin – entered,
dressed in long black robes.

The Cap'n began a speech in English: 'For our foreign guests,
today is a very good day. We remember Mr Vujay Tossoy, one of
our greatest composers, and expert especially in military song and
mystical music so we will have a short concert. Immediately after
the concert we will go to our whirling ritual.'

In his diary Andersen describes Sufi music 'as if a musically
gifted savage had heard an Italian singer for the first time and
now in his own way was trying to imitate him'. It reminded me
of the occasions in infants school when we were all given an
instrument to bash while the teacher played the piano. Except
here there was no teacher on piano. When the concert finally
ceased, there was no applause. It was followed by some a cappella
vibrato warbling – the kind of music that sounds exotic and eerie
when you pick it up late at night on Long Wave just left of Radio
Luxembourg, but live is something of an endurance test.

The musicians filed out of the room.

Just as I was beginning to lose the will to live, we got our
first glimpse of a dervish. A man in white robes, a cummerbund
and dervish turban entered the arena and solemnly laid a fluffy
red fleece on the floor. Six more emerged wearing long black
capes, turbans and leather slippers, among them the Captain
(who I think was representing the moon – Feyzullah's role), an
Omar Sharif lookalike (the only one, incidentally, who came at
all close to looking deranged throughout the proceedings), and
a couple of the musicians who had played earlier, one of whom
could easily make a living as a Keanu Reeves-alike. They all

bowed to the fleece. A straggler, dervish number seven, followed a few moments later. The Captain kissed the red fleece and then stood on it, the rest knelt and kissed the floor. One man began chanting.

They walked, taking one deliberate step at a time, followed by a three-second pause (rather like the walk I do in museums to suggest I am deep in thought), anti-clockwise around the ring, bowing to each other when they reached the red fleece. They repeated this one more time and then lined up in their original positions. Throughout it all, the musicians played a tuneless lament from the balcony above.

On an inaudible command, the dervishes shed their black cloaks in unison, revealing white shirts, white cotton jackets and black cummerbunds above pleated white skirts. They folded their arms across their chests, placing each hand on its opposite shoulder, bowed for the umpteenth time and walked, one by one, over to the Captain. He kissed them tenderly on the back of the neck and then slowly, rather majestically in fact, the spinning began.

With a seamless, swaying smoothness each dervish moved away from the Captain, uncrossing their arms as they went, and then began turning away, off around the arena. One arm was raised higher than the other; one hand pointed down; one, rather elegantly, pointed up (Omar remained on the sidelines, scowling). Their eyes were closed, their heads tilted languorously to one side. As they built up speed, to around 45 rpm, their skirts, which were weighted like expensive curtains, span outwards and upwards like a fairground ride. It was unexpectedly graceful, hypnotic almost, but made quite a draught.

The dervishes' footwork was especially impressive. Their feet were a blur yet, Omar aside, they never once looked like they might lose their balance or have a dizzy spell. (Back in my hotel room that night I had a go at spinning myself, and nearly broke the television. Hardly surprising, dervishes train for three years to get this right.)

It was all as Andersen had described in his diary for 30 April 1841:

> They held their arms out and span on the spot and around each other; two in the middle, the others around them and around themselves. A priest walked very quietly among the two in the centre, and the others. They were very pale, one could hear song and music. Suddenly they stopped and stood still for a moment, then the same dance began all over again. They seemed lifeless like dolls, they were representing the movement of the planets.

I later learned the significance of the clothes: The hat, called a *sikke*, represents a tombstone, to remind the dervish that life is just a passage. The black cloak, or *tenure*, symbolises the material world, shedding it as they begin to turn signifies the transition to the spiritual world: the white shirts revealed beneath are a symbol of the shroud and of purity. The high priest, or *sheikh*, represents the sun around which the dervishes – the stars – revolve.

The correct name for the whirling ritual is *Sema* and it is based on the concept that everything in the world travels in a circular fashion, from the blood in our bodies, to the planets to the contents of an atom. By whirling, participants – *semazen* – aren't supposed to be trying to seek enrapturement, but they can get a little trancey if they achieve a state known as *Fenafillah* – a 'dynamic concentration' similar to the Hindu nirvana.

They span, giddyingly, for about twenty minutes, before slowly winding down, re-crossing their arms and bowing to a stop. After a short meditative break, they repeated the procedure twice more. Omar, the runt of the litter, joined in occasionally with some jerky, 'ranting tramp' spinning, much to the amusement of some Australian tourists sitting next to me, who giggled openly.

Finally, the dervishes knelt in a row on the far side of the floor. At this point events took a worrying turn. The Captain stood up suddenly and began chanting a prayer to which virtually everyone in the room except me and the Australians responded, holding their hands out, palms up. Embarrassingly, even the girl I had rolled my eyes at while we were waiting was chanting along. I suddenly felt like the hero in a 1950s sci-fi movie who finds himself in the middle of an entire village brainwashed by aliens. The Australians had stopped laughing.

At the end of the prayer, the Captain crossed the arena, turned, and bowed to the other dervishes, and backed out of the room. They followed in the same manner.

Outside the congregation gathered around a table of tea and cakes, as congregations do. I smiled and nodded at a couple of elderly ladies in the cake queue, and they smiled back. But though I had paid for a ticket, I felt like an intruder, and left after just four date muffins and a couple of buns.

That night in his diary Andersen records that he is feeling 'sensual' – his code for randy. This may have been down to the dancing, but he also mentions another meeting that might explain it: 'After dinner, a visit from a young, blond Russian fellow, Aderhas. He's from the Caucasus and staying here at the hotel, travelling to Egypt and then home over Copenhagen – feeling sensual.' The next day, he gives us perhaps more information than is strictly necessary: 'Sensuality is a thrilling, tingling through the nerves as you release a drop of your vitality.'

Good grief! Just what did he and Aderhas get up to in that hotel room? Nothing physical, I'm sure, but might it have been the beginning of something beautiful? After all, his diary entry a few days later reports that the two of them took what sounds like a very romantic evening stroll by the waterfront, with the floodlit minarets above them: 'The stars were twinkling in a southern sky. The moon was bright . . . The minarets stretched upward like colossal flowers of fire on white stems. It was a lovely sight out over the cemetery . . . The evening was so mild; it was a fairy tale . . . we walked beneath the cypresses. At nine o'clock cannon shots from all the ships and from the coast, so that the windows rattled.

Shot after shot.' Sadly, we hear no more of the Russian; he and Andersen were just passing ships.

After Constantinople, Andersen is, for a while, uncertain of his next step. The voyage up the Danube by steamship and, for the non-navigable stretches of the river, horsedrawn carriage, is rife with risk and he is in doubt up until the last minute. Upriver navigation of the Danube had only been made possible by the advent of steamships in 1830 and, though there were sailings to Vienna every two weeks, it remained a treacherous route.

On 2 May he writes in his diary: 'Disturbances in Rumelia, Thessaly and Macedonia. People say it would be dangerous for me to take the Danube route. I've a mind to travel home over Siros.' The entry ends with an odd juxtaposition of sex and death: 'Encountered another corpse today, a Greek woman. An Asiatic sensuality is torturing me here. Oh, how I'm burning with longing!'

The next day he is still fretting about the trip: 'Slept restlessly last night; anxious about the trip via the Danube; struggle and uncertainty. News has come today that the Austrian steamer *Stambul* has struck a rock in the Black Sea fifty-five miles east of Amasra. The Passengers were rescued . . . Thinking of taking the Danube route.' However, by the time he came to write up his almanac entry for the same day he had made up his mind: 'Decided to take the Danube route home.'

This was genuinely uncharted territory, and not just for Andersen. Thirty years *after* he travelled up the river, the French explorer Lejean wrote that less was known of the countries of the lower Danube than those of the Nile. 'If we were not killed,' Andersen writes in his diary, 'we should at least expose ourselves to a hundred annoyances.' But, he adds, 'it is a passage which, in anticipation, interested me in a high degree'.

Eventually, he hears from the Austrian Internuncio, Baron Stürmer, that he can accompany two Austrian officers, a Colonel Philippovich and a Major Tratner, who will be taking post and a large sum of money to Vienna. 'The voyage was therefore now fixed,' writes Andersen in *A Poet's Bazaar*, 'and from that moment all fear was gone.'

The fact that a man who travelled everywhere pushing a wheelbarrow of neuroses before him could countenance such a dangerous journey is still one of the most striking of all Andersen's many paradoxes. These days, when Richard Branson can fly you across Europe in the same time and for the same cost as your weekly supermarket visit, it is difficult to appreciate how massive an undertaking it was simply to reach Constantinople in 1841, especially travelling alone.

Even with all the luxuries and conveniences of twenty-first-century travel the journey was beginning to take its toll on me. Travelling by yourself has its benefits; you don't have to bother affecting an interest in shoe shops and modern art, for instance, but you do eventually begin a gradual slide towards insanity.

The most troubling manifestations of this are the endless, circular conversations you begin to have with yourself, initially in your head, then, after a while, out loud. Other side effects of travelling alone include delusional paranoia about things like the hotel staff rifling through your smalls and people talking about you in foreign languages, but there are more tangible risks too. Having yet again, in Naples, found myself at the mercy of a nefarious taxi driver who, if I hadn't complied with his request for a fare that was at least five times what it should have been, would almost certainly have beaten me senseless and left me as a pile of pulped matter on the pavement, I wondered how Andersen coped with this kind of thing.

My Greek Andersen expert Myrto had part of the answer when she said he travelled in a kind of fairy-tale bubble, as if the perils of the real world were something that happened to other people. Though he relishes fantasising about worst-case scenarios and is never afraid to turn the volume up for the sake of a good story, it could well be that he never really believed the dangers were as real or as threatening as even he made them out to be; either that or he felt some kind of divine immunity from them.

Writing in *The True Story of My Life* specifically of his decision to continue on from Constantinople up the Danube to Vienna (a journey of roughly 800 miles/1,300 kilometres), he gave one explanation of his peculiar bravery: 'I do not belong to the courageous,' he writes, 'I feel fear, especially in little dangers; but in great ones, and when an advantage is to be won, then I have a will, and it has grown firmer with the years. I may tremble, I may fear; but still do that which I consider the most proper to be done . . . I had a strong desire to become acquainted with the interior of the country, and to traverse the Danube in its greatest expansion. I battled with myself; my imagination pointed to me the most horrible circumstances; it was an anxious night . . . [but] from the moment I had taken my determination I had the most immovable reliance on Providence, and flung myself calmly on my fate.'

Old-fashioned fatalism is one explanation for how Andersen came to terms with the dangers of this leg of the trip, but it doesn't really explain why he wanted to risk everything in the first place. Surely Malta, Athens and Constantinople had furnished him with more than enough new and exotic experiences. Why was it so important for him to risk everything and continue?

Could it be that Andersen was driven onward through ever more dangerous territory and to take ever greater risks by a rogue strain of machismo? Andersen loved the idea that he was travelling further than his fellow Danes – particularly, of course, the other writers – and it gave him a kick that he would be the one to return to tell everyone about the amazing things he had seen. There was, for him, great kudos to be gained from this journey. In a letter to Henriette Collin, for example, he proudly boasted, 'Princess Carl of Prussia was in Sicily. It was my description of Malta that decided her also to make a visit there.'

But who in particular was he trying to impress? Certainly he had something to prove to Heiberg and the literary critics who had mocked him as a feminine fop. This would show them what he was made of, that's for sure. Throughout his life Andersen would do everything he could to impress the Collin family too, but, of them all, it was Edvard, Jonas Collin's middle son, whose opinion still mattered the most, even after all these years.

It was Edvard, not Jenny Lind or even Carl Alexander of Weimar, who was the abiding love of Andersen's life. Even though, by 1840, Edvard's marriage to the ever-tolerant Henriette had dampened Andersen's ardour considerably, he remained a focus of frustrated love.

Andersen first got to know Edvard in 1827 when he moved from the school in Helsingør to Copenhagen. 'Something in you drew me early on,' Andersen wrote to Edvard. 'Many things I respected and found attractive; you expressed an interest in me, and I wanted this interest to increase, I wanted to gain you as a friend, of a sort of which only a few exist.'

Just what kind of friend it was that Andersen sought in Edvard has provoked a great deal of speculation. Many Danish Andersen scholars have described their relationship as brotherly. But the truth, as betrayed by countless letters written by Andersen over the years, is that he was deeply in love with his benefactor's son. In one letter to Edvard, Andersen himself described the relationship as more than filial: 'My own dear Edvard! Oh how I am thinking of you! Yes, I am dearly fond of you! More than if you were my brother!'

Edvard, a solid, respectable and, I suspect, terrifically dull man, stubbornly refused to reciprocate. 'I, full of affection, threw myself upon him with my whole soul,' Andersen once wrote of Edvard, 'and he passed on calmly and practically through the business of life.' Edvard was an archetypal product of his class and education. His self-contained, methodical approach to life was the antithesis of Andersen's exuberant emotionalism, although that never stopped Andersen trying to capture his heart.

If you are looking for evidence of Andersen's homosexuality, you could make a fairly good case from his letters to Edvard, but in truth Andersen's feelings were rooted as much in his desperate need for affection and love as in physical desire. In letters written throughout the early 1830s he employed his entire arsenal of techniques, from simple declarations of longing: 'How I long for you, my dear Collin, long to speak to you from the heart and in friendship, alone, up in that poetical little room'; to promises of discretion: 'I will tell you, that I am so dearly fond of you, perhaps more so than you think; with all my soul I cling to you . . . Fear not, I have a loose tongue, but not concerning my own affairs . . . If only I could truly tell you everything'; to unbridled petulance: 'No one have I been so angry at as you! No one have I wanted to hurt as much, no one has brought more tears to my eyes, but neither has anyone been loved so much by me as you.'

Andersen did begin to get the message when Edvard announced his engagement in 1833 but even the letter he wrote offering congratulations was, in reality, yet another self-pitying tirade: 'Every day you distance yourself more and more from me . . . but my pride gives in to my love for you! . . . What is there in my character that you dislike? . . . I wish you well! In your new position you will acquire many friends but none who will love you as I do.'

Though he is often painted as the villain of the piece by Andersen fans (mostly because of his Stalinist approach to the editing of Andersen's papers after his death – removing all traces of his affection for men), you have to feel a little sorry for Edvard. The best he could manage in response was to offer Andersen practical assistance, which he did. In the early days, he would point out to him, for instance, that, actually, now might *not* be a great time to launch into a poetry recital – 'If you recite so much as a single poem I shall leave!' he once told him. Later he took care of Andersen's finances, even buying his lottery tickets for him (after a lifetime trying, Andersen won five hundred *rigsdaler* in 1873); and he acted as proofreader for many of Andersen's later works, transcribing and then editing his 1846 autobiography. Though he was actually three years younger than Andersen, Edvard seems to have adopted an almost fatherly role, offering Polonius-like advice and admonishments – often to Andersen's great irritation. He became Andersen's toughest critic; he clearly had Edvard in mind when a hen says to the Ugly Duckling: 'When I tell you harsh truths it's for your own good, and this way one can know one's true friends.'

Harsh truths were Edvard's speciality, as we have already seen from his critique of '*Agnete*' and *The Moorish Girl*, but it is not as if Andersen was particularly sensitive to his friend's needs either. When he heard of the death of Edvard's first child, a daughter, Andersen managed to turn the tragedy into a personal one in which he felt excluded from Edvard's grief and snubbed because he had forgotten to send him birthday greetings. To Jonas he wrote: 'Even if I am not fortunate enough to be among the friends to whom he turns for consolation in his sorrow, he might all the same, once this grief is relieved, remember me by writing a few words.'

A few years later, when Edvard suffered a second, terrible loss of a child, Andersen visited a few weeks afterwards to read his latest story – 'The Story of a Mother' – about a mother who goes on a quest to find the soul of her dead child. Hardly the most tactful choice; he had to be asked to stop as he had reduced Edvard's wife Henriette to tears.

The pivotal moment in their relationship came in 1831, with a desperate, pleading, all-or-nothing letter that Andersen wrote to Edvard while on his first trip to Germany. The letter was about a pronoun; its bitter consequences would rumble on for decades after.

In Danish, as in French, there are two pronouns for 'you' – the formal 'De' and the more personal 'Du'. Though 'De' is still used today in some circumstances – institutions, such as banks, still address their customers using 'De', for instance; and Danes just love it when an Englishman uses it – it is very rarely used in speech. Back in 1831, however, the very foundation of personal relations hinged on the use of these words. And when the relations are between an uppity poor-born poet and the son of the Minister of Finance their use became a symbol of class division, mutual respect and even, in Andersen's hands, love.

'Of all human beings you are the one I consider my true friend in every respect, please, be that to me always, my dear Collin, I do so need an open heart,' wrote Andersen. 'I have an important request, maybe you will laugh at me, but if sometime you really want to make me happy, to let me truly have evidence of your respect – if I am worthy of it, then – Oh! Please do not be cross with me – say "Du" to me! Face to face I should never have been able to ask you, it must happen now that I am abroad . . . I shall never ask you again, of course . . . Are you annoyed with me? You cannot imagine how my heart is pounding while I write this, although you are not here.'

He waited, agonising, for the reply. It came immediately. Edvard, desperate to keep a distance between the two of them, was against the idea for reasons he could not, or was not prepared to, articulate: 'There are many trivial things against which people have what I think is an innate dislike; I knew a woman who disliked wrapping paper so much that she was sick whenever she saw it – how does one explain such things? . . . Why this change in our relationship? Is it to give others an external sign of our friendly relationship? But that would be unnecessary and of no significance to either of us . . . Let us speak no more about it. I hope we shall both forget this mutual exchange.'

Fat chance.

Like a terrier with an old shoe, Andersen would return again and again to the 'Du–De' issue, both in his letters to Edvard and others; in his diaries; and even in his work. In 1833, feeling slightly contrite at the fuss he had made, Andersen wrote: 'Now I see clearly how right you were when you did not give in to my childish demand that we should say "Du" to one another . . . it has often made me cry, I have been more grieved than you think, but now I clearly see that it would not have been appropriate.' But when he sent Edvard his latest poetry collection he made clear again his desire to be on intimate terms: 'We know deeply each other's soul and thoughts, we share with each other pleasure and pain, and faithful heart knocks against heart. But the lips express the formal "De".'

In 1835 he wrote to Edvard on the subject again: 'At the moment no icy cold "De" comes between us, I say "Du", and your lips greet me with the same sound as you shall utter first in the next world. Oh, if only I were rich, we would then both fly to Italy, the wonderful Italy which I have not enjoyed at all. Oh, if only we were there together, if only for a month! Edvard, I have many young friends, yet I love no one like you . . .'

Thankfully he never actually sent this letter. Unfortunately, soon after, he did send this one: 'I am longing for you, indeed, at this moment I long for you as if you were a lovely girl from Calabria, with dark eyes and passionate glance. I never had a brother, but if I did I could not have loved him as I love you . . . God give that you become very poor and I very rich, distinguished, a nobleman. Then I would properly initiate you into the mystery, you would learn to appreciate me more than now. Oh, is there an eternal life . . . there we shall learn to understand and appreciate each other . . . there we shall be equal.' (In fact, part of this came true towards the end of Andersen's life, when he became very wealthy and loaned large sums of money to Edvard's children to buy houses.)

The 'De–Du' issue was immortalised in the autobiographical wish-fulfilment novel Andersen was writing at the time, OT (for Odense Tugthus – or gaol). Its two protagonists are Otto and Wilhelm – who are, essentially, Andersen and Edvard. In this instance it is Otto who has the hang-up about using 'Du' and Wilhelm who uses it more casually. On one occasion the two meet at a fancy-dress party. Wilhelm is dressed as a woman (how the alarm bells must have rung for Edvard when he read this); he approaches Otto, who doesn't realise who he is, and throws himself into his arms. 'The blood rushed to his [Otto's] cheeks when the fair one threw her arms around him, and laid her cheek upon his . . . Otto felt his heart beat as in a fever; it sent a stream of fire through his blood: he thrust her away, but the fair one continued to overwhelm him with caresses ... Of the kisses which Wilhelm had given him, of course, they did not speak; but Otto thought of them . . .'

Fifteen years later, in 1846, Andersen would rake over the coals of the 'Du–De' controversy all over again in 'The Shadow'. Here Edvard takes the role of the shadow, refusing his victim's pleas to use 'Du' in almost exactly the same words that he used in the original letter. 'Some people cannot touch grey paper without feeling ill,' says the Shadow by way of explanation. 'It gives me the same sort of feeling when you're familiar with me.'

Thirty years later Andersen was *still* banging on about it, but Edvard never did consent to their using the informal 'Du'. It was little consolation that Andersen managed to persuade Edvard's son, Jonas, to use it during one of their foreign trips together at that time.

Instead, Andersen was left to pounce on the rare crumbs of encouragement that occasionally spilled from Edvard's pen – most often when Andersen was a safe distance away, travelling. When he had heard how far Andersen had travelled in the letter he had written from Constantinople in 1841, Edvard was gratifyingly impressed: 'You are a damn good traveller! The way you have managed to carry through this journey is something not many others could have done, and if you haven't got courage then at least you have shown a firm determination, which is equally good; that certificate will be given to you by yours faithfully, who is not in the habit of flattering you.'

A measure of the enduring importance of Edvard's praise to Andersen is the diary note written the day he received the letter, 28 June 1841: 'Received from the Collins two letters that were so loving and filled me up with bliss, so that this was the happiest evening of the journey, I read them at least six times . . .'

All the dangers, inconveniences, hardships and expense of the Danube trip had been worth it for those few lines.

As it transpired, for the most part the fears and dangers that gave Andersen so many sleepless nights in Constantinople never really materialised on the last leg of his journey home. At one point on the river at Nicopoli in Bulgaria a heavily armed Tartar comes on board and reports an attack on himself and his companions, who have been abducted; while at Turtucan they hear that on the other side of the Balkans revolt and death were raging, but the journey is otherwise unhampered by massacre or revolution.

All my enquiries prior to arriving in Istanbul had led me to believe that there was no longer a ferry from Istanbul to the Romanian Black Sea port of Kustendje (today Constanta), from where Andersen had proceeded by carriage to the Danube. The ferry service had ceased running the previous summer and I was assured that, currently, the best way to get to Constanta, where I was to join a river cruise, was to take an overnight, eighteen-hour train – with no sleeping compartment – from Istanbul to the Romanian capital, Bucharest and then another three-hour train ride to Constanta. Not an appealing prospect.

Resigned to this, I had even taken an afternoon cruise up the Bosphorus as far as the Black Sea in an attempt to go as far as I could by water in the direction of Constanta, knowing full well that the ship would turn around at the mouth of the Bosphorus and sail right back again. But I had not counted on Istanbul's endless capacity for surprises. While browsing the Romanian tourist board website to find a place to stay in Bucharest, I discovered that, miraculously, a direct ferry service had just that week recommenced from the old harbour buildings near Galata Bridge to Constanta. A ferry would be leaving that Saturday night at ten o'clock, arriving by nine the next morning. My ride up the Danube would be leaving the following Tuesday, which did mean a longer stay than I would have wished in Constanta, but it was still a significant improvement on eighteen hours lying rigid with fear of theft or worse on a third-class train across Bulgaria.

All this I had discovered on 2 April – Andersen's one hundred and ninety-ninth birthday. He had, it seemed, had his eye on me after all.

Chapter Nine

THE DANUBE

As we moved slowly away from the banks of Pera, its evocatively distressed old harbour buildings (where Andersen's ship had also anchored) fading from view, I went up on deck for my last view of Istanbul. The evening was warm and still. Seagulls whirled above the dunce's cap roof of the Galata Tower and as I looked across to the dark ramparts of the Topkapi Palace and the floodlit minarets beyond, the deep-blue sky erupted with fireworks. This seemed to set off a chain of touch papers as the sky above Asia also now combusted with kaleidoscopic pyrotechnics. They really shouldn't have.

Glimpses of lacy, fairy-lit palaces and wooden nineteenth-century *yalis* (Bosphorus mansions) passed by the portholes as I made my way to the lounge where the handful of other passengers had been summoned to show their passports. I joined a large, late-middle-aged man perched, like a sack of potatoes on a pogo stick, at the bar. Out of the corner of my eye I could see he was wearing yellow cords, a blue dogtooth sports coat and a striped shirt, its buttons stretched to bursting by a belly that seemed intent on escape. Besides his wine glass he had placed his wallet, as over-stuffed as his shirt and splayed like a spatchcocked chicken with gold and platinum wings. I didn't even need to look at the name on the cards (let's call him Alastair), to know that he was English, ex-public school, wealthy, and that he would have a story or two to tell.

He heard me order a glass of wine: 'Ah, English? One of the

FO boys, are you?' I turned to look at his face, a ruddy, puffy globe topped with a greased helmet of grey.

'Yes. Hello. FO?' I said.

'Foreign Office; there's a lot of them about,' he said cryptically. I had, it seemed, walked into a Graham Greene novel after all.

Alastair claimed to be working for the FO himself, though the details he gave were sketchy. He was, he said, in Istanbul acting in an advisory capacity, helping an English firm with a factory in Turkey sort out some 'patent infringement issues' – which could have meant anything from legal advice to leg-breaking. He was on his way to Bucharest where, he said, the gambling was good. I explained my mission and we made small talk for a while but, as so often happens with enforced, prolonged encounters with strangers you meet while travelling, the small talk soon turned confessional.

It turned out that Alastair was escaping a tricky domestic situation at home. His current wife – his fourth – had apparently turned against him in the most spectacular fashion, outmanoeuvring him to take over the two companies he had set up running nursing homes specialising in dementia in Cardiff; he claimed the business was worth close to three million pounds (there has to be a Welsh joke there, but I'm damned if I am going to deal with the hate mail).

'I tell you, I was absolutely distraught when I found out,' he said. 'She had got me trussed up like a chicken, I had not got a clue what to do.' Apparently his wife had made herself director of the company but, due to some legal loophole that I was, by that time, too sloshed to fully understand, Alastair was eventually able to outmanoeuvre *her* by getting the company that formed his company (are you still with me?) to create thousands of shares in the Cardiff company, enough to give him the casting vote on the 'Board'.

Alastair had fled England before his wife had discovered all this but he showed me several vicious text messages that suggested that the penny had now dropped: 'I was only 1 + u fkd me', said one. 'U b sorry you fat fuck', was another, and a third, slightly more mysteriously, read: 'Bitch wont b there in 2 yrs.'

I asked him what they meant. 'Oh yes, she thinks I was having an affair as well; I wasn't. Well, not an *affair* as such. Listen, I am not the one to come to for marital advice, that I can promise you.'

In the ship's restaurant we were joined by one of the few other passengers, a Turkish man who told us, in very broken English, that he was on his way to sell shoes in Bucharest. When he heard I was going to be staying in Constanta his eyes lit up: 'In hotel you press button, they send girls!' he said, but other than that he mostly just grinned at us.

I told Alastair about how I was using Andersen's travels as an excuse to escape Denmark. 'You're a bit of a poof, aren't you?' said Alastair. 'Letting your wife do that. None of my wives could ever control *me*.' He carried on in this vein for some time, throwing in a few casual insults – 'Your eyes are too close together, aren't they? You must get told that all the time'; 'Does Bob the Builder know you've stolen his trousers?' – then correctly assessing my income (or lack of it) to within a thousand pounds, and making sweeping assumptions about my political and religious beliefs.

'You are a bit of an arse really, aren't you?' I said eventually. He hesitated, not so much offended as weighing up the truth of this.

'Yes, I *suppose* you are right; it has been said. I was beginning to doubt your sperm count until you said that, but yes.'

To be fair, Alastair was entertaining company. There seemed to have been no scam beneath his moral yard stick, no barrel he wouldn't scrape. He claimed, for example, to have introduced aversion therapy to the UK, setting up a Belgian doctor of dubious bona fides in premises on Harley Street to place patients in baths full of cigarette butts where they would be given electric shocks to help them quit smoking. ('Trouble was he kept banging the patients and then refunding them the money. We only found out when we saw the bank statements.') Then there was a faked heart attack insurance fraud, and the inevitable partnership in a garage that welded wrecked cars together. Alastair had also hosted a show on television in the early 1970s. I had never heard of it but he assured me it had been 'massively popular'. 'Oh yes, I had a chauffeur-driven Bentley, knew Michael and Roger [Caine and Moore, not Fish and Whittaker presumably], went to Tramp, all of that. You ask anyone, they all knew me.'

For all his insults and his arrogance, it was hard not to like Alastair. He was candid and charismatic. He was also well aware of his foibles and, occasionally, flattering. I was, he said, the kind of 'young Turk' he had once been. 'You know I am more and more impressed by you by the minute,' he said. 'You remind me of Hemingway or one of those chaps, I bet you've got a big knob.' He was also touchingly, if misguidedly, solicitous of my well being, advising me to 'open a garage or start a vanity publishing house. Do something that ring fences some income for you away from your wife.'

Eventually, after several gallons of Turkish Chardonnay, we staggered off to our cabins.

Andersen met an idiosyncratic Englishman on this leg of his journey too – a rather more agreeable one than he had met while travelling in Italy. This was William F. Ainsworth, cousin of the novelist W. Harrison Ainsworth; the two became good friends during the time they spent together on the journey up the Danube to Budapest, walking together on the beach at Constanta, collecting interesting stones, and, further up river, biding time reading together in their shared rooms in quarantine – a ten-day hiatus imposed on all travellers arriving from Asia at the Austro–Hungarian border.

As he did with all of the notables he met on his travels, Andersen asked Ainsworth to write something to remember him by in his scrapbook. Ainsworth noticed Andersen's predilection for collecting famous names – Thorvaldsen, Heine and Mendelssohn were already there and over the years the scrapbook would gain many more, including Dickens, the famous French actress Rachel, Georges Sand, Schumann, Lord Palmerston, Dumas and Hugo. (In a later travel memoir, *A Visit to Spain* (1862), Andersen noted, with the professional envy of a true celebrity stalker, that he had met a man who collected famous teeth: 'He had a whole "tooth-album", including a tooth of a bandit who had been executed long ago, a tooth of a well-known singer and a tooth of the barber of Sumalacárregui – his celebrities were at least a very mixed lot.')

Ainsworth wrote:

Orsova, Day of Ascension of our Lord, 1841.

There is so much vanity in introducing my unknown name among those of so gifted and illustrious individuals; but this is compensated for by the pleasure of doing so, when requested by so amiable and kind hearted, as well as, intellectual a person, as Mr Andersen.

William Ainsworth
Lately in Charge of an Expedition to Kurdistan, sent by the Society for Promoting Christian Knowledge and the Royal Geographical Society of London.

In 1846, when Andersen's fame had spread to England, Ainsworth was asked to write a short piece for *The Literary Gazette* about their meeting.

Full well do I remember the poet Andersen. [He was] a tall young man, of prepossessing appearance, pale colour, yet somewhat delicate; brown hair and sharp nose and features, with a very slight slouch in his gait, and the sidling movement of an abstracted man. He was friendly and cheerful in conversation, although restless and preoccupied; but there was an extreme simplicity in his manners and confidence

in others that made it impossible not to entertain feelings
of regard and interest for him at once . . . We had ten days
of intimate acquaintanceship; and I certainly rejoiced very
much in the good fortune that had given me so pleasant,
and in every respect so gentlemanly a companion in durance
vile . . . Although always cheerful and companionable, there
was never anything light or frivolous in his conduct. As we
used to write all the morning, we did not meet much till
dinner time. 'Do you know,' he said to me one day, 'how
this Hungarian soup is made? By leaving water for a week
in the pantry where the meat is kept,' he answered, upon
my acknowledging my culinary ignorance. Certainly the
soup served up in the quarantine deserved to be so considered. Herr Andersen was naturally of pious turn of mind,
and observed the Sabbath strictly, putting by his papers, and
doing no work on that day. 'These people,' he said to me
of some Wallachians [modern day Romanians], who were
boisterously enjoying the Sabbath morning in the quarantine, 'by putting on their best clothes, think that it is Sunday.'
One evening we had a severe thunder-storm: 'I have learned
to despise the dread of thunder as a superstition,' he said,
in his peculiar nonchalant manner, 'since I have learned to
feel and appreciate the goodness of God.'

This is precisely as I had imagined Andersen – companionable,
fidgety and with a 'nonchalance' that was probably a by-product
of his own, peculiar kind of self-confidence. It also confirms that
there was an irresistible charm about the man. People warmed
to him. That said, the overbearing piety that can sometimes grate
in his stories was also in evidence.

Ainsworth also notes Andersen's susceptibility to illness, particularly when travelling: 'Unluckily Herr Andersen was so unwell,
and so much indisposed by the rude jolting of the car, that
before he had got a mile he gave the journey [to a bath house]
up, as being quite beyond his strength, and returned on foot.'

And he casts an envious glance at his social-climbing skills later in the trip: 'At Pesth I began to lose sight of him, for he had provided himself with introductions, whereas I was a mere bird of passage.'

Much to Andersen's delight, Ainsworth later used his drawings of a whirling dervish in his book (they appear on the back cover of this book too). I've mentioned his drawings a few times already and I carried several photocopies of the sketches he had made during his travels in my rucksack to help me track down various sights. He was in fact a remarkably talented and expressive draughtsman, although his untrained style was wholly at odds with the artistic conventions of his time. His pictures always look slightly autistic to me – in a good way – and they are only now beginning to be recognised as works of art in their own right.

Andersen had begun drawing during his first trip to Germany in 1831 and had dashed off 150 sketches on his travels through France, Switzerland and Italy in 1833–34. 'I was hardly aware of it before the pencil was moving in my hand and sketching the tremendous scene in my diary. I became a draughtsman without ever having had an hour's teaching,' he wrote. His drawings were mostly made on small scraps of paper, no larger than a postcard, which he then overlaid with ink. He often used them to capture scenes he wanted to write about later, but he also drew from existing paintings. He continued drawing on this trip, recording Breitenburg Castle, the dervishes, the quarantine house in Orsova, and scenes on the river, in Athens and Constantinople.

Many of his artist friends were dismissive of these naive doodles. When Andersen proudly boasted to the painter J.A. Jerichau that he had never had a lesson, Jerichau answered: 'Yes, that is quite obvious!' Anton Melbye, who taught Pissarro and was a friend of Corot, once tried to teach him a little technique by copying a sketch Andersen had made from his window in Via Sistina. I've seen both pictures and Andersen's is by far the better – full of life and energy, compared to Melbye's sterile rendering.

With hindsight you can pick out traces of everything from

Impressionism to Cubism, and the styles of artists like Chagall, Klee, Matisse and Van Gogh in Andersen's drawings. Andersen once did a drawing of a room he was staying in en route to Rome that is strikingly similar to Van Gogh's painting of his hospital room, painted a few years later – complete with wonky chair. Tantalisingly Van Gogh, who was twenty-two when Andersen died, was a fan of his stories and once wrote to a friend: 'Don't you find Andersen's fairy tales very fine? It is certain that he also draws . . .' He told his brother he was sure Andersen had an artist's mind.

Ainsworth, Andersen and the rest of the passengers arrived in Kustendje, in Romania, on 6 May to find a town little rebuilt since the Russians had ransacked it thirty years earlier during one of their regular scuffles with the Turks (which culminated in the Crimean War of the mid-1850s): 'Everything appeared as if this destruction had taken place a few weeks ago; miserable, half-fallen-down houses formed the main street,' writes Andersen. 'As far as we could see around, we could discern nothing but sea or an immense steppe, not a house, not the smoke from a herdsman's fire; no herds of cattle, no living object; all was an interminable green field.'

As they wait to take a carriage overland to meet the Danube at Czerna Woda, circumstances are already conspiring to worsen Andersen's mood. The houses are either 'wretched' or 'like a dunghill', the landscape is 'monotonous' and the locals 'wild men'. The travellers are forced to suck water from puddles, using their handkerchiefs as filters to strain out the insects. Then there are the poverty-stricken children: 'Most of the little ones were quite naked; one certainly had a sheepskin cap on its head, but that was its sole article of raiment; another boy had his father's large caftan about him, but the caftan stood open, and we could see that he had nothing on but that.'

For Andersen a further, distressing symbol of the town's squalor and decay is the sighting of a dead stork on the shore. 'A super-stitious thought crossed my mind – and no one can certainly say that in his whole life he has been free from superstition – perhaps I also shall just reach across the sea, and my life's career is ended,' he writes.

Storks were a sacred bird for Andersen, he often employed them in his stories (notably, of course, in 'The Stork') as a symbol of dignity and renewal, and, indeed, of himself – his physical resemblance to the bird was noted by more than one friend.

A family of storks act as a kind of participatory Greek chorus in 'The Marsh King's Daughter', one of Andersen's longest, most ambitious and, frankly, more bewildering tales in which an Egyptian princess goes in search of a miracle cure for her dying father, using swan's wings to fly to the north, only for her evil sisters to cut off her wings as they pass over marshland. The princess is forced to bear the Marsh king a daughter. The girl, Helga, is rescued by a stork and adopted by a Viking woman. Helga is what you would call a 'problem child' – by day she is a beautiful but cantankerous girl, by night a placid but hideous frog (the pre-Freudian aspect of this duality has been noted by many). Helga the frog girl becomes an improbable superhero, however, when she frees a Christian priest who has been captured by the heathen Vikings. To cut a long short story short, the storks eventually help rescue Helga and her mother, and return them to Egypt.

Andersen returned to the dead stork the next day while out shell-collecting with Ainsworth. It has been joined by, of all things, a dead poodle: 'A sea and air romance might be written about these two,' proposes Andersen. 'Of the last we have none, but we shall have them soon, now that balloons are so plentiful.'

Constanta has, of course, grown exponentially over the last hundred and sixty years, although the boom time of the Soviet era has long passed and it now, once again, wallows in a state of forlorn decrepitude. The harbour looks like the place where old cranes come to die, while the rest of the city has a lawless, Wild West feel, with unmade roads, mostly single-storey houses – aside from a cluster of daunting tower blocks in the centre – and a sorry array of shops. Many of the buildings look to be held together by the diligence of the local spider population alone and, generally, there was a faintly menacing air about the place. No street corner was left unadorned by a gang of unshaven men hanging around smoking in purple nylon tracksuits.

Halfway through the first day the horrible thought struck me that the staff of my hotel probably assumed I was a sex tourist, as many single western men visiting Constanta are. I set about trying to find some distractions, anything to get me out of the room and away from the back-to-back repeats of *The Persuaders* on Romanian TV. (I never did figure out why this Roger Moore–Tony Curtis crime-caper series was so-called. Seems to me they did little by way of actually *persuading* anyone to do anything, and more just flirting with dolly birds while wearing turtlenecks and wrestling half-heartedly with stuntmen.)

With the rain rendering the Black Sea's popular resort beaches a rather too bracing proposition, all I could do, I decided, was to eat myself happy as Andersen had done (he even names the innkeeper in *A Poet's Bazaar* and recommends it to anyone passing – 'The viands were excellent'). I took myself off to the nearby Shaft Pub, a log cabin whose English menu featured tempters such as 'spitted sucking pig', 'green cucumbers', the mysterious 'spitted wether', and bear. As I waited for my food, I looked around the room with its open fires, hunting trophies and those chandeliers made from fake cartwheels you get in . . . wait a minute . . . this all looked rather familiar. Yes, I had inadvertently strayed into the Romanian equivalent of a Harvester.

The bear tasted like horse, by the way.

Needless to say, I was waiting on the quayside two days later with the eagerness of a Harrods sale bargain hunter, a good couple of hours before the MV *Prinzessin* was ready for boarding. I was already unpacked and leaning nonchalantly against the sundeck railings, cocktail in hand, when my mother arrived with the rest of the passengers from Constanta airport.

Taking one's mother along is not, I realise, something intrepid travel writers are supposed to do. Tim Cahill's Amazon adventures would have been seriously compromised by having Mrs Cahill snr wiping snake venom from his face with a spittle-damped hankie. Mamma Theroux wouldn't fit in the canoe and Bruce Chatwin's mother would almost certainly never have allowed him to get away with all those fibs. Among the travel-writing aristocracy, a mother is strictly taboo. Even admitting you have a mother is probably deemed a bit wet.

Luckily, as far as the travel-writing aristocracy is concerned, I would probably rank somewhere between the woman who plucks the pheasants they kill while out on their metaphorical travel-writing-aristocracy shoots, and the dog that retrieves them, and besides, a cruise up the Danube had long been my mum's dream holiday. When she heard that I was to undertake this journey, the ensuing hints, pleading and then awful, harrowing emotional blackmail would have been enough to weaken a far more resolute man than I.

I realised early on, too, that my mother would make a useful 'beard' aboard a ship full of elderly folk and it only took a brief glance at our fellow guests to see that I had made the right decision. Everywhere I looked on this four-deck river cruiser (essentially a scaled-down version of your traditional cruise ship, complete with bird-bath-sized swimming pool), I was surrounded by people so aged they made Nancy Reagan look like a prom queen. I felt like I had walked onto the set of *Cocoon II* as, up on the sundeck, ladies with suspiciously heavy hair and shirtless men displaying a medical encyclopaedia of surgical scars lounged on deckchairs or clunked behind their Zimmer frames like the animated figures from a Ray Harryhausen film. The vast majority of the passengers also happened to be German, so blue and purple rinses, a variety of woven footwear and all too revealing Speedos were de rigueur. Evening wear was, typically, salmon-pink sports jackets and Joan Collins' cast-off frocks, with the coat hangers apparently still stuck in the shoulders.

Without my mother I would have been as out of place as a toddler in a strip club; at least with her I might elicit envious glances. 'Oh, if only we had a son who loved us enough to accompany us on an eleven-day cruise,' I imagined them thinking, although the truth was probably closer to: 'Hey, check out Norman Bates!' The crew, made up of hard-bitten Slavs, Slovaks, Hungarians and Bulgarians, eyed me equally suspiciously, trying to figure what might possibly lure a young-ish man to go on holiday with a group of people more than twice his age. I had, it seemed, gone straight from being a suspected sex tourist to a potential gold-digging gigolo out to snare a Bavarian sauerkraut millionairess, before upping her dosage.

At least, I thought to myself as I trudged to dinner in the suit my mum had kindly brought with her so that I might conform to the evening dress code, in a 'women and children first' scenario I would have a fair chance of being counted among the latter.

In fact, the suit left me in no position to cast any sartorial stones. The idea that one would be told what to wear while on holiday was a new one on me, but my mother had read the small print and managed to unearth the suit I had worn to my first office job from her attic. As was fashionably prescribed by Hepworths back in those days, this was a Teflon-shiny, double-breasted Prince of Wales check. Fifteen years on, the cuffs were frayed, a button was missing and the sleeves finished, in an unintentional tribute to Don Johnson, a quarter of the way up my forearms.

'Why on earth should I be told what to wear on holiday?' I whined as we made our way through the nylon-carpeted, brass-columned lobby to the dining hall.

'Well, if you've paid all that money you don't want to be surrounded by builders' bums at dinner, do you?' said my mum, wiping something only she could see from the corner of my mouth with a dampened hankie.

I wondered how Andersen and his mother might have got on had she accompanied him on his journey. It is a fairly preposterous notion, I know, but it does give me the excuse to tell you what little is known about Anne Marie Andersen.

When Andersen returned to Odense after his first term at school in Slagelse, he recalled that his mother 'rejoiced over me', but little else is recorded of her reaction to her son's remarkable success. In *The True Story of My Life* he is far more anxious to impress upon us his fast-growing fame: 'Everybody knew how remarkably well things had fared with me . . . some old women in the hospital below, who had known me from childhood, pointed up to me.' Perhaps he was already conscious that he had left her way behind; that Anne Marie the washerwoman could never hope to comprehend his new life. Perhaps he was ashamed of her; perhaps he worried that she would embarrass him in front of all his posh new friends.

By the time Andersen returned to Odense in 1825 Anne Marie had lost her second husband, was living in the poorhouse and was well on her way towards the pointy end of the slippery slope of alcoholism. Illiterate, she often persuaded others to write begging letters to her son, and he replied with small sums of money. He doesn't seem to have tried to do much else to help her, and I can't help feeling that the many idealised representations of doting, dedicated mothers in his fairy stories were in part motivated by guilt at his failure to help her.

Her death warrants only a passing, inevitably self-reflective mention in his autobiography: 'There was a letter from Collin senior; it reported my mother's death. My first reaction was: Thanks be to God! Now there is an end to her sufferings, which I haven't been able to allay. But even so, I cannot get used to the thought that I am so utterly alone without a single person who must love me because of the bond of blood.' He then moves swiftly on to the critical reaction to his *singspiels* by Heiberg.

So Andersen doesn't appear to come out of his relationship with his mother with a great deal of honour, but I don't believe this apparent coldness is wholly representative of her importance in his life. Though he had more in common with his father, Andersen had been close to Anne Marie. It was she who had done so much to protect this fragile boy in the early years. She was his chief protector and her love for him burns through his descriptions of his childhood. While his father introduced him to literature, Anne Marie and her washerwomen friends gave him something of equal consequence as far as his future career was concerned. It was in the company of these peasant women that he first heard the timeless folk tales that were to form the basis of many of his early short stories. Their stories featured trolls and princesses, witches and fools, soldiers and kings – the repertory cast of fantastical characters that Andersen would draw on throughout his career. They gave him the foundation on which to build, develop and ultimately transform the genre.

Anne Marie was clearly an incredibly strong woman physically as well. She earned her living washing other people's clothes in the river that runs through Odense, and this she did year-round. The cold must have been unimaginable, and, ultimately, it drove the poor woman to the gin bottle to keep the blood flowing.

Andersen fictionalised his mother's terrible fate in his powerful autobiographical story, 'She Was No Good', describing an incident in which a son takes a bottle of gin to his mother as she washes clothes in the river: 'He turned down by the street corner, into the little lane that led to the river, where his mother stood by the washing bench, beating the heavy linen with the mallet . . . "It is a good thing that you are come," she said, "for I have need to recruit my strength a little. For six hours I have been standing in the water. Have you brought anything for me?" The little boy produced the bottle, and the mother put it to her mouth and took a little. "Ah, how that revives one!" she said. "How it warms!"' The mother ends up drinking herself to death, earning her the eponymous rebuke of her neighbours. It is one of the most moving of all Andersen's stories and, I suspect, closer to the reality of his childhood than anything in his autobiographies.

For all his hypochondriacal tendencies and supposed frailty, Hans Christian inherited his mother's physical strength. The man had stamina, of that there is no doubt. He was an Olympic *flâneur* who could walk to the ends of the earth; he thought nothing of walking thirty miles in a day and on the *Poet's Bazaar* journey he often jumped out of the carriages he rode in to walk or even run ahead to see the view. In 1831, on his first trip to Germany, he walked forty-eight miles to Eisleben to pay homage at the birthplace of Martin Luther; in 1834 he had leaped like a lanky mountain goat up Mount Vesuvius, knee deep in volcanic dust, way ahead of his friend, the porcine Henrik Hertz. He began taking swimming lessons in 1838, and, as we have already discovered, learned to ride in Athens. Far from being the delicate, fairy-boy he is often portrayed as, Andersen was quite the Marlboro Man.

As well as this Anne Marie is at least partly responsible for her son's unquestioning adoration of royalty (having worked at Odense Castle, home of the Crown Prince) and, more usefully, his survivalist's pragmatism regarding money. She remarried after the death of Andersen's father, most probably out of financial necessity, but it was this remarriage – to another shoemaker, also younger than she, who died four years later – that most likely soured Andersen's love for his mother in later life.

The first evening on board the *Prinzessin* ended, as so many would, with a 'folkloric' performance. As the cruise continued I came to dread the appearance of the guest artists who would board late in the afternoon in civvies carrying odd-shaped music cases, and later that night reappear in elaborately embroidered national costume to run around shouting and singing for a bit before leaving, dropping hints that they expected a tip as they went.

On one occasion, in Romania, the folklore artists persuaded us that it was the tradition for the audience to stuff money into an artificial chicken that they paraded round on a silver salver, which we duly did. These were all quality acts, no doubt, and the German passengers seemed to like them – at least those who managed to stay awake beyond 8 p.m. – but if you have seen men in skirts slap each other about a bit once, then that is enough. 'German entertainment, German language and comforts, made us think that we were removed, by magic, from the East into the midst of Germany,' Andersen had written while staying in Constanta. Only, *he* meant it in a good way.

To relieve the tedium of watching mile after mile of dense, low-lying woodland glide by during the first two days of our voyage up the Danube, there were organised excursions. The first trip was to see for ourselves the megalomaniacal excesses of Ceausescu's Bucharest, much of it uncannily reminiscent of Manchester's Trafford Centre mall. We were told by our English-speaking guide, Vlad, that the only person to have given a speech from the balcony of the never-used parliament building (the second largest building in the world after the Pentagon; building it cost the equivalent of the Romanian GDP for three years), was Michael Jackson. The King of Pop used this auspicious privilege to say the following words: 'Hello Budapest!'

We ended our second day's sightseeing at Vidin, one of Bulgaria's oldest cities where Andersen had counted twenty-five minarets. Going ashore (by now he is aboard the 'big and beautiful' steamship *Argo*, sailing first class), he remarks upon the inconsistency of Bulgaria's quarantine rules: 'Every one of us that wished to walk about in the town must first go into this house and be smoked through, so that the infectious matter in our clothes and bodies might be driven out. It was somewhat difficult to hold one's balance on the loose boards from the ship. The steps were pretty steep; but the good-natured Turks took us by the hand and helped us down. They then let go directly, and we were smoked that we might not infect them. Philippovich, whom they already knew was on board, and who was to have an audience with the Pasha, was not smoked at all, for it would have detained him.' He adds: 'We landed, and were smoked, but all the goods, even woollen bags, entirely escaped this fumigation.'

For the first few days we sailed with Bulgaria on our 'left' (as I believe seafaring folk actually say, when no one's listening) and Romania on our 'right'. I busied myself, as Andersen would have, by getting to know my fellow passengers. I joined two of the other English passengers, Bill and Ben, on the sundeck. I couldn't help notice that Bill was reading a biography of Hitler. It was called *Hitler* and had a picture of the Fuhrer on the front.

'Brave choice for this trip,' I said, nodding at our fellow passengers.

'Yes,' said Ben. 'He does this to me every time. Last time we went to Spain he was reading a biography of Franco.'

Bill and Ben were regular travelling partners – former colleagues, now retired, from a Newcastle insurance company. This was their twelfth cruise, they told me. When I assumed they were gay, Bill visibly blanched. Ben spluttered: 'Gay, goodness no, gosh! No! We most certainly are *not* gay we just go travelling together, we're not gay, God, no, ha, ha!' I apologised for any offence I might have caused, but they eyed me suspiciously for the rest of the cruise.

As we talked I could hear my mother, not for the first or last time, completely undermining all my prior hard work pretending to be a grown-up. '. . . Yes! I caught him eating it. So I pulled down his trousers right there in the street and I said, "Michael, if I catch you doing that again I'll tell your father . . ."' As the days went by I would hear several of these well-worn family legends – like the time I vomited over the mayor during the opening of the new library; the time my sister dressed me up like Orphan Annie with gingham dress, pigtails and rosy cheeks, and took me shopping; and the time I urinated in the paddling pool while my brother and sister were still in it. (I was provoked.)

Beside me on the sundeck a German woman in shorts clambered aboard one of the boat's two exercise bikes. She pumped and clunked and wheezed for a few minutes, during which time I became strangely, hypnotically drawn to the Alpine roadmap of veins on her legs. In fact, so hypnotised was I that I fell asleep, missing the fruit-carving demonstration in the lounge.

Happily, I woke just in time for the mid-afternoon cake break. I had learned quickly that if I timed things accurately I could get two helpings of cake by starting early downstairs in the lounge, and then sauntering nonchalantly up onto the sundeck where a different lot of guests were being served the same dazzling array of sponges. Other than that there was little else to do apart from browse among the displays in the Swarovski crystal shop or work my way slowly through the cocktail list. It was the closest I would come to the grinding tedium Andersen had endured during his ten days' enforced quarantine in Orsova (although as far as I know they had no fruit-carving classes).

Things were rather more lively aboard Andersen's steamship, the *Argo*. At Nicopolis they took on board some French leech salesmen who had been harvesting their stock in Bulgaria. While rinsing their charges on deck some of them escape: 'One of the cabin boys limped about with bleeding feet, for a leech had laid fast hold of him,' Andersen notes. (Leeches remain a highly valued commodity and tons of the little suckers are regularly shipped up the river from the Danube delta to foreign medical companies.)

In between bouts of eating and sleeping I went onto the bridge to interview our captain, a Hungarian (as most Danube captains are) named Zoltan Kun. He seemed a friendly fellow. Like Andersen's captain Dobroslavich, I could easily imagine Zoltan treating his crew 'like dogs, and yet was inwardly beloved by them'. He did not speak English and, as my Hungarian was slightly rusty, I had enlisted Katalina, the Slovenian entertainment officer, to interpret.

According to Zoltan every captain has a different way of navigating the river but shipping companies are legally obliged to take pilots on board who have local knowledge of particular stretches to help them. Water levels were the key to navigating the river, he said. Despite the damming of the Danube, which had a great calming affect on the river – raising water levels, submerging rocks and taming the tricky current – the Iron Gate (the nickname given to a system of gorges and valleys that was, for centuries, the gateway to Europe) was still the most problematic stretch. It is not as treacherous as it was when Andersen had sailed this way – he described 'whirlpools that have swallowed up boats, and broken vessels in pieces, round about in the foaming stream are to be seen black rocks stretching their crushing fingers into the air' – but Zoltan told me that, as the world's climate has become less predictable, so has the river. It can turn, in a season, from a rushing torrent to being so dry you can cross it on foot.

It helped to build up a good relationship with one's ship. 'My ship has vibrations, every ship has special vibrations. I have sailed this river with her for eighteen years. I know her better than I know my wife. She talks to me.' (Later the hotel director told me that around ten years ago, Zoltan had considered changing to another ship but just could not make the break, and remained faithful to this day.)

Zoltan could remember the river before many of the locks and dams were built, back when it ran a similar course and had a similar character to Andersen's day. He could also remember the steamship that was moored permanently in the Iron Gate from the 1870s to the 1960s and was used to winch other ships upriver. It now lies rusting on the river bed.

When Andersen passed through the Iron Gate his ship was 'dragged up against the stream by fifty or more Serbians with a rope and iron chain, walking on a pathway and hauling it along. A number of river vessels lay under the shore, the poor Serbians had to spring like gazelles from ship to ship, haul and haul, then jump into their light boats, and with the rope around their waists, row themselves and us forwards.' He reports that in the middle of the river are several falls, so the ship hugs the coast, but at Gladova things become too dangerous and all the passengers disembark, leaving the captain and two sailors to navigate the remaining miles.

In 1972, however, the geography of this part of the Danube was changed beyond recognition with the arrival of the Djerdap Dam, 943km upstream from the Black Sea. The dam raised the river level by thirty-five metres, submerging many of the treacherous rocks that had created the mid-river falls, as well as several towns and inhabited islands. The dam provided an endless source of cheap electricity for Presidents Tito of Yugoslavia (now Serbia, on the south bank) and Gheorghiu-Dej of Romania (on the north bank). Each country still operates a kind of time share on the dam – one week Romania gets the power, the next week Serbia gets it (presumably they bath-share and burn furniture on alternate weeks).

I hesitated before asking my final question. Zoltan had a stern, captainly bearing that suggested he didn't suffer fools' questions gladly. 'So, is the Danube ever blue?' Katalina rolled her eyes and translated the question.

'No, never.' Zoltan laughed. 'The legend is that when the Turks were thrown out of Hungary their bodies were thrown into the river and the blue dye in their uniforms coloured the water.'

'Either that or the composer was drunk,' added Katalina. (Actually, Johann Strauss the younger pinched the title from the writer Karl Isidor Beck. You can send my share of your pub quiz winnings via my publisher.)

Shortly after Gladova, Andersen and his chums disembarked once again, this time to serve their gruelling ten-day quarantine period (intended to prevent the spread of cholera and typhus) in Orsova. They are greeted by the Pasha, 'a powerful man about forty years of age, with blue military surtout, large gold epaulets and fez'. As they travel on to their prison, they see the Pasha leaving to spend the night with his wives: 'We went to our fenced prison, he to flowery terraces,' laments Andersen. 'The lot of man is different in this world – that is the moral of the story.'

For the ever-restless Andersen it is an agonising delay. Of the prison-like quarantine quarters he writes: 'The whole building is a sort of box within a box . . . every chamber within has a little yard. The first day in quarantine goes on excellently well: we get a good rest after travelling; the second, third and fourth day, we write letters, the fifth and sixth we become accustomed to the place, and read a good book, if we have one; but the seventh day we are dis-accustomed again, and find that the seventh day, but not the whole seven days, ought to be a day of rest. I began to find it desperate.' He resorts to, first, tree hugging, then actually climbing trees to catch a glimpse of the outside world: 'It looked like a little paradise – for there people were free.'

Even within the quarantine camp they had to be alert to outside contact: 'We had to look about us, and see that the wind did not bring a little feather over the wall, that might fall on our shoulders; see that we did not tread on a thread that any one had lost, for in that case the quarantine was lengthened.'

Feathers and threads successfully avoided, the final day comes and Andersen is packed and raring to go. Unfortunately the Pasha is predisposed: 'At length our hour of freedom struck, but the Pasha had a dinner party, or something of the kind. All of us, therefore, were obliged to wait a whole hour beyond our term of imprisonment – a whole hour, which seemed like a day, before we could depart; and then it was not with mirth, as when we came. We were exhausted. We, who had pleased ourselves so much with the thought of liberty, were out of practice, and could scarcely lift our wings.'

With the higher water levels, post-1973, I held out little hope of seeing any of the sights Andersen recalls in the infamous Kazan (Cauldron) Gorge, the narrowest part of the Danube where the waters were once so rough they were said to boil. But the first encouraging sighting was of Trajan's slate, a large engraved slab carved into the perpendicular limestone cliff face on the Bulgarian side. (It was made by the Romans to commemorate the Emperor Trajan's successful Dacian campaign that expanded the empire as far as the Black Sea.) The Veteranis cave, where Austrian soldiers once held out against marauding Turks, came soon after. Though mostly submerged, the triangular peak at its entrance was still clearly visible on the Romanian side of the rocky cliffs.

It was inside this cave that Andersen had his fortune told by a gypsy girl, her words translated for him by a young man from Bucharest. 'The augury seemed to have been more applicable to a rich Englishman than a Danish poet,' he recalls in *A Poet's Bazaar*, '"Thy silver shall become gold, and thy possessions increase year by year," she had said.' This actually came to pass, though Andersen is more intrigued by her next prediction: '. . . She had said I should have the least comfort in my daughters. And there she had certainly hit the right nail on the head, as it regards the poet, for 'Agnete' and *The Moorish Girl* have brought me but little comfort. I must, therefore, always strive to have boys.'

This is an anxious time for the travellers who, at this point, are making their way by land through an area not covered by the quarantine. Even the slightest contact with the locals and they might have risked picking up an infection again and would have to return to quarantine in Orsova: 'The tails of our horses were bound up that they might not, untimely whisking them, touch the rope . . . The poor Serbian peasants placed themselves as close to the bank of the river as they possibly could, and yet we were not more than a foot from them . . . if even the whip-lash had touched the skirt of one of their coats, we should have had to return to the quarantine in Orsova.'

Quite where all this caution disappears to just a few para-graphs later when Andersen goes out walking alone and meets some more gypsies is a bit of a mystery. One of them, a young boy, impresses Andersen so much with his manners and appear-ance that he wants to take him home with him: 'There was something so innocent in his whole behaviour, something so noble, that I am certain if I had been rich I should have adopted the boy.' Showing apparently no regard for the quarantine rules that had caused him such hassle on the journey so far, he instructs the boy to collect some flowers for him, which allows him to give the boy some payment in return (later on he blithely mentions that he was supposed to have washed his money in vinegar before giving it to anyone). He also gives the boy his card and invites him to visit him in Copenhagen should he ever succeed in his ambition of becoming an officer. Just in case the plague spores have not had quite enough opportunity to pass between them, he shakes the boy's hand. Reflecting on the encounter in *A Poet's Bazaar*, Andersen writes: 'Never has any boy made such an impression on me . . . He must be an officer . . . and I here bow to every noble, rich Hungarian dame who may perchance read this book, and perhaps have a friendly thought to spare for *The Improvisatore* or *Only a Fiddler*, and I beg her – the poet begs her – if he has, unknown to himself, one rich friend in Hungary or Wallachia, to think of Adam Marco [the boy's name] near Drencova, and help her little countryman forward, if he deserves it.'

And if, one presumes, he hasn't died from some terrible business-card-borne disease.

Actually, this entreaty to his well-heeled readers was not as far fetched as it sounds. It was probably inspired by something the philosopher Stiegler's wife had said to him back in Munich – that if she ever met a young, poor boy with a great talent she would support him. A couple of years later, while travelling in Saxony, Andersen met a wealthy woman who, inspired by his novel *Only a Fiddler* – about a poor but musically talented boy's doomed attempts to make good – had paid for two young musicians to attend a conservatorium.

The Kazan Gorge is the most spectacular part of the lower Danube and, at 53m deep, one of the deepest stretches of river in the world. Looking ahead upstream, its forested, mountainous banks – steaming as the morning sun finally seeped through the dark, rowdy clouds – looked like massive theatre wings. On the right were the Carpathians in Romania, on the left, in Serbia, the Balkans.

With this more dramatic scenery, plus the uncorking of a table full of very large Weiss beer bottles in the lounge, the atmosphere on board the MV *Prinzessin* had grown notably bubblier, as had the river, where white foaming snakes on the surface now betrayed the strong currents beneath.

The hulking, nine-towered stone fortress of Gobulaza and the rhino-horn rock mass opposite – which Andersen says is called Babekey – marked the end of the gorge and, as the river opened up into a vast inland sea, I went onto the sundeck to fend off my impending deep-vein thrombosis. We were passing a submerged forest, its leafless, drowned trees scratching upwards in hopeless defiance of their sub-aquatic fate. Overcome by that strange compulsion we all have to wave at complete strangers from moving waterborne vessels, some of the passengers were 'you-hooing' at a group of locals winding their way up the steep, cobbled main street of a village on the Romanian bank. It was a funeral procession. They didn't wave back.

We passed through Belgrade that night, but weren't stopping as, even with Milosevic languishing hundreds of miles away in his Hague cell, the cruise company was concerned for our safety. The Nato bombing of 1999 did little to endear the people of western Europe to the Serbians and, virtually since the Balkan conflict kicked off – after Slovenia and Croatia declared themselves independent in 1991 – a motley mob of war criminals (Arkan and Knezevic, to name two who met their end in the lobbies of Belgrade's five-star hotels) have roamed these parts. It was hard to imagine US jets strafing the cosy chalets and riverside mansions, and knocking out bridges from here to Novi Sad (blocking the Danube in the process), but it happened, in Europe, only moments ago. Of course the Balkans remain about as stable as one of those Doodlebugs they occasionally still dig up in the East End. The ethnic frictions that date back to the Turks' occupation are still sparking, and some say it is only a matter of time before the region erupts again.

★　★　★

In 1841 Belgrade was the name given to the fort here, which was still occupied by the Turks. The neighbouring town was Semlin, which, like the rest of Serbia, had been under the control of the revolutionary Prince Milosch since the 1820s.

Andersen mentions this only in passing, which is fairly remiss as, actually, he is witnessing nothing less than the end of seven centuries of the Ottoman Empire and the emergence of Balkan nationalism. At that time the Danubian territories from the Black Sea all the way to Budapest were a seething mass of revolutionary discontent, directed either at the Sultan in Constantinople (desperately and often brutally trying to hold together a disintegrating empire) or the dribbling fool of an emperor, Ferdinand V, in Vienna (doing likewise with the Hapsburg territories). It was one of the great news stories of his era – but you would hardly know it from *A Poet's Bazaar*.

On this journey he had already swanned blithely through Italy oblivious to the emerging movement towards unification and impending war. In *A Poet's Bazaar* he does mention meeting some people just outside Mantua who spoke of the expected conflict between France and Germany and seeing ammunitions convoys and Austrian cavalry but, as was usually the case, Andersen brushes away the geo-political turmoil of his time with his customary airy fatalism: '. . . In the great events of life, where I cannot do anything myself, I have the same firm belief as the Turks in a directing Providence; I know what will happen, happens!' Tell *that* to the Marines.

In Greece, meanwhile, he had reacted to the patent absurdity of a Bavarian teenager being imposed on the Greeks as monarch by having a shouty conversation with him about hills, while in Constantinople he offered no opinion on the barbarity of the Ottoman Empire, and, again, seemed oblivious to the signs of its impending demise.

Critics of *A Poet's Bazaar* were not slow to point out this inherent weakness in Andersen's journalism. M.A. Goldschmidt, writing in the Copenhagen journal, *Corsaren*, wrote: 'We had expected [something], particularly from H.C. Andersen, whose struggle of poverty against richness, who knows what suppression and subjugation are: from him we had expected a feeling for the people, for their poverty, for their suppression.'

Andersen's response came in his autobiography: 'I felt no . . . necessity to mix myself up in such matters; for I then believed that the politics of our times were a great misfortune to many a poet. Madame Politics is like Venus: they whom she decoys into her castle perish. It fares with the writings of these poets as with the newspapers: they are seized upon, read, praised, and forgotten . . . Politics is no affair of mine. God has imparted to me another mission: that I felt, and that I feel still.' It is a fair defence as far as fairy-tale telling is concerned, but rather weak when it comes to a topical travel memoir.

The truth is Andersen was hopelessly out of step with the revolutionary ethos of the mid nineteenth century. While the rest of Europe was sending its royals into exile or locking them up, he was fawning over them in the most inexcusable manner – and he got far, far worse as he got older. Right up until his death he was revelling in the various awards and honours that flooded in to his rooms on Nyhavn from all over the world.

Though I would not for a minute think of comparing the horrors of a bloody ethnic war to what I suffered that night as we passed Belgrade, I will say that, in the same way that whispering the word 'Saigon' into the ear of a Vietnam veteran can sometimes trigger raging psychosis, the phrase 'Cruise Show' will now send me scurrying for the cupboard under the stairs, from where I will only be tempted out by Valium on a stick. Nothing can convey the full, spirit-shrivelling agony of watching a bunch of eastern European waiters present ship-themed 'skits' and 'funny songs' to a bilingual audience while dressed, variously, as ballet dancers, prostitutes and policemen. As if this wasn't torture enough, every 'joke' had to be translated for the English audience *after* it had wrung its laugh from the German contingent.

Here, for example, is an example from the MV *Prinzessin* News Sketch: 'This late news just in: due to economy measures we will not be able to wash your bedding every day. Instead, we would ask cabin number 243 to change bedding with cabin number 235, and for cabin number 468 to change bedding with cabin number 470, and so on.'

The show also featured wave after wave of those oompah singalongs that make up roughly ninety per cent of the German TV schedules, and ended with the engine crew performing 'YMCA' dressed in tutus. It is branded on my memory for eternity.

That night my mother and I had dined with a German couple, Horst and Julia. He was an architect, she a teacher. We chatted about grandchildren and architecture (I impressed with my newly gleaned knowledge of Camden Sainsbury's). They seemed a nice, liberal pair. He was a Rotarian and she did charity work for a local school for the disabled.

But then the mood changed. Julia returned from the dessert buffet and sat down.

'Did Horst tell you what we saw this morning in the river?' she asked breezily.

Horst's face dropped, he leaned forward and in a soft voice said, 'A baby.'

'What do you mean, a baby? Are you sure? Could it have been some wood or something?' I asked.

'We had binoculars. It was stuck on some tree for a while.'

'But could you be mistaken? On a scale of one to ten, how sure were you that it was a baby?'

Horst looked me in the eye. 'Seven. If it wasn't a baby, it was a very lifelike doll. It could have been a doll, I suppose. It was bloated. It was floating face down with its bottom up, the head was underwater. The head is about a fifth of a baby's body weight, you know. As soon as I saw it I had a terrible feeling in my stomach and I called Julia over.'

I wondered why they hadn't called the captain. 'Well, what

could he have done? What would have happened? By the time they had stopped the boat the current would have taken it away. And what if we had made a mistake?'

'And,' added Julia, 'it would only have got the mother into trouble, and she probably had many problems. There was no point, the baby was dead. Someone else will find it.'

The conversation switched seamlessly back to grandchildren. The boat sailed on, but all I could think about – and the image still returns – is the face of a child looking down as the riverbed flowed beneath it.

Our next stop, like Andersen's, was Budapest. He arrived two days prior to the city's fair and his steamer is packed with travellers. On two occasions fellow passengers steal his bed and he kicks up a fuss. 'Today a Jew took *my* bed,' he writes in his diary. 'I am annoyed . . . The deck looked like a battlefield after a terrible fight.' He notes, with obvious satisfaction, that the bed thief later loses all his money at cards.

Later he notes, 'A Turkish Jew who had come down from Semlin had the best of it. He continued to keep the place he had first taken; he sat on a carpet he had spread out, and held a large keg of wine between his legs. Every moment he drank a toast, nodded and sang, crowed like a cock, and sighed like a maiden; he was the pantaloon for the whole company, and merry enough he was.'

I should stress that, though it may occasionally seem otherwise, Andersen was no anti-Semite. He spent a large part of his later life as a house guest of two of Copenhagen's most prominent Jewish families, and when accused of this crime by the editor of the London *Literary Gazette* he wrote back, furiously: 'I must protest against an accusation brought against me in one of your articles, viz that I am always against the Jews. Now, that is not so. I have often seen how they were unjustly treated.'

Things are hardly better in the first-class lounge: 'The gentlemen sat unceremoniously amongst the ladies, and played a very high game at hazard . . . Champagne corks flew about; there was a smell of beefsteaks! And in the evening it was worse still; they had to sleep on tables and benches, nay, under the tables and benches, even in the cabin windows; some lay in their clothes . . . The ladies' cabins were equally overfilled; a few of the eldest took courage, and a manly heart, as we call it, and sat down within the door of our cabin with us!'

We reached Budapest that evening. Searchlights scanned the sky. High above Buda, the hilly part of the city on the left bank, hovered a massive glowing white light – an airship. Altogether everything you could wish for from an arrival in a new city.

I disembarked and went for a late-night walk. The air was warm and heavy, there were courting couples everywhere and I promptly fell in love with the place. I even saw two tram drivers blow kisses to each other as they passed. Any travel writer who ever likens another European city to Paris should immediately leave his keyboard, unfold the longest blade of his Leatherman and hurl himself upon it, but there *is* plenty that is Parisian about Budapest – from its winding river bank to the broad, tree-lined avenues, to its casual, unaffected romance.

Perhaps this was the kind of thing that got Andersen all worked up again as, in his diary from Budapest, he notes that he is 'wild in the blood' and 'sensual mood. Uhsa!' (I assume 'Uhsa' is kind of Pacino-esque 'hoo-ha!')

My mood was shattered, however, by the bellowing of English stag-weekenders. 'Look at the arse on that!' they shouted (not at me, at least I assume not) as they slouched outside a bar. Is there any sense in which these people have even the slightest shred of self-respect or humanity, I wonder? A nightclub tout approached another group of prowling simians. 'No flat tits, no fake tits, no long tits, just good Russian tits!' he said, with a practised persuasiveness doubtless born of a familiarity with his clientele.

I went to a new bar that a friend had recommended. It was one of those ice-cool Scandinavian-style places that could have been in Barcelona, London or Stockholm, with the same crowd of ever-hopeful middle-aged men in sports jackets and jeans, and girls in tight T-shirts smoking Marlboro Lights. There were sexy waitresses and a DJ playing music that sounded like a stuck record. Everyone knew each other and I felt rather lonely. Eventually I think my Droopy impression began to deter trade as the waitress hinted I should leave. (I say 'hinted', what she actually said was: 'If you don't want another drink you can leave now.')

With just one day in the city, I had a full programme of Andersen sights that I was eager to cram in and the next morning I set off early on foot. I first crossed to Buda to try to find a sixteenth-century remnant of Turkish rule – the tomb of the dervish saint and friend of Suleymain the Magnificent, Gül Baba, to whom Andersen had carried 'a greeting from the East to the Turkish saint!' I found this tranquil shrine, a marble octagon crowned with a gold crescent and surrounded by a colonnaded garden, up a steep, unmarked cobbled street, and then a winding flight of steps. Fountains tinkled and the air was filled with the smell of freshly cut grass and blossoming roses.

A half-hour walk away on Castle Hill – Buda's squeaky-clean tourist ghetto – I spent some time in the Museum of Budapest, its striking lack of artefacts a testament to the thoroughness of Turkish plunder. Tucked away in a corner I did find a poster advertising a *dampfboote* (steamboat) service on the Danube from 1841. Though it wasn't the exact boat Andersen sailed on, judging from the schedule, he would almost certainly have passed it going in the other direction.

A drawing of the waterfront at Pesth in 1834 showed what Andersen describes as a 'bridge of boats', a kind of floating pontoon walkway that looks like one of the challenges from *It's a Knockout*. This was the only thing connecting Pesth with Ofen, the German name Andersen uses for Buda. In fact, construction of the original stone Chain Bridge began soon after Andersen's visit in 1841 and this first permanent crossing of the river in

Budapest became a potent augur of the Hungarian age of Reform. The bridge was the idea of Count István Széchenyi, the mastermind of Hungarian reform – which was in full flow when Andersen visited. Széchenyi is also credited with bringing flushing lavatories to Hungary, and introducing steamships to the Danube in 1833. As Andersen mentions in *A Poet's Bazaar*, by 1841 his fame had already spread to Denmark by way of his definitive book on his great passion, horse racing.

Andersen met Széchenyi, briefly, many years later at a gathering at Széchenyi's brother's house in Vienna. 'This short meeting I account one of the most interesting events of my stay in Vienna,' Andersen wrote. 'The man revealed himself in all his individuality, and his eye said that you must feel confidence in him.' Sadly Széchenyi died soon after, before he could see his dream of a united Budapest fulfilled. He shot himself in the head while incarcerated in a lunatic asylum.

I walked back to Pesth across the milky-tea river via the current Chain Bridge, rebuilt after the Second World War. Excuse the digression, but I was keen to see Andrássy út 60, once the most feared address in all of Budapest, home, first, of the Hungarian Nazis, then of the notorious communist terror organisation the ÁVO and its successor the ÁVH. Today the building houses a stunning museum charting the panoply of totalitarian wrongdoing that plagued Hungary for most of the twentieth century. The basement is the most unnerving part; here the torture cells have been preserved just as they were in the fifties and early sixties. It is the small details that I found most chilling – the drainage hole in the middle of the cell floor and a single cosh hanging on a wall. What with the dripping-water sound effects and piped staccato cello music my stomach was in knots by the time I emerged into the daylight.

I crossed Andrássy út to my original goal, the former apartment of Andersen's old chum, Franz Liszt, above the Hungarian Music Academy of which he was once president. Ferencz Liszt (Germanicised to Franz when he became famous) was a child prodigy who became a kind of proto rock star, with shoulder-length hair, swooning female fans and a demonic way with the ivories. It is not such a quantum leap from Liszt to, say, Jerry Lee Lewis, particularly when you learn that he had a ravenous appetite for women, fathering a number of children with other men's wives.

After his death in 1886, George Bernard Shaw said of Liszt that he was 'a man who loved his art, despised money, attracted everybody worth knowing in the nineteenth century, lived through the worst of it, and got away from it at last with his hands unstained'. After seeing him play at the concerts described at the beginning and end of *A Poet's Bazaar*, Andersen became good friends with Liszt, meeting him both in Copenhagen and at his home in Weimar, and collaborating on a libretto. In person, Andersen reported that Liszt was as fiery as his stage persona. '[He] can instantly warm you up,' he wrote of the man who had, by that time, courted further controversy by shacking up with Princess Carolyn Sayn-Wittgenstein, 'but if you draw close you get burned.'

I spent the rest of the day wandering around Pesth. I spotted buildings still pockmarked with bullet holes, spent an hour deciding which kind of paprika to buy in the market and had a glorious goulash in a small corner café. A small wooden cup with three dice inside was presented with the bill. I looked at it questioningly. 'Three sixes and it's free,' said the waiter. I didn't throw even one six, but it was a nice touch all the same. My beer was less than a pound, incidentally, which explains the stag-night grotesques I had seen the night before.

We set sail again early the next day (honestly, I don't know where these pensioners get their stamina from), passing Bratislava shortly after. 'I like this city,' writes Andersen, now sailing on the *Maria Ana*, 'it is lively and motley. The shops appear to have been brought from Vienna!' The next sight to glide by was the ruins of Theben (also known as Devin). The fortress here is now a major tourist attraction, but in 1841 it was smouldering following clashes between the Turks and the Hungarians. Andersen prefers not to dwell on the 'misery' and the 'many mothers . . . seeking their children' that he sees on the shore, or the burned horse limping away over the bridge. 'We hurry past. We are in Austria!' he exclaims, lifting the current-affairs carpet and brushing yet another major news story of 1841 underneath.

As we passed into Austria, the scenery became immediately more mountainous – it was easy to see why the Turks struggled to come much further up river than this. The water grew more turbulent too, with white crests nearer the banks and whirlpools beneath us. The boat slowed, labouring against the current.

As a more familiar Europe approaches, Andersen begins to think of his impending return to Denmark: 'All the unpleasantness of home came back to me,' he writes in his diary. 'I could feel this German–Danish atmosphere – I wish I had died in the Orient. Went to bed in a bad mood.' For the next few days his diary is full of comments like 'I thought a little bitterly about home'; 'Bitterness towards Heiberg; it is first awakened here'; 'In a bleak mood about my financial outlook back home, thought a great deal about Heiberg and how best I might have my revenge'.

'A dejection of spirits crept over me, and pressed on my heart – a prediction of something evil!' he bleats in *A Poet's Bazaar*. 'In our little Denmark every person of talent stands so near the others, that each pushes and treads on the other, for all will have a place. As regards myself, they have only eyes for my faults! My way home is through a stormy sea! I know that many a wave will yet roll heavily over my head before I reach the haven! Yet this I know full well, that posterity cannot be more severe to me than are those by whom I am surrounded.'

Years later, writing in his autobiography, he recalls the sense of doom he felt as the *Maria Ana* approached Vienna: 'The sight of [Vienna's] towers, and the meeting with numerous Danes, awoke in me the thought of being speedily again at home. The idea bowed down my heart and sad recollections and mortifications rose up within me once more.'

The thought of returning home was looming in my mind too, but I had begun to look on Denmark in a slightly different light since I had left four months earlier. Andersen once wrote: 'Ah, at home, when you go round the corner the sawdust blows in your eyes, everything is quite accursed, you are robbed of your share of the pavement, jolted on the arm, and you get your new clothes greasy. But abroad! Then you remember the Danish songs, the Danish woods and close fields and storks – all the happy and affectionate things! All sharp memories have lost their sting, but the sweet still have their flavour, and so everything is perfect at home.'

I wouldn't say I yet felt that everything was perfect in Denmark, and I can't say I missed the Danish songs (nor, for that matter, do I ever recall ever having seen a stork), but I did pine for my wife and, thankfully, her acceptance of my apologies on the phone for all the terrible things I had said about her country indicated that she probably had not changed the locks. And, much to my surprise, I had actually begun to *miss* some aspects of Denmark. I missed the security, the clean streets, and the fact that I could make myself understood without recourse to embarrassing hand waving. Besides which, it was now spring – the most energising and beautiful of all the Danish seasons. The leaves on the beech trees would be sweet and tender (the Danes use them in salads), the café tables would be moving outdoors (they are keen alfresco diners) and the long-legged girls would be wearing see-through, nightie-type dresses while riding bicycles once more.

Other than the mountains, the first real sign that we were in Austria was a man sweeping the pavement in the first town we passed. He wasn't a street cleaner, you understand, just an everyday, house-proud local with time on his hands and a bee in his bonnet – unthinkable in any of the countries we had so far passed through.

At this precise moment, a thought occurred to me. Just why *are* the Austrians so rich? I looked it up and Austria has the ninth highest GDP per capita ($23,400) in Europe, ahead of big hitters like the UK, Germany and France, as well as tax havens like Liechtenstein and San Marino. It is only beaten by the usual suspects like Switzerland, Luxemburg and, of course, Denmark. Yet 'Made in Austria' is not a label I can ever recall having seen. It is not a notable banking centre or tax haven and, other than for skiing, it is not a major tourist destination either. Austria doesn't have the landscape for large-scale agriculture and the Austrians are hardly big players in the international entertainment or sporting arenas. Unless they are keeping awfully quiet about it in order that they can hold the world to ransom when Saudi Arabia runs dry, they have few mineral resources.

Can lederhosen and Mozart chocolates really be such lucrative exports? Maybe the Austrians are funding their swish German convertibles and Hugo Boss suits by economising; perhaps they eat pasta and ketchup for dinner and have amassed a huge collection of Co-op stamps (although the fact that I saw lobster on the menu in a fish-and-chip shop in Vienna suggests this is unlikely). Answers on a postcard please.

By now the sun had coaxed its worshippers away from the macramé demonstration in the lounge. Poolside was once more a Himalayan range of teak bellies and, oh god no, *please no*, a topless grandmother. ('If the WI saw that, they'd have a fit!' said Mum. 'Except those ones who did that calendar of course.') Thankfully that particular sight was short-lived as a sudden hailstorm, with stones the size of broad beans, made the Danube go all fizzy, and sent us scurrying for cover.

That night we arrived in Vienna. It had taken Andersen thirty days to travel here from Constantinople – including the ten days' quarantine; I had done the same journey in fifteen days, including the enforced three-day hiatus in Constanta.

I took an unnecessarily orange underground train into the centre of the city (the Danube was diverted to the outskirts of

Vienna decades ago), where it soon became clear that the Viennese are shamelessly devoted to self-indulgence, whether it be epicurean, musical, theatrical or just pitching the woo. The shop windows were piled high with liqueur chocolates, monumental cakes and pâtisserie; on every street corner I met men and women carrying odd-shaped musical instrument cases, on their way to giving a concert (either that or the Mafia is a stronger presence than you'd suspect); and the kissing-couple count was unprecedented.

Though many of its public buildings are preposterously grandiose, there is a feminine delicacy, a graceful other-worldliness to the Austrian capital that quite took me by surprise. Set against a slate-grey sky the town hall, for example, looked straight from Gotham City, but its spiky, Gothic splendour was underscored by the nearby Volksgarten, ablaze with roses, dripping with new-fallen rain and bursting with perfume.

Andersen had been to Vienna before – on his way back from that first visit to Italy in 1834 – but, as with the chapters on Germany and Italy with which *A Poet's Bazaar* begins, his writing lacks some of the vigour of his later descriptions as the book and his journey draw to a close. He allows just a few paragraphs for Vienna, and they are mostly dedicated to shameless name dropping.

The Volksgarten is the setting for one of the best 'drops' (not to mention another of the book's ever so slightly over-extended metaphors): 'In the midst of a great orchestra stands a young man of dark complexion; his large brown eyes glance round about in a restless manner; his head, arms, and whole body move; it is as if he were the heart in that great musical body, and, as we know, the blood flows through the heart: and here the blood is tones; these tones were born in him; he is the heart, and all Europe hears its musical beatings; its own pulse beats stronger when it hears them: the man's name is – Strauss.' (This, it turns out, is Johann Strauss the elder not his more celebrated son, the Waltz king.)

This, my only full day in Vienna, was Corpus Christi, a holiday in Austria so, sadly, the Swarovski flagship store on Graben was closed. Still – praise the Lord! – the cake shops were open and there was something of a carnival atmosphere on the streets. Vienna's venerable Gothic cathedral, Stephansdom was packed for the early-morning service. Outside thirty horse-drawn carriages waited beside their drivers, dressed in bowler hats (the drivers, not the horses), while near by 'hilarious' human statues 'entertained' the crowd, and guides dressed as Mozart touted for business.

Andersen finds a different kind of local touting for business outside the cathedral on his fourth day in the city. 'A young poor girl lay and begged in the rough weather,' he writes in his diary. 'Her figure was beautiful, it moved me, but a little later I thought that maybe she just lay there to show the figure and catch a knight. I got angry at myself over that evil thought.' (Later on he runs into more temptation: 'Walked over the bridge, on the way three *donnas* [an Italian euphemism for hookers], the place is swarming! and none pretty.')

A few steps away from Stephansdom is the hotel König von Ungarn where Andersen stayed when he first arrived in Vienna, before moving to Rauhenstein Gasse just around the corner. After all my detective work in Germany, Italy, Greece and Turkey, this was the first of Andersen's hotels I had come across that was actually still a hotel (as a bonus, Mozart had lived next door from 1784 to 1787). Very much excited by this, I went in and asked the receptionist if he knew anything about Andersen's stay. He began looking up Andersen on his current guest list. When he finally decided to make the effort to listen to the words I was saying instead of picking on a couple and then devising his own sentences, he curtly suggested I speak to the manager . . . who was off today on account of it being a holiday.

A ten-minute walk from here was the Augustinerkirche, home to Andersen's favourite Viennese sculpture – the memorial to Maria Theresia's daughter, Maria Christina, by Canova – a ghastly, kitsch, white marble faux-crypt in the shape of a pyramid. Ranged around the entrance are, variously, *ever* such a sad lion who appears to be weeping, a sexy angel lolling its head dolefully on its mane, and six theatrically miserable mourners queuing on the left. All of this leads me to believe that, were he alive today, Andersen would be an avid collector of Franklin Mint figurines.

Across the courtyard outside the church is the Spanish Riding School. I have never really understood why Vienna has such a thing. Was it part of an exchange? Did Spain get an Austrian Skiing Academy? As I stood pondering this mystery (a mystery whose bottom I could probably quite easily have gotten to if I had paid the exorbitant entrance fee), an improbable procession of costumed adults and children entered the square, did a lap and then came to a halt in front of the church. It was a First Holy Communion. However, a Viennese First Communion would seem to be something adults tell themselves they are doing for the kids, while actually being an excuse for them to dress up silly and parade around. Thus, the small group of children about to receive the body of Christ for the first time were outnumbered ten-to-one by men dressed as eighteenth-century soldiers, various priests and bishops in all their get-up, and women in *Flash Gordon* head-dresses.

There were nuns too, of course, so I hastened away to another *objet* I was particularly keen to see in Vienna. Even though it had nothing to do with Andersen, I was sure he would have appreciated the grisly story behind it.

The siege of Vienna (1683) was one of the defining confrontations between East and West. The Turkish army, enough to fill twenty-five thousand tents, amassed outside the city walls under the leadership of the Grand Vizier Kara Mustapha. The Viennese, led by Charles of Lorraine, were helplessly outnumbered, but with the help of the Poles, triumphed (a Turkish victory here is one of the great 'what-ifs' of European history). The Turkish leader was eventually forced back to Belgrade and knew his time was up when he received a package from the sultan in

Constantinople. It contained a silk cord – as used on the necks of those who had displeased the sultan in the past. Without a word, the vizier knelt down on his prayer mat and was executed by one of his soldiers.

In his dauntingly highbrow literary history of the Danube, the Italian scholar Claudio Magris mentions that the Pasha's head, which was dug up by the Austrians some years afterwards, is on show in the Museum of Viennese History. I wandered around for over an hour trying to find it only to be told that it had been put into storage because it scared the children. Andersen, that serial child scarer, would definitely not have approved.

For lunch (I know you are wondering), I went to Plachetta, a traditional Viennese restaurant whose speciality is Tafelspitz, a dish of boiled beef said to be the favourite of Emperor Joseph. It arrived in a gigantic copper pan, brimming with broth and accompanied by huge side orders of fried potatoes, spinach, apple sauce and freshly shredded radish. The waiter ladled the broth first and then fished a mammoth steak from the depths of the pan. It was deliciously tender and I finished the lot. As I did, reclining in my chair in that satisfied way one does when one has consumed something the size of a suitcase, the waiter returned and hooked another steak, just as large as the first, from the broth, and then piled more spinach and potatoes alongside it on my plate. He then removed some cross sections of bone from the pan too, and indicated that I should scrape the marrow from them and spread it on some toast. It seemed impolite not to finish everything and order dessert, seeing as they had gone to so much trouble.

On my waddle back to the boat, bloated to bursting with *sachertorte* and beer, I passed the intriguing looking Head Shop. I could see bright lights shining through a gap in the blinds and peered in. Inside was row after row of what I initially took to be tomato plants, until I noticed the bongs and Bob Marley posters everywhere. Vienna as the next Amsterdam? Having rather fallen in love with the place and had all my preconceptions of the city comprehensively overturned, I wouldn't rule it out.

'Do you remember reading any Andersen to us as kids?' I asked my mum back on the ship that night.

'Oh yes, don't you remember that gramophone record we had of "The Ugly Duckling", who was it that sung it? Olivier's boyfriend . . . Rock Hudson?'

'Danny Kaye.'

'Yes, that's right, of course. You loved that, wouldn't stop screaming until we put it on and rocked backwards and forwards for hours on the sofa to it. Drove us all mad listening to it over and over. Your father wondered if you were autistic.'

'What about the stories?' I asked, changing the subject. 'I knew so many of them but I can't remember how I knew them.'

'We did have a book of his stories, don't you remember? It had a scary white queen on the front – you would never let us leave it in your room at night. You loved the one about the king with no clothes,' said Mum, 'but then you were quite an exhibitionist . . . [the author has removed a long anecdote, which he hardly feels is relevant here, concerning nudity at a summer fête]. My own favourite was "The Snow Queen" I loved that as a girl.'

Mum asked me about Andersen and what kind of a man he was. I told her about the neurotic behaviour, the sensitivity to criticism, the raving ambition and his incessant moaning about Denmark.

'Ooh, but he sounds just like yo—'

'I know, I know,' I sighed.

Her eyes lit up when I described the affect St Peter's had had on me and that I had seen the Pope (my mother lives in eternal hope that I will return to the Church) and she was very impressed by my trip to the embassy in Rome – although I may have slightly exaggerated the reception given me by the ambassador. Sandra caused some consternation, of course ('I hope you washed your hands'), but I think I managed to convince her the visit was justified.

I said goodbye to my mother the next morning. She would stay aboard as the *Prinzessin* continued on to Passau in Bavaria, but as Andersen had headed north to Prague so must I. Despite the childhood anecdotes and the various loaded references to relatives with 'proper jobs', it had been wonderful to spend so much time with her. Neither of us had ever imagined we would undertake such a journey at this stage in our lives, but I am glad we did.

When *A Poet's Bazaar* came out the Danish critics were incandescent that Andersen had dedicated various chapters of it to eminent personages he had met on his trip and, at the risk of invoking critical ire myself, I would hereby like to dedicate this chapter to my mum (and also use this as an opportune moment to own up to the fact that, yes, it was me who burned down the garden shed, not Simon from next door, as I claimed at the time).

Reading *A Poet's Bazaar* you get the distinct impression that Andersen really loses all interest in his travel memoir at this point – perhaps his mind was already on the next volume of fairy stories. He dashes off the trip from Vienna to Copenhagen in a few pages, excusing his cursory mention of both the Czech capital and Dresden by claiming he is 'bent on speed' and anxious to return to Copenhagen.

'Music sounds; rockets ascend! Farewell! Over the swelling sea to the green islands!' is all we get of his journey from Hamburg to Copenhagen, for instance, although the truth is that, far from heading directly back to Copenhagen, he actually spent a week meandering through Denmark before finally alighting in Copenhagen, where he attended an audience with the king. But, again, Germany was such familiar territory that he seems unable to dredge something new from it.

He was strangely blasé about his next stop, Prague, writing: 'Why does the inelegant, ungraceful, unhandsome, fix itself so

strenuously in the mind? Prague has so much that is characteristic and beautiful!' Was it another eastern European stag-night
Mecca then too? I wondered as I read this, sitting in a café on
the Old Town Square, desperately pretending not to be English.

These days the square is essentially a giant, open-air beer hall,
which reverberates to the sound of drunken men belching to
each other, like Brontosauri calling across the Jurassic valleys of
the Gobi, from Thursday to Sunday every week. It is easy to tell
the stag groups as one of their party is invariably wearing a floral-
print summer dress or carrying a street sign, while the rest laugh
exaggeratedly while wearing rugby shirts. The incongruity of all
these lunks louting about in such elegant surroundings is akin
to seeing a herd of wildebeest at the ballet. I know the beer is
cheap, but why Prague? The beer is even cheaper at Asda. Could
it be that, beneath the belching and the loutish behaviour, these
men are secretly here to nourish their passion for baroque architecture? 'I say, Gary you wanker, don't you find those rococo
architraves a touch whimsical?' 'Yes, Darren, but exquisite Gothic
cornices, don't you think? I love you. Do you want a fight?'

Of the weekend he spent in Prague, Andersen describes only
his visit to the grave of the Danish astronomer, Tycho Brahe
(who was enticed to Prague by the Hapsburg king Rudolph II).
Brahe lies buried in the Church of Our Lady Before Týn, and
Andersen's pilgrimage to his grave prompted an odd little passage,
written in the third person, but with an obvious, self-justifying
subtext:

> The Dane wanders through the aisle to the right; a large
> red-brown stone, in which is carved a knight in armour, is
> set in the pillar. Whose bones lie mouldering within? A
> countryman's! A Dane's! A master-spirit! Whose name sheds
> a lustre over Denmark! The land which expelled him . . .
> The Dane weeps by Tycho's grave in a foreign land, and
> becomes wrathful against an undiscerning age. Denmark,
> thou hast hearts in thy shield; have one also in thy breast!

He now, even more oddly, turns on himself, using his narrative voice to berate the aforementioned 'Dane'. 'Be still, son of a younger race; perhaps thou thyself, hadst thou lived in his time, wouldst have misjudged him like the others; his greatness would have stirred up the sediments of thy vanity, and thou wouldst have cast it into his life's cup. Race resembles race – therein consanguinity betrays itself.' He then proceeds to burst into tears on behalf of the exiled Brahe (hardly a role model, Brahe lost his nose through alcohol abuse and died when his intestines burst through over-eating).

The church is only open half an hour before Mass but I assumed that would still give me plenty of time to find the grave and, who knows, maybe have a little weep myself. Contrary to Andersen's description of it, the twin-towered church (circled by bats at night) is quite sizeable. With Mass about to start I still hadn't found him and was beginning to despair when I noticed a stone tablet on the floor with simple gold lettering that read: Tycho Brahe. Looking up, I came face to face with the familiar false nose on a red marble plaque facing the altar on one side of a pillar. It dawned on me: Andersen had actually shed tears here.

Silly bugger.

Andersen's fame, it seems, was spreading across the continent. Early in the journey, when travelling from Leipzig, he mentions in his diary that he travels with a man who says he is honoured to be sharing a carriage with 'such a great man as me'. And again now, on the steamer from Prague to Dresden – a route that had only begun operating a month earlier – Andersen's vanity is tickled when a doctor spots his luggage tag and asks if he is the famous poet, while another fan greets him and writes him a poem. In his diary he also notes 'a coquettish lady [who] knew The Improvisatore and Only a Fiddler. She made eyes at me a great deal, but I was so affected that I didn't want to talk to her.' (Go tiger!) Of course, nothing could please him more than this burgeoning international recognition.

No one on the train I took to Dresden seemed familiar with my short history of the bikini for the *Radio Times*, or if they were, they were too shy to approach. I had only planned to spend the afternoon in Dresden before heading for Hamburg and home, but this was Sunday night, so there was no connection until the next morning.

'But I am bent on speed!' I pleaded with the ticket lady.

'What is this bent you are saying? I do not understand. Please having your ticket goodbye.'

Inexplicably for a city of so few attractions (the Hygiene Museum, anyone?), and even fewer charms, Dresden has three massive Ibis hotels standing in a row in the heart of its windswept, Croydon-esque 1970s city centre. I checked into one, dumped my rucksack, and headed off towards the fragments of historic Dresden that Bomber Harris missed.

Actually, I am being incredibly unfair on poor old Dresden. Andersen described it as 'Northern Germany's Florence', and it still boasts one of the greatest art collections in Europe. Here are dozens of Dutch masters (Youngers and Elders), Van Dycks, Canalettos, Holbeins, Dürers, a Bronzino, Botticellis, Titians and, most famously, Raphael's *Sistine Madonna*, with its iconic cherubs leaning on their elbows at the bottom of the frame, looking for all the world like two bored kids out shopping with Mum. This particular painting had bewitched Andersen on his first visit to Dresden in 1831, where he had seen it in the Zwinger Castle: '[*The Madonna*] is innocence personified,' he notes in his diary. 'The others say they could not fall in love with but only show respect to such a woman; indeed, I could love her, love her blissfully in my mind and spirit, with hot kisses and embraces.'

From Dresden Andersen travelled by train to Leipzig, where he heard Mendelssohn play once again. Ottilie von Goethe, the writer's daughter-in-law, is there, thus enabling a memorable name-drop triple-whammy in a letter to the Collins: 'My table is covered with calling cards from all the noted artists here in Leipzig . . . Brockhaus [his German publisher] has given a dinner

in my honour and tonight I sat in his loge with Mrs von Goethe.'
Together they hear the great composer giving a recital on the
same organ that Bach had played.

I had already tasted Leipzig's many pleasures – most of them
fried in a vat of butter – and had no great desire to seek out
Brockhaus's loge, so the next morning I took the fastest train I
could directly from Dresden to Hamburg.

I'm not sure why, but I love catching Andersen out with his
little white lies (I think, perhaps, I like to imagine him squealing
with laughter at being caught out, as he used to when the Collins
exposed his exaggerations). A notable fib occurs at the very end
of *A Poet's Bazaar* where he neatly bookends his journey by
claiming to have attended another concert by Franz Liszt in the
same venue he had seen him in eight months earlier in Hamburg.
'Liszt is here,' he writes. 'I shall hear him again in the same saloon
as when I departed . . . Shall I not think that my whole travelling flight was only a dream, under Liszt's rushing, roaring, fuming,
foaming fantasias? Not months, but only minutes have vanished.'
The truth is, he actually saw Liszt perform in Copenhagen after
his audience with the king, dining with the composer the next
day. Smug? Me?

I managed to avoid the teams of wild horses they have on
standby at Hamburg station to drag tourists into town and, so
I pressed straight on to my final destination, Odense, where
Andersen had also stopped en route to his royal rendezvous in
Copenhagen. He was in no hurry to return home; after all, he
literally had no home to go to, having given up his rented rooms
on 31 October – something he often did to save money while
travelling.

By coincidence he arrived in Odense just in time for St Knud's
Fair and was tickled when an elderly lady met him in the street
and told him: 'I am very glad that you have arranged your journey
so as to come to the fair. I see that you remember Odense; that
I have always said.'

The last time Andersen visited his home town, in 1867, it was for an even more noteworthy event. He travelled there by train to receive the freedom of the city. The ceremony took place in the evening but, as he stood by the open window of Odense Town Hall, the toothache that had plagued him all his adult life erupted once more. The entire experience, which ought to have been the crowning glory of his life, was a living hell. 'The icy air which rushed in at the window made it blaze up into a terrible pain,' he wrote afterwards, 'and in place of fully enjoying the good fortune of these minutes which would never be repeated, I looked at the printed song to see how many verses there were to be sung before I could slip away from the torture which the cold air sent thought my teeth.' It is an archetypal bittersweet Andersen moment.

Lissen was waiting for me at Odense station and we walked, talking without catching breath, to my Andersen footstepping terminus: the tiny corner shoe box on Hans Jensensstræde where he was born.

Or not.

In fact, there are significant doubts concerning the authenticity of the house claimed to be his birthplace, which makes up a corner of the lavish Hans Christian Andersen Museum. Certainly he denied it, protesting that he could never have been born 'in that hovel', and there are no records of Anne Marie and Hans ever having lived there either (although Hans' aunt was registered as residing there). But none of this stops the local authorities promoting the house as his birthplace and, today, it is part of a small, olde worlde ghetto that lies close to the concert hall where all this began.

As we arrived, an elaborate stage show featuring an Andersen lookalike and a group of costumed children was in full swing in the gardens. Families had gathered on the sloping lawns and we joined them for a brisk run-through of his best known stories.

I did a brisk run-through of my journey too – not on stage, you understand, but quietly to Lissen – describing my visit to

Sandra, my courageous face-off with three car-rental heavies, and how I had befriended ambassadors, religious gurus and internationally famed actresses along the way. She seemed impressed.

As *A Poet's Bazaar* ends Andersen builds to one last, emotional crescendo:

> I have never known home-sickness, unless when the heart has been filled with a singular love at thinking of the dear friends at home, an endless pleasure, which pictures forth the moment that we see them again, for the first time, in the well-known circle. Then the picture comes forth so life-like, that tears come into the eyes; the heart melts, and must forcibly tear itself away from such thoughts! Is this home-sickness? Yes! Then I also know it. The first moment of arrival at home is, however, the bouquet of the whole voyage.

He learns on his return that, since he has been away, Copenhagen has got its first omnibus and his nemesis Heiberg has begun to have international success. Since I have been away, Lissen tells me, Copenhagen has got its first metro, and, in the run-up to the bicentenary of Andersen's birth, Roger Moore has been named an official Hans Christian Andersen Ambassador.

EPILOGUE

'Aren't you already again – according to your letter to Father – thinking of writing another travel book? Who do you think wants to buy a book in several volumes about your journey, a journey which a thousand people have made, and two thousand eyes cannot have missed so much, I suppose, that you can fill up two volumes with new and interesting material. It really is extraordinarily selfish of you to assume such an interest in you among people, and the fault is undoubtedly yours.' This was Edvard Collin's characteristically encouraging message to Andersen on the subject of travel memoirs. Though it was written in 1834, it doubtless summed up his view of *A Poet's Bazaar* before it was published in 1842.

But Edvard was wrong. As Andersen gloated in his autobiography, the book was a great success, earning him more money than any other work up to that point. Though it is all but forgotten now, *A Poet's Bazaar* (at one time he planned to call it *My Evenings in the Orient*), contributed greatly to Andersen's fame, which spread rapidly across Europe during the 1840s: '. . . the "Bazaar" was much read, and made what is called a hit. I received much encouragement and many recognitions from individuals of the highest distinction in the realms of intellect in my native land. Several editions of that book have since been published, and it has been translated into German, Swedish and English and it has been received with great favour.'

Of the criticisms concerning his fawning dedications to Prokesch von Osten, Liszt, Thalberg and others, he was dismissive:

'These dedications were, in my native country, regarded as a fresh proof of my vanity. I wished to figure with great names, to name distinguished people as my friends . . . the newspaper criticism in Copenhagen was infinitely stupid . . . There is something so pitiful in such criticism that one cannot be wound up by it; but even when we are the most peaceable of men, we feel a desire to flagellate such wet dogs, who come into our rooms and lay themselves down in the best places.'

I tend to side with the wet dogs on this one, but the fact remains that *A Poet's Bazaar* is not just Andersen's finest travel book; it deserves to rank with his greatest stories and his finest novel, *The Improvisatore*, as among the best of his writing. Its lively mix of reportage, interspersed with his trademark flights of fantasy and an, at times, revealing memoir contributes something utterly unique to the genre.

That said, the journey itself was perhaps even more important than the book that resulted from it. It was nothing less than a delayed coming of age for Andersen. It galvanised his sense of purpose as an artist, and gave him tremendous confidence as a man: 'The journey had strengthened me both in mind and body,' he wrote, looking back on the trip years later. 'I began to show indications of a firmer purpose, a more certain judgement. I was now in harmony with myself and with mankind around me.' To his friend Ingemann he claimed that the journey helped him to find his 'poetic voice'.

The trip took quite a while to digest, and many years afterwards he was still ruminating on its impact on his life: 'It was now as if a new life had risen for me, and in truth this was the case; and yet if this does not appear legibly in my later writings, it manifested itself in my views of life, and in my whole inner development. As I saw my European home lie far behind me, it seemed to me as if a stream of forgetfulness flowed over bitter and rankling remembrances: I felt health in my blood, health in my thoughts, and freshly and courageously I again raised my head.'

It is surely no coincidence that some of his finest stories followed closely on its heels. Stories like 'The Nightingale', 'The Ugly Duckling' (1843); 'The Fir Tree', 'The Snow Queen' (1845); 'The Shadow' (1847), and 'The Little Matchgirl' (1848) revealed a new maturity, and an increasing inclination to write for his adult audience. These stories brought him virtually unalloyed adoration from the Danish critics, as well as massive sales and further international recognition.

Andersen would travel again, of course. In fact his need to escape, to search and to seek stimulation, never diminished and he travelled incessantly for much of the rest of his life. He visited Germany many times; England twice; and made it as far north as Scotland, and as far south as Spain, from where he took a brief trip to Tangier – always managing to hook up with people of note, invariably finding endless cause for complaint and usually wishing he was somewhere else. He wrote three more travel books, on Sweden, Spain and Portugal. None offer quite the blend of exotic experiences and youthful zest of *A Poet's Bazaar*, but the neuroses and vanities of their author shine through, as ever, and his eye for local colour remained keen.

He found Spain, which he visited in 1862, as primitive as Italy had been twenty years earlier. At one house he was forced to go to the loo in a hole in the corner of the garden: 'As I was squatting there, a yellow dog came by – I thought it was a lion!' he wrote. *A Visit to Portugal* in 1866 is blessedly free of the name dropping and toadying of *A Poet's Bazaar*, simply because he met virtually no names worth dropping. 'At one moment I was of a mind to stay in Portugal and see what time would bring,' he recalled of his time with the O'Niels. 'Then I remembered the old proverb, that the dearest guest becomes a bore if he stays too long in another's house. I had, so far as I knew, never yet tested the truth of this and certainly had no desire to do so.'

Famously, he had in fact done just this some years earlier when visiting Charles Dickens at his home in Kent. He had met Dickens on his first visit to England in 1847 – 'we seized both each other's hands, gazed into each other's eyes, laughed and rejoiced. We knew each other so well, though we met for the first time.' The English novelist invited him to stay at Gad's Hill, which he did on his return in 1857. But Andersen proved to be a wearisome house guest – demanding that Dickens' sons shave him, finding it difficult to communicate, and outstaying his welcome to the extent that, after he left, Dickens pinned a sign to the door of his room that read: 'Hans Andersen slept in this room for five weeks – which seemed to the family AGES!'

Unlike Dickens, Andersen never made it to the States, despite several invitations from his US publisher. The death of his great friend Henriette Wulff at sea while en route there in 1858 put him off long journeys by steamer for ever. He visited Italy several more times though, on the third occasion writing to a friend: 'I am growing here into the very ruins, I live with the petrified gods, and the roses are always blooming, and the church bells ringing – and yet Rome is not the Rome it was thirteen years ago when I was first here. It is as if everything were modernised, the ruins even, grass and bushes are cleared away. Everything is made so neat . . .'

In Rome once more in 1861 – in the company of Edvard's son Jonas – Andersen met Robert Browning and Henry James. James recalled the small gifts – tin soldiers and other toys – that children had begun to bestow on Andersen at that time, writing: 'Beautiful the queer image of the great benefactor moving about Europe with his accumulations of these relics.' Elisabeth Barrett Browning wrote of him that 'he seemed in a general VERVE for embracing. He is very earnest, very simple, very childlike'. She even made Andersen the subject of her last poem (though obviously she didn't realise it was such at the time), 'The North and the South':

> The North sent therefore a man of men,
> As a grace to the South,
> And thus to Rome came Andersen.

Later in life Andersen preferred to travel with young, male friends – more often than not one of Jonas Collin's grandsons. In return for covering their travel costs, Andersen expected them to attend to his needs – both practical and emotional – but with the exception of Edgar, who seems to have been a genuine help when they travelled together to Germany and Switzerland in 1855, Andersen invariably fell out with these strong-willed young men who, quite reasonably, found this effeminate, accident-prone hypochondriac something of an embarrassment. 'Harald is difficult to rouse in the mornings and awkward to have around. He won't call on people, won't speak German, very heavy-going like Viggo,' Andersen wrote of two of the grandsons following their tetchy trips. He reserved the most vitriol but, ultimately, the greatest affection, for Jonas jnr, who, following their trip to Spain together, he called 'an insolent little brat on whom I have wasted the kindness of my heart'. Jonas had much in common with his father, Edvard. And, though entirely lacking in empathy for the highly strung writer, he could be relied upon when the going got rough and he was among those who nursed Andersen towards the end of his life. Andersen appears to have doted on him – perhaps even fallen in love with him – despite their many tiffs. Though Andersen had by then apparently given up hope of forging a romantic partnership with anyone – male or female – he does seem to have grown quite attached to these boys, becoming jealous if they stayed out late at night, for instance.

Another of Andersen's later travelling companions, the theatre director William Bloch, also recalled his behaviour in terms redolent of a jealous lover. One night, Bloch returned to their hotel room half an hour late. 'So there you are at last!' stormed Andersen. 'How can you behave so impudently . . . didn't you say you would be back at eleven o'clock? It is half past now. I thought you had been run over, and I was on the point of telegraphing your family. You have behaved very badly.'

'Half an hour later,' writes Bloch, 'he was begging to be forgiven for the outburst.'

(Bloch wrote a wonderful book – sadly, only available in Danish – about life on the road with the ageing Andersen. Andersen seems to have spent the entire time flying into rages at incompetent waiters and hotel staff, and moaning about his health like some valetudinarian aunt.)

Andersen's last foreign trip was to Switzerland with the writer Nicolai Bøgh in 1873. He went seeking a cure for a mystery illness – stomach pains and nausea – that had struck a few months earlier, and would later develop into terminal liver cancer. A doctor in Berne diagnosed 'excessive excitability' and Andersen returned more ill than ever. 'I shall never be well again, and death is slow in coming,' he wrote in his diary in November of that year. 'I want to die, and at the same time I fear it.'

But the desire to travel remained strong. Two weeks before he died, on 4 August 1875, when he must have been in considerable pain and virtually unable to walk, Andersen was still contemplating a trip to Montreux (the plans were later found scrawled on the back of a letter Carl Alexander had written to him congratulating him on his newly awarded status as Privy Councillor).

'My doctor thinks that in the spring I may recover in health and strength, and then I want to travel. I very much long to visit England and my friends there, but I am afraid this will be too exhausting for me; I think I must go to the mountains in the south,' he wrote to a friend.

But by the end Andersen was dosed up on morphine and unable to leave his bed. The last few entries in his diary were made by Dorothea Melchior, who nursed him at her home, Rolighed (meaning Calmness). 'He says,' she writes in one of the final entries, '"Don't ask me how I feel, I don't understand anything now."' The diary ends on 4 August 1875: 'Now the light has been extinguished. What a happy death! At 11.05 our dear friend breathed his last sigh.'

Andersen had lived to the ripest of old ages and, for all his hypochondria, made it to his eighth decade with few physical ailments aside from the recurring toothache. He even lived long enough to see himself depicted in chocolate at the Copenhagen Industrial Exhibition of 1872.

He survived virtually all of his critics, including Heiberg – which must have been a satisfaction in itself – but he also watched most of his friends die. With characteristic bloody mindedness, Edvard outlived Andersen by eleven years and inherited his estate and papers, carefully sifting the latter for content that might prove embarrassing, before publishing his own memoir of life with the great writer.

Andersen was never particularly bothered about possessions or about amassing great wealth but, despite this, and the fact that writers' copyright was not properly enforced during his lifetime (and not, in fact, until the Berne Convention of 1896), he still left a considerable estate: 30,000 *rigsdaler* plus the rights to his work, which sold for another 20,000; all in all, a fortune roughly equivalent to £500,000 today.

Andersen requested that Edvard and his wife be buried along-side him when their time came, and so they were. But a few years later Edvard and Henriette were disinterred and taken to the Collin family plot. Today Andersen lies alone in Assistens Kirkegård in Nørrebro, Copenhagen. Many of his friends and enemies, like Ørsted, Kierkegaard and Heiberg, as well – though he never knew it – as his forgotten half sister Karen Marie, lie close by, but Andersen's grave remains the star attraction: a place of pilgrimage for countless tourists from around the world, just as he would have wished.

THANKS

Solveig Ottosen and her colleagues at the Hans Christian Andersen Centre in Odense generously opened their archives to me and tolerated many days of ill-informed questioning on the topic of Hr Andersen and his life, so to them many thanks. Thanks also to Malene Sejer Larsen, who spent an equal amount of time patiently explaining the nuances of the Danish language to me, and thus saving me even greater embarrassment than I have doubtless heaped upon myself with my 'instinctive' readings of various Danish texts in this book. I was touched by the trouble Dirk Heisserer took in arranging his whistle-stop tour of literary, nineteenth-century Munich; likewise, Bruno Berni, Poul Skytte-Christoffersen, Mrs Schmidt at Breitenburg Castle and, of course, the wonderful Myrto Georgiou Nielsen – not to mention virtually every librarian and archivist from here to Istanbul unfortunate enough to be on duty the day I passed through – all gave me their attention for far longer than I deserved. The Turkish Tourist Board, the Pera Palace Hotel, the Maltese Tourist Board, the very, very nice Meridien Phoenicia Hotel in Valletta, Europcar and Peter Deilmann Cruises all helped me keep within at least the same stratosphere as my original budget, and it is to my eternal shame that, in the case of the latter, I repaid their graciousness with cheap shots and low, ageist abuse (Deilmann Cruises are, I should stress, the best in the business – my mother had a great time – and you should book immediately). I will forever be indebted to Peter and Karen Marschall for their tremendous support during my travels; while, finally, 'this book would never have happened without . . .' thanks must also go to my agent, Camilla Hornby at Curtis Brown, for encouraging words given precisely when they were needed most.

SELECT BIBLIOGRAPHY

Andersen, Hans Christian: *Almanakker 1833–1873*, Copenhagen 1971.

Andersen, Hans Christian: *Andersen's Fairy Tales – Complete and Unabridged* (translator unknown), Ware 1993.

Andersen, Hans Christian: *Fairy Tales* (date and translator unknown), London.

Andersen, Hans Christian: *The Improvisatore* (translator Mary Howitt), London 1878.

Andersen, Hans Christian: *In Sweden and Other Stories* (translator unknown, probably Mary Howitt), London 1869.

Andersen, Hans Christian: *A Poet's Bazaar*, Copenhagen 1842 (plus translation by Grace Thornton, New York 1988; and Mary Howitt, New York 1871).

Andersen, Hans Christian: *The True Story of My Life* (translator Mary Howitt), London 1847.

Andersen, Hans Christian: *A Visit to Portugal 1866* (translator Grace Thornton), London 1972.

Andersen, Hans Christian: *A Visit to Spain 1862* (translator Grace Thornton), London 1975.

Andersen, Hans Christian: *Collected Works* (translator Mary Howitt), New York 1870.

Andersen, Hans Andersen: *En Biografi*, Copenhagen 2002.

Anderseniana 1933–2004 – an annual collection of essays on Andersen, published by Odense City Museums.

Barber, Robin: *The Blue Guide to Athens*, London 2002.

Behrend, C. and Topsøe-Jensen, H. (eds): *HC Andersen Brevveksling med Edvard og Henriette Collin*, Copenhagen 1933.

Bloch, William: *På Rejse med HC Andersen*, Copenhagen 1942.

Bredsdorff, Elias: *HC Andersen set med engelske øjne*, Copenhagen 1954.

Bredsdorff, Elias: *Hans Christian Andersen, A Biography*, London 1975.

Buzard, James: *The Beaten Track: European Tourism, Literature and the Ways to 'Culture' 1800–1918*, Oxford 1993.

Capelli, Rosanna: *National Archaeological Museum of Naples Guide*, Naples 1999.

Collin, Edvard: *HC Andersen og det Collinske Hus*, Copenhagen 1882.

Conroy, Patricia L. and Rossel, Sven H. (eds): *The Diaries of Hans Christian Andersen*, Washington 1990.

Dent, Bob: *Blue Guide City Guide Budapest*, London 1996.

Dreyer, Kirsten (ed): *HC Andersen's brevveksling med Lucie og BS Ingemann*, Copenhagen 1997.

Dulcken, H.W. (translator): *The Complete Illustrated Stories of Hans Christian Andersen*, London 1989.

Fiore, Kristina Herrmann: *Guide to the Borghese Gallery*, Rome 1997.

Flint, Kate (ed): *Charles Dickens, Pictures From Italy*, London 1998.

Fossi, Gloria: *Uffizi Gallery: The Official Guide of all the works*, Florence 2003.

Freely, John: *Blue Guide City Guide Istanbul*, London 2000.

Freely, John: *Galata: A Guide to Istanbul's Old Genoese Quarter*, Istanbul 2000.

Gallico, Sonia: *Vatican*, Rome 1999.

Grønbech, Bo: *H.C. Andersen*, Copenhagen 1980.

Helweg, Hjalmar: *H.C. Andersen En Psykiatrisk Studie*, Copenhagen 1927.

Macadam, Alta: *Blue Guide City Guide Florence*, London 2001.

Magris, Claudio: *Danube* (translator Patrick Creach), London 1989.

Marx, Harald and Weber, Gregor: *The Old Masters Picture Gallery*, Munich 2001.

de Mylius, Johan; Jørgensen, Aage and Pedersen, Viggo Hjornager (eds): *Hans Christian Andersen Centre: Hans Christian Andersen, A Poet in Time: papers from the Second International Hans Christian Andersen Conference*, Odense 1999.

Nielsen, Myrto Georgiou: *Once Upon a Time there was an Andersen*, Athens 1994 (unpublished, though it really ought to be).

Olsen, Kåre and Topsøe-Jensen, H. (eds): *HC Andersen's Dagbøger 1825–1875*, Copenhagen 1973.

Oxenvad, Niels (ed): *Jeg er I Italian!: HC Andersen på rejse 1833–34*, Copenhagen 1990.

Prince, Alison: *The Fan Dancer*, London 1998.

Roess, Emily: *A Child's Recollection of Hans Christian Andersen*, publ. *Munsey's Magazine*, New York, 1905.

Schirò, Joe and Sørensen, Sven: *Andersen and Malta*, Valetta 1991.

Schroeder, Veronika: *Museum Guide: Neue Pinakothek*, Munich 1999.

Sjøberg, Erik: *H.C. Andersen og Prostitutionen*, Odense 2001.

Thomson, David: *Europe Since Napoleon*, London 1957.

Toksvig, Signe: *Life of Hans Christian Andersen*, London 1933.

Topsøe-Jensen, H. (ed): *HC Andersen og Henriette Wulff. En Brevveksling*, Odense 1959.

Withers, Carl Lorain: *The Private Notebook of Hans Christian Andersen*, publ. *The Forum magazine*, 1927.

Wood, Annie: *Andersen's Friendships*, publ. in *Temple Bar Magazine*, London 1877.

Wullschlager, Jackie (ed): *Hans Christian Andersen Fairy Tales*, London 2004.

Wullschlager, Jackie: *Hans Christian Andersen: The Life of a Storyteller*, London 2000.

INDEX

www.randomhouse.co.uk/vintage